Toronto, ON   M8V 1K8

MW01122526

Humber College Library
3199 Lakeshore Blvd. West
Toronto, ON   M8V 1K8

The Unorthodox Guitar

The Unorthodox Guitar

A GUIDE TO ALTERNATIVE
PERFORMANCE PRACTICE

Mike Frengel

HUMBER LIBRARIES LAKESHORE CAMPUS
3199 Lakeshore Blvd West
TORONTO, ON.   M8V 1K8

OXFORD
UNIVERSITY PRESS

OXFORD
UNIVERSITY PRESS

Oxford University Press is a department of the University of Oxford. It furthers
the University's objective of excellence in research, scholarship, and education
by publishing worldwide. Oxford is a registered trade mark of Oxford University
Press in the UK and certain other countries.

Published in the United States of America by Oxford University Press
198 Madison Avenue, New York, NY 10016, United States of America.

© Oxford University Press 2017

All rights reserved. No part of this publication may be reproduced, stored in
a retrieval system, or transmitted, in any form or by any means, without the
prior permission in writing of Oxford University Press, or as expressly permitted
by law, by license, or under terms agreed with the appropriate reproduction
rights organization. Inquiries concerning reproduction outside the scope of the
above should be sent to the Rights Department, Oxford University Press, at the
address above.

You must not circulate this work in any other form
and you must impose this same condition on any acquirer.

Library of Congress Cataloging-in-Publication Data
Names: Frengel, Mike.
Title: The unorthodox guitar : a guide to alternative performance practice /
Mike Frengel.
Description: New York, NY : Oxford University Press, [2017] |
Includes bibliographical references and index.
Identifiers: LCCN 2016026705 (print) | LCCN 2016030153 (ebook) |
ISBN 9780199381845 (cloth : alk. paper) | ISBN 9780199381852 (pbk. : alk. paper) |
ISBN 9780199381869 (updf) | ISBN 9780199381876 (epub)
Subjects: LCSH: Guitar—Performance. | Guitar—Instruction and study.
Classification: LCC MT580 .F74 2017 (print) | LCC MT580 (ebook) |
DDC 787.87/143—dc23
LC record available at https://lccn.loc.gov/2016026705

9 8 7 6 5 4 3 2 1

Paperback printed by WebCom, Inc., Canada
Hardback printed by Bridgeport National Bindery, Inc., United States of America

CONTENTS

PREFACE

Throughout the 20th century composers and performers from practically all genres of Western music have sought to expand the available palette of musical sounds. No doubt, finding fresh and interesting ways to organize music around the same 12 pitches and established rhythmic schemes proves challenging. Novel sound materials offer an alternative path forward—one in which the salience of pitch is diminished, instead directing the ear toward less conventional sonic attributes: the way a sound unfolds over time; the inharmonicity of a resonant spectrum; the acceleration of a spinning object coming to rest. Rather than conforming to traditional musical concerns, these newfound sonic dimensions often imply alternative organizational strategies. It is ultimately what new sounds suggest in terms of music's organization that most challenges conventional norms, and equally, what makes these sounds so inviting to experimentally minded composers and performers. Indeed, novelty runs the risk of becoming gimmick unless it inspires new and interesting musical relationships.

Traditional instruments have historically provided the sounding materials of music. Their standardization allows for the development of well-established performance practices, along with communities of players that devote years of training to the refinement of skills on their instruments. A pursuit of novel sound materials built on instrumental tradition allows this wellspring of performance potential to be harnessed. This is not only important for the projection of virtuosity, a central component of live performance, but it is also necessary if a work is to be performable by the larger community of musicians. On the other hand, it is difficult to obtain new sound materials from an instrument designed and constructed to produce the 12 pitch classes of common practice tonality. Getting a traditional instrument to speak in novel ways requires an unorthodox approach. To this end, new music practitioners often employ extended techniques, instrumental preparations, and/or electronic processing and augmentation.

Extended performance techniques involve engaging a traditional instrument in unusual ways. Some expand behavioral possibilities while using more-or-less conventional sounding materials. The use of both hands to hammer the strings of the guitar against the fretboard—so-called touch technique—provides an example; the resultant materials sound like the expected equal tempered pitches of a guitar, but the technique offers a degree of polyphonic freedom otherwise unattainable on the instrument. Other extended techniques lead to more adventurous-sounding results: a string can be pushed off the fretboard and joggled to obtain a wobbly, unstable pitch; adjacent strings can be crossed and attacked together to achieve a buzzing effect; strings can be scraped or rubbed to create noise-like effects ranging from smooth whistles to aggressive striated textures. Added to this, found objects such as bolts, sticks, brushes, dowels, fans, string bows, and percussive beaters can be used to engage the strings or body of the instrument, leading to a seemingly endless array of sound types that are far removed from the expected output of a guitar.

Not only can instruments be played in unorthodox ways, but they can also be altered to provide new possibilities. The guitar offers a robust platform for experimentation with such instrumental preparations. Found objects can be attached to the instrument so that they interfere with the normal vibrations of the strings, leading to inharmonic timbres, buzzing ornamentations, rattles and bouncing behaviors, and a wide variety of non-pitched materials. Prepared sounds often have morphologies that deviate from the expected attack-decay of a plucked string. They may bounce or rattle against the strings, imbuing the sound with an intrinsic rhythm that does not conform to a regular pulse or metric view of time. And the placement of such sounds in time is often guided more by the temporal profile of the previous sound than any overriding pulse of meter. Again, these sounds invite us to think of music's organization along different lines.

Electronic technologies offer tremendous potential for expanding the timbral and performance capabilities of a live instrument. Such extensions come natural to the electric guitar, with a wide range of sound-altering stomp boxes and hardware processing devices on the market. Acoustic guitars can take advantage of these same devices using a transducer such as a pickup or microphone to obtain an analog signal. Today, however, the average laptop computer can handle real-time signal processing, and there are robust platforms available for experimentation with sound, including virtual pedalboards that emulate hardware effects and even include amplifier modeling. Computer-based systems offer possibilities far beyond signal processing: sounds can be electronically generated, either through file playback or synthesis; sensors can be attached to the instrument or performer to obtain data streams that are mapped to processing parameters; interactive performance systems can be developed in which the computer listens and responds to a performer's actions or instrumental output; systems based on artificial intelligence can act as virtual musicians in an improvisational context. Indeed, the role of a computer in live performance can be multifaceted—at times fusing with and extending an instrument's sound, while at other times contributing a distinct voice to the musical texture.

The Unorthodox Guitar is a comprehensive guide for experimentally minded guitarists and composers wishing to write for or perform on the instrument in new ways. This is not a methods book; rather it is intended to serve as a resource, reference, and source of inspiration. It is unique among guitar books in that it focuses primarily on non-standard approaches to the instrument, including alternative tunings, extended performance techniques, instrumental preparations, and electronic augmentations. Of course, even works entrenched in unorthodox techniques are likely to also employ conventional materials. To that end, common practice techniques and issues of standard notation are covered.

Considering the degree to which steel string guitars prevail in popular music genres, and the fact that the vast majority of young guitarists opt for steel string models, it is surprising that works for steel strings have been practically non-existent in contemporary classical music until relatively recently. Even today, their contribution to the repertoire remains marginal. A survey of steel string guitar techniques employed in genres across the board makes it clear that such underrepresentation can in no way be attributed to a lack of instrumental potential. To the contrary, the steel string guitar has proven to be highly versatile, capable of a wealth of timbral contrasts, extended performance techniques, alternative tunings, and instrumental preparations. Nowhere is this versatility better exemplified than in the electric guitar, where the potential to transform the sound of the instrument electronically offers a range of timbral and behavioral possibilities that are perhaps only surpassed by the synthesizer.

The steel string guitar is equally underrepresented in books on contemporary guitar performance. The few comprehensive publications on the subject—John Schneider's *The Contemporary Guitar* (1985) and Seth Josel and Ming Tsao's *The Techniques of Guitar Playing* (2014), as informative as they are—focus primarily on the nylon string instrument and its role in contemporary classical music.[i] *The Unorthodox Guitar* distinguishes itself from these others in that it gives steel string instruments, both acoustic and electric, as much attention as the classical guitar.

The Unorthodox Guitar is also unique in its stylistic pluralism. Techniques and examples are culled from a broad range of musical genres, including contemporary classical, blues, folk, country, jazz, rock, and non-Western idioms. Much of the impetus for this project was to encourage an exchange of ideas across stylistic lines. There are idiomatic playing techniques associated with each type of guitar, and distinct techniques have developed within diverse musical styles. As a result, techniques common to one style of music often seem unconventional in the context of another. Yet many of these techniques are perfectly viable on all guitar types. By discussing them collectively, the hope is that readers are not only encouraged to consider the techniques, but more generally, to consider other musics.

The Unorthodox Guitar comprises nine chapters that can be taken in any order. For the most part, considerations of electronics have been separated from those of instrumental techniques and preparations. However, discussions of nylon string, steel string acoustic, and electric guitars are purposely mixed to encourage a cross-pollination of practices and techniques across stylistic lines.

Chapter 1 provides an overview of guitar types, identifying characteristics and idiosyncratic properties of each. Common acoustic, electric, steel string, and nylon string instruments are considered, as well as a number of variants on traditional designs. Individual hardware components are examined, including bridges, saddles, tailpieces, necks, nuts, headstocks, tuners, pickups, and volume and tone knobs, always with a concern for how design options affect the tone, integrity, and performance potential of the instrument. Modern developments such as sustainer systems, hexaphonic, and MIDI pickups are also examined. This chapter is particularly valuable to composers who are not guitarists themselves, but it includes an abundance of information that guitarists should also find enlightening.

Tuning is the subject of Chapter 2. The six strings of the guitar can be tuned in any way, and the ease with which their tensions can be adjusted makes the instrument a fairly flexible platform for experimentation. Deviations from standard tuning are often employed for practical reasons, such as to allow certain pitches or pitch combinations to be obtained. When using a bottleneck slide, for instance, guitarists often employ open tunings so that a major or minor chord sounds when the strings are stopped in a straight bar configuration. Changes in tuning can also help guitarists to step outside of their own playing tendencies, as the pitches on the fretboard are relocated. A large number of 12-tone equal-tempered tunings are presented in this chapter, including transpositions of standard and open tunings, Nashville, ostrich, and specialized configurations. A more adventurous approach to tuning abandons the 12-tone equal tempered system altogether, replacing it with a new collection of pitches. Just a few of the possibilities are 19-tone equal temperament, 24-tone equal temperament, and just intonation. Such alternative tuning systems often necessitate a re-thinking of the harmonic language itself, as the concerns present in 12-tone equal temperament may not be relevant given a different pitch collection.

Guitar notation is notoriously inconsistent in practice. Chapter 3 provides an overview of basic notation for the instrument, identifying best practices and introducing conventions used throughout the book. Experienced guitarists may find this content remedial. However, composers interested in writing for the guitar who are not guitarists themselves should definitely take notice of the material covered here.

Chapters 4 and 5, taken together, present a rich catalog of extended performance techniques. Chapter 4 focuses on methods of attacking the strings, while Chapter 5 expands the discussion to techniques involving the left hand.[ii] Practical concerns related to sound projection and reliability of the technique, either on a single instrument or across instrument types, are addressed. Notation is critical whenever novel techniques are employed since there is not an established performance practice that the player can rely on for guidance. The notation of extended techniques often involves the creation of new symbols and terminology that need to be defined and explained in instructions that accompany the score. Numerous notation examples are provided in this chapter. Some are from published works, while others are hypothetical. The examples are merely suggestions; they represent one way of notating the techniques at hand. More important, they are meant to reflect the thought processes and concerns that guide the development of new notation in general.

Almost any found object can be attached to the guitar in a way that yields an interesting and musically useful sound. Chapter 6 aims to define a typology of preparations, which includes mutes, rattlers, bouncers, string attachments, string coupling, third bridges, buzzing bridges, cross-stringing, percussive sounds, and soundboard modifications. Numerous specific preparations are given as examples within each category, with the broader aim to develop a general understanding of the sonic qualities and mutable nature of the category. Equipped with this conceptual knowledge, guitarists and composers will be better able to get the most out of their own found objects.

Chapter 7 covers important components of a live guitar rig, namely, amplifiers and hardware effects. A catalog of common guitar effects is presented, with descriptions of the important parameters of each. Common and experimental uses of effects are also discussed. Throughout the chapter, special concern is given to preservation of the guitar tone as equipment is added to the chain. Although the chapter is oriented toward the electric guitar, the same processing techniques and considerations are available to acoustic instruments, assuming that a pickup or microphone is employed to obtain an analog signal.

Chapter 8 explores the potential that the personal computer offers for real-time processing and instrumental augmentation. Not only are commercial software applications available that mimic traditional hardware effects, but audio programming environments such as Cycling '74's Max allow for the creation of sophisticated and interactive processing algorithms in which controllers can be mapped to the various parameters, enabling the performer to engage the effects directly as part of the performance. The discussion then shifts to means by which an instrument can be augmented with sensors or portable controllers. Various types of control signals are examined, followed by discussions related to mapping control signals to sound parameters, the relationship between physical and sounding gesture, and the role of virtuosity and fallibility in live performance.

Chapter 9 examines practical issues related to the performance and recording of mixed works. It begins with a classification of relationships between live and electronic components, arguing that such relationships are more salient in the mixed work format precisely because the source of the electronics is unseen. Methods of live sound amplification and projection for both live and non-live sources are considered, including the use of guitar amps, microphones, acoustic guitar pickups, and direct signals. Procedures for minimizing ground hum and extraneous noise are also offered. The chapter ends with a discussion of recording strategies for the guitar in the context of mixed works.

In a period of music's history largely marked by innovation, the antiquated distinctions between so-called musical sounds and noises have been largely abandoned, and practitioners are now looking to new sound materials for creative inspiration. To that end, new technologies are increasingly being employed that not only change how we make music, but more important, the music that we make. The guitar shines in this environment, offering a robust platform for experimentation and a community of players eager to work outside of established norms. The contents of this book—alternative tunings, extended performance techniques, instrumental preparations, and the integration of electronics into guitar performance—are all a means to an end, that is, of making new music.

ACKNOWLEDGMENTS

Many friends and colleagues have helped shape this book, and I am deeply grateful to all of them. In particular, I would like to thank Mark Applebaum, Clarence Barlow, Gilbert Biberian, Georg Hajdu, Daniel Hjorth, and Larry Polansky for making their music and ideas about it available to me. To Robert Ward for his advice on the classical instrument and its associated performance techniques. To Tolgahan Çoğulu, Aaron Green, William Greenwald, and Dan and Bryan Swords for making their instruments available. To Giacomo Fiore for his insight on the just intonated works of Polansky, Harrison, and Tenney. To Bruce Hamilton for his guidance with photographs. And of course, to John Schneider, Seth Josel and Ming Tsao, Bart Hopkin and Yuri Landman, and Peter Yates and Matthew Elgart for their important contributions to contemporary guitar practice.

ABOUT THE COMPANION WEBSITE

www.oup.com/us/theunorthodoxguitar

Oxford has created a Web site to accompany *The Unorthodox Guitar: A Guide to Alternative Performance Practice*. Materials that cannot be made available in a printed book, such as audio, video, and software examples, are provided here. The reader is encouraged to consult this resource in conjunction with the chapters. Examples available online are indicated in the text with Oxford's symbol ⊙. In addition to the called out examples, the website contains supplementary software and example materials to support the reading.

The Unorthodox Guitar

1

Instruments and Their Hardware

The Acoustic Guitar

An acoustic guitar employs a hollow body to amplify and project its sound (Fig 1.1). While the strings are the sole source of the sound, they are very soft on their own. Attached to the body, however, a string's vibrations are transferred through the saddle and bridge to the soundboard, which is constructed out of thin wood and made to vibrate freely. With such a large surface area, the soundboard moves enough air for the instrument to be heard at a reasonable level. Although the soundboard plays a primary role in projecting sound, the entire body, including its shape, size, materials, and construction, affects the tonal quality of the instrument. We might think of the body as an acoustic equalizer that imposes a uniform spectral contour on all sounds that pass through it, imbuing the instrument with a coherent timbre throughout its range.

The Nylon String Acoustic Guitar

In the English-speaking world, the nylon string guitar is often associated with classical music and for that reason it is sometimes referred to as a "classical" guitar, differentiating it from its steel string relative. On the global stage, however, nylon strings are far more ubiquitous, serving as the norm in folk and popular genres worldwide. Indeed, the history of the guitar is principally a story of the nylon string instrument, as steel strings were not developed until the 20th century.

Guitar strings were originally made of catgut, a type of cord derived from fibers found in animal intestines.[1] In the mid-1940s, string maker Albert Augustine began to develop nylon strings, which proved to be more durable and consistent in terms of timbre and intonation, as well as sounding louder. In modern nylon string sets, the three treble strings are made of a single nylon filament; the lower three strings consist of a core of nylon threads that are wound with bronze or silver plated copper wire.

Nylon string guitars can be divided into three broad categories: the classical guitar, the flamenco guitar, and hybrid nylon models. Each has its own set of design concerns and characteristic sound quality. As the names imply, the type of guitar that a player chooses tends to fall along musically stylistic lines, with hybrid models found mainly in jazz and folk genres. We'll now look at each in turn.

Figure 1.1

Anatomy of an acoustic guitar (a Martin D-18).

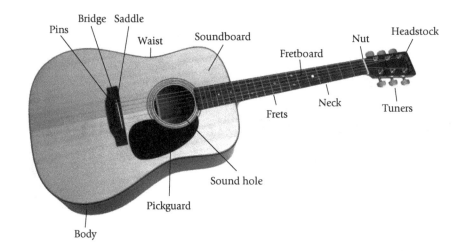

Pins

Bridge Saddle

Waist

Soundboard

Fretboard

Nut

Headstock

Neck

Frets

Tuners

Sound hole

Pickguard

Body

Figure 1.2

A Pepe Romero nylon string classical guitar (No. 218, 2013).

The Classical Guitar

The modern classical guitar derives its design from the 19th-century Spanish luthier Antonio Torres Jurado, who brought the instrument to its current dimensions, employed a thinner soundboard, and introduced fan bracing to the interior of the body (Fig. 1.2).[2] Today, body dimensions vary slightly from one maker to the next, with the Torres style representing the smaller end of the scale. On the larger end is the Madrid-style body, which favors volume, warmth, and sustain. If compared to a steel string dreadnought acoustic guitar, the classical body is slightly smaller and has a tighter waist.

The neck of a standard nylon string guitar has 19 total frets, joining the body at the 12th with no cutaway. Fretboards are flat and the action is set relatively high to ensure clear and unobstructed tones. Classical technique is characterized by a right hand that plucks individual strings with the fingers. To this end, a wide two-inch nut is standard, offering ample room for the fingers.

The Flamenco Guitar

The flamenco guitar is derived from the classical instrument but constructed around concerns for the aggressive strumming and integration of percussive slap and golpe techniques associated with the idiom. These instruments have shallow bodies with less bracing, a thinner soundboard, tighter string spacing, and a lower string height, all of which contribute to a tight and punchy sound. The soundboard is usually equipped with tap plates (golpeadores) above and below the strings, providing surfaces that can

Figure 1.3
A 1933 Santos Hernandez flamenco guitar with golpeadores installed above and below the strings (photo from www. trilogyguitars.com).

Figure 1.4
A Taylor 812ce hybrid nylon string guitar (photo from taylorguitars.com).

be tapped percussively with the nails without tarnishing the wood's finish (Fig. 1.3). Temporary protective surfaces made of static-cling film are commercially available for the classical instrument. These can be used on steel string guitars as well and turn out to be useful when one is working with instrumental preparations on a valuable instrument.

The Hybrid Nylon String Guitar

In recent years, manufacturers specializing in steel string guitars have ventured into crossover instruments, combining elements of both steel and nylon string designs (Fig. 1.4). These guitars are often played with a pick and have necks and body styles resembling those of a steel string instrument, including a cutaway to access the higher frets. Some have as many as 22 frets, with a range comparable to that of an electric guitar. In addition, many are equipped with built-in electronics for amplification. Such hybrid instruments are largely marketed to folk and jazz players who desire the sound of nylon strings, but crave the comfort and playability of a steel string design.

The Steel String Acoustic Guitar

The steel string acoustic guitar emerged in the United States in the early 20th century, largely in response to a growing demand for more affordable instruments. No maker has had more of an impact on the instrument's development than the C. F. Martin Guitar Company. German luthier Christian Frederick Martin immigrated to the United States and established the C. F. Martin Guitar Company in 1833, originally specializing in European-style guitars with gut strings. In response to a growing public demand for inexpensive instruments, Martin introduced X-bracing to the body construction, which was quicker and cheaper to manufacture. Advances in wire production at the turn of the century made steel strings considerably cheaper to produce than gut. Steel strings also gave the instrument more volume, which would become increasingly coveted as the instrument began to appear in ensembles. As luck would have it, Martin's X-bracing was ideally suited to handle the additional tension posed by the metal strings, and by the end of the 1920s steel strings were standard on Martin guitars. Other makers would soon adopt Martin's designs. Figure 1.1 shows a modern Martin D-18 with a dreadnought body style.

Steel strings sound bright and thin when compared to nylon. While perfectly suitable for melodies, fingerstyles, and virtuosic passages, these instruments are largely designed with strumming in mind. Compared to the nylon string instrument, they have a lower string height with a narrow neck and tight string spacing. Steel string acoustics typically have 21 total frets, with the neck joining the body at the 12th or 14th fret. Some newer instruments have cutaways for easy access to the higher frets.

Body Styles

The evolution of the steel string acoustic body has been marked by a gradual increase in size as manufacturers have sought ever-louder instruments. Today, steel string acoustics are made in a variety of body shapes and sizes, many of which are modeled after early Martin designs (Fig. 1.5). Of these, the dreadnought is by far the most prevalent and also one of the largest. As a general rule, larger bodied instruments produce more volume and

Figure 1.5

Common steel string acoustic body styles.

Body Style	Description
Parlor Size 1 and 2	 The smallest of the modern full-scale instruments, the parlor guitar produces a soft and light sound that is best suited for fingerstyle playing in intimate settings.
Concert Size 0	 The 0 body style is slightly larger than a parlor guitar and was originally designed for use in concert settings. At some point, companies began marketing the concert body as a parlor guitar, a practice that continues to this day.
Grand Concert Size 00	 The 00 is slightly larger than the concert in terms of body length and width, with a slightly wider neck. It is well suited to fingerstyles.
Auditorium Size 000	 The 000 is similar in design to the grand concert, but with a slightly wider and deeper body. The sound is louder with more bass response. This body offers a good compromise for both for fingerstyle playing and strumming.
Orchestra Model Size OM	 The orchestra model has the same body as the auditorium, but with a slightly longer scale length and wider string spacing. It is well suited for fingerstyles.
Dreadnought Size D	 The dreadnought has a large, deep body with less-pronounced waists. Dreadnoughts are loud and have a heavy bass response. Combined with their narrow neck, they are ideal for strumming and flatpicking.
Super Jumbo	 Gibson's "super jumbo" is the largest of the common acoustic body styles, providing even greater volume and bass response.

a thicker tone with increased bass response. Smaller bodies, on the other hand, provide a more even balance between bass and treble strings and offer greater control at soft dynamics. To a large extent, the choice of body style comes down to whether the player will be strumming chords or playing with the fingers. Conventional wisdom is that smaller body styles are better suited for fingerstyles and solo playing, while larger-bodied instruments are better for strumming accompaniment or playing with other instruments.[3]

The Archtop Acoustic Guitar

Orville Gibson began making steel string mandolins in the late 19th century. Inspired by the design of the violin, his instruments had arched tops and backs with f-hole vents on the soundboard. In 1902 he founded the Gibson Mandolin-Guitar Mfg. Co., Ltd. In addition to a variety of mandolins, Gibson offered the L-1 guitar, which was based on a similarly arched body design but with a conventional round sound hole. Unlike Martin guitars, these instruments were not inexpensive; Gibson marketed their guitars as instruments of the finest quality and craftsmanship. Although Gibson eventually began manufacturing less expensive flat top guitars that were essentially based on Martin designs, the company retained an interest in the archtop instrument and continues to make them today.

Working for Gibson in the 1920s, Lloyd Loar made significant improvements to the archtop design, introducing the notion of a harmonically tuned soundboard and back, carved from a single piece of wood and "tuned" by tapping on it at various places as it was thinned to ensure a consistent sound. He also replaced the circular sound hole with the characteristic f-holes already in use on Gibson mandolins, added a truss rod and adjustable bridge, and implemented a lighter bracing pattern using only a couple of longitudinal tone bars (Freeth & Alexander, 1999). These developments first appeared in Gibson's L-5, released in 1922, upon which many subsequent archtop guitars have been modeled. Figure 1.6 shows a modern Gibson L7-C.

Acoustic archtop guitars are designed to allow the soundboard to vibrate as freely as possible. In addition to lighter bracing, the instrument is assembled so that nothing touches the soundboard except for the bridge. The strings are typically anchored to a trapeze tailpiece attached to the heel of the instrument and suspended over the soundboard so as not to interfere with its vibrations. If there is a pickguard it will also be attached to the side and suspended over the soundboard. Even the bridge is "floating," meaning that it is not fixed to the soundboard but simply rests on it, held in place by the tension from the strings.[4]

Figure 1.6
A Gibson L7-C acoustic archtop guitar (photo from Gibson.com).

Figure 1.7
Ovation Elite
C2078AX-5
acoustic-electric
guitars (photo from
ovation.com).

In terms of sound, archtops are softer than many of the larger-bodied acoustic instruments and generally have less sustain. However, they have a focused, nasal tone quality that blends well with other instruments and is capable of cutting through an ensemble without cluttering the overall sound.

The Acoustic-Electric Guitar

An acoustic-electric guitar is an acoustic guitar that has been fitted with transducers and built-in electronics for amplification. In addition to volume controls, many are equipped with an onboard preamp, equalization capabilities, and if multiple pickups are installed, a mixer for the different signals. Many acoustic-electric instruments are essentially based on conventional steel string designs, with added electronics. Others, however, are designed with concerns for amplification. One notable example is the Ovation Roundback, developed by Charles Kaman in 1966 (Fig. 1.6). These instruments have a shallow body with a contoured back made of Lyrachord, a fiberglass material impregnated with tiny glass beads. The material and body shape maximizes sound projection while minimizing feedback when the instrument is amplified. Many newer Ovation designs replace the traditional circular sound hole with a number of smaller holes positioned around the perimeter of the soundboard or on the sides, as can be seen in Figure 1.7.

The Electric Guitar

George Beauchamp, co-founder of National Stringed Instrument Corporation and Rickenbacker Guitars, developed the first commercially available electric guitar in 1932.[5] Referred to as the "Frying Pan," it had a round body just large enough to mount the bridge and pickup. Gibson and Fender guitar manufacturers soon entered the market with their own electric models. By the 1930s the electric guitar had become an established instrument in popular music ensembles, most notably big bands, where it could compete with brass sections and trap kits. With the guitar empowered by this newfound dynamic range, its role also shifted from accompaniment to one of soloist in ensembles.

Over time, a performance practice developed that is quite distinct from that employed on the nylon string instrument.

The electric guitar is extremely versatile, capable of accompaniment as well as virtuosic solo passages. It has the greatest range of all standard guitar types, with at least 21 frets and cutaways in the body. Furthermore, the dynamic range of the instrument is limited only by the power of the amplifier, and as such, the electric guitar is able to compete in practically any ensemble context. Perhaps the most distinctive attribute of the electric instrument, however, is the ability to alter the sound by means of effects processing, giving the instrument unparalleled timbral variety. A typical electric guitar is shown in Figure 1.8.

Body Styles

Because the electric guitar relies on pickups for amplification, the body is designed around concerns that are quite distinct from those of the acoustic instrument. Consider that a string fixed at both ends will have maximum sustain if all the energy traveling along it hits the end points—the bridge and nut—and is reflected back into the string. In practice, however, some of the string's vibratory energy escapes. If proof is needed, simply observe how a solid body guitar vibrates when played; the energy responsible for those vibrations is energy not redirected into the string. All other factors being equal, an instrument that is firmly constructed out of solid woods should have less energy loss from the strings and therefore greater sustain than one that is not as solid. In addition to affecting sustain, a vibrating body also sets the end points of the string in motion, which distorts the shape of the waves when reflected from them, thereby affecting timbre. In an effort to minimize vibrations, electric guitar bodies are made of hard woods, often mahogany, ash, poplar, or alder.

Electric guitars are available in solid body, semi-hollow body, and hollow body varieties. Solid bodies are most common, and as the name implies, are made of solid wood (Fig. 1.8). They come in a wide variety of shapes, ranging from conservative to far-out

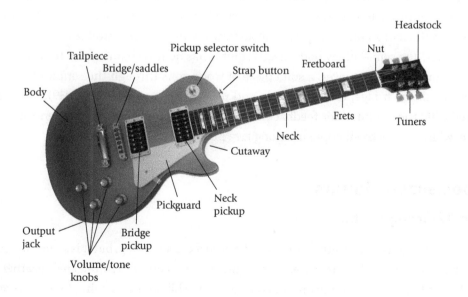

Figure 1.8

Anatomy of a solid-body electric guitar (a Gibson Les Paul).

Figure 1.9
A Gibson ES-335 semi-hollow body guitar (photo from Gibson.com).

Figure 1.10
A Gibson Songwriter Deluxe Studio 12-string guitar (photo from Gibson.com).

Figure 1.11
E-standard tuning for the 12-string guitar.

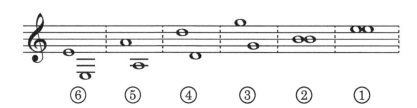

designs. Most, however, are modeled after traditional Fender or Gibson instruments. The hollow body electric guitar is completely hollow, essentially based on an acoustic archtop design with added electronics. Hollow bodies can be "full-bodied" or "thinline," the latter being more shallow to minimize feedback when amplified. Hollow body instruments produce sufficient sound to be played acoustically, although the thinline body is considerably softer. The semi-hollow body electric guitar has hollow chambers on both sides with f-holes for venting. However, a solid piece of wood runs through the center of the body, upon which the bridge, tailpiece, neck, and pickups are mounted (Fig. 1.9). In addition to reducing the potential for feedback, this body style gives these instruments a mellow tone, which makes them popular among jazz players.

Specialized Guitars

The 12-String Guitar

The 12-string guitar is essentially tuned and played like a six-string, but it is strung in courses (i.e., pairs of strings) that are placed close enough to each other to be fingered together (Fig. 1.10). The higher two courses are tuned in unison, while the remaining four are tuned in octaves (Fig. 1.11). For courses three through six, it is common to place the higher string in

Figure 1.12
A Dobro Hound
Dog Deluxe Square
Neck single-cone
resonator guitar
(photo from
epiphone.com).

each pair above the lower string, leading to a slightly brighter timbre during downstrokes. However, some instruments—most notably Rickenbacker guitars—reverse this order and place the higher string below the lower. In either configuration, the 12-string guitar is characterized by a thick sound with a natural chorus effect due to slight intonation differences between the unison and octave doublings. These instruments provide lush chordal accompaniment when strummed. Fingerstyles and lead parts, however, sound less defined.

Seven-Stringers and More

Guitars with seven, eight, or nine strings are available from private luthiers as well as some major manufacturers such as Ibanez. These instruments are available in acoustic and electric models, the latter being most prevalent. The additional strings are typically placed below the sixth in successive fourths to extend the lower range. The tuning of the seven-string guitar is thus B1-E2-A2-D3-G3-B3-E4; the eight-string is F#1-B1-E2-A2-D3-G3-B3-E4, and the nine-string is C#1-F#1-B1-E2-A2-D3-G3-B3-E4.

The Russian Guitar

Developed in Russia in the 18th century, the Russian guitar is an acoustic instrument with seven nylon strings that resembles the appearance of a classical guitar. The additional string is placed below the sixth to extend the lower range. The instrument typically employs the open G tuning D2-G2-B2-D3-G3-B3-D4 and is played with the fingers, both strumming and plucking. The Russian guitar plays a prominent role in Russian music up to the present day.

Resonator Guitars

The resonator guitar, also referred to as a Dobro or resophonic guitar, is an acoustic instrument in which the sound is amplified by one or more metal cones built into the body (Fig. 1.12). The bridge sits atop the cones and transfers energy from the strings directly to the metal, giving these instruments a characteristic twang that has won favor among blues and country players. The body of a resonator guitar may be made of metal or wood, the latter sounding slightly warmer, yet still with a distinctive twang.

Resonator guitars come in square neck and round neck models. The square neck instrument is intended to be played as a lap steel and cannot be held in the normal manner. It has a raised string height and reinforced neck, the latter allowing the strings to be tuned higher while also providing increased sustain. The round neck instrument can be played either way, but if used as a lap steel guitar it helps to raise the strings with a nut extension (Fig. 1.15).

There are three resonator cone designs, each giving the instrument a distinct timbre. The original tri-cone design consists of three separate metal cones joined by a T-shaped bar that distributes energy from the bridge to the cones. Tri-cones are generally more costly to produce but have a smoother and more complex tone quality with great sustain. The single-cone biscuit bridge design replaces the three separate cones with one large cone, with the bridge transferring energy to the cone through a single point of contact. The result is louder and more metallic than the tri-cone. The single cone spider bridge, on the other hand, employs a web-shaped system to distribute the energy from the bridge to the cone, producing a tone that is more nasal than the other designs.

Fretless Guitars

The fretless guitar has a smooth fretboard without raised fret wires, similar to a bowed string instrument. For visual reference, some have indications as to where the frets would be. Because the strings are stopped directly with the fingers, notes on the fretless guitar sound characteristically dull and have little sustain, reminiscent of a plucked double bass. The morphology of these tones is unique and can provide contrast when juxtaposed against fretted notes on a standard instrument. More often, however, fretless necks are chosen for their ability to produce smooth and continuous portamento effects impossible on the fretted instrument. They may also be advantageous when alternative tuning systems are used since the neck is not fixed to any particular intonation. For such tuning systems, colored tape or chalk can be used to mark the position of pitches on the fretboard, offering a simple visual guide to the player.

Fretless guitars can be purchased from major vendors and specialist luthiers in both nylon and steel string models. One can also be made at home by removing the fret wires on a standard neck, filling the grooves with epoxy, and then sanding the fretboard until smooth. The string height usually ends up excessively high once the frets are removed, which causes the strings to wrap around the fingertip when depressed, damping the notes considerably. Lower action is needed to get significant sustain, which is likely to involve lowering both the nut and saddle.

The Baritone Guitar

The baritone guitar sits registrally between the conventional guitar and the bass. Its longer neck allows the strings to be tuned lower without being overly slack. Figure 1.13

Figure 1.13
A Gretsch® G5265 Electromatic Jet Double Neck guitar, comprising a baritone neck and a conventional neck (photo from gretschguitars.com).

shows a Gretsch G5566 Jet Double Neck electric instrument, comprising a baritone and a conventional neck, clearly illustrating the different scale lengths. Acoustic baritones can also be found but are less common. The baritone is usually tuned a fourth below a conventional guitar, resulting in the open strings B1-E2-A2-D3-F#3-B3. Tunings a fifth or major third lower are also employed. The instrument produces a deep, rich timbre that is well suited to melodic activity in the lower register. Guitarist Pete Anderson uses a baritone in precisely this way on Dwight Yoakam's "Little Ways" (1987).

The Steel Guitar

The steel guitar is laid face up and played by plucking the strings with the right hand while stopping them with the left using a tone bar or "steel," a solid metal implement that functions like a bottleneck slide and gives the instrument its characteristic portamento sound. Purpose-built steel instruments are commercially available in a variety of forms. Lap steels are literally rested across the legs of a seated performer and have a single six-string neck (Fig. 1.14). Larger console and pedal steels are mounted on stands, have more strings, and often have multiple necks for different tunings. Added to this, the pedal steel has foot and knee levers that alter the tension of individual strings. Electric steel guitars are typically played with a volume pedal, used delicately to increase sustain.[6] Designed specifically for the unique steel playing technique, steel guitars have very high action, no raised fret wires, relatively wide string spacing, and reinforced necks able to withstand higher string tensions, all of which prohibit the instrument from being played like a normal guitar.

Steel technique actually developed on the standard instrument, and guitars continue to be employed as lap steels in country, bluegrass, Hawaiian, and experimental genres. Simple alterations to a standard instrument make steel technique much easier. The string height could be raised to avoid the tone bar knocking against the fret wires as it is moved along the neck. Extension nuts can be purchased that are designed to sit over a standard nut for precisely this purpose (Fig. 1.15). Heavy gauge strings are recommended for improved sustain, and depending on the tuning, they may require a mix of gauges not typical to a six-string set. Open tunings are usually employed on steel guitars, as the use of a tone bar makes it impossible to stop the strings in shapes other than a straight or slanted barré. In many cases, these are the same open tunings that are used on the standard instrument. Some, however, are unique to the lap steel, such as C6 tuning: C3-E3-G3-A3-C4-E4.[7]

Modeling Guitars

Modeling guitars represent a true evolution in the electric instrument's design. Rather than using a conventional electromagnetic pickup, they have distinct pickups under

Figure 1.14
An Eastwood Airline lap steel.

Figure 1.15
A Tyler Mountain extension nut installed on a Fender Telecaster.

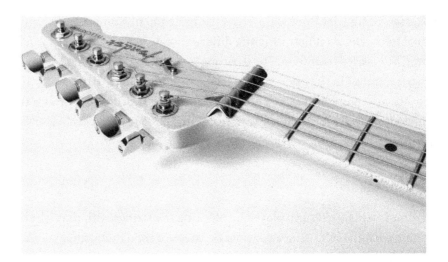

each string to capture and digitize the signals independently. With a rotary dial a player can emulate the sound of various classic guitar tones, as well as a few other stringed instruments such as the banjo and sitar. The sound transformation is accomplished using signal processing techniques, as opposed to synthesis or sample playback, an important point that distinguishes modeling instruments from MIDI (musical instrument digital interface) guitars. In addition, string pitches can be changed electronically, allowing for virtual alternate tunings or a virtual capo. Modeling guitars are great for the working musician who needs to obtain a wide range of tones and tunings on stage. A particularly attractive quality of these instruments is that they are not susceptible to buzz and hum interference like a traditional pickup. Line6 is a leading manufacturer of modeling instruments.

Sustainer Systems

Sustainer systems utilize a controlled electromagnetic field to continuously sustain the strings of an electric guitar, similar to the way that an EBow functions.[8] In contrast to the handheld EBow, however, sustainer systems are built into the instrument and capable of sustaining all six strings simultaneously while freeing the hands to engage the instrument normally. The Moog Guitar and the Fernandez Sustainer offer two examples of commercial sustainers.

The Moog Guitar

The Moog Guitar, developed by Paul Vo in 2008, contains special pickups that utilize magnetism in order to affect the sustain of the strings. More sophisticated than other sustainer devices, the Moog Guitar offers a number of operational modes: "Full Sustain Mode" provides infinite sustain on every string and at every fret; "Mute Mode" electromagnetically dampens the strings to produce a variety of staccato effects; "Controlled Sustain Mode" provides sustain to the strings being used while damping the others; "Harmonic Blend Mode" accentuates upper harmonics, which can be shifted using a foot pedal provided with the instrument. The guitar also comes with a built-in Moog resonant filter that can be manipulated by a foot pedal.

The Fernandez Sustainer

Fernandez Guitars sells a kit called the Fernandez Sustainer, which is installed in the neck pickup position of the guitar. It offers three modes of operation: "Natural Mode" sustains the fundamentals of any stopped pitches; "Harmonic Mode" sustains a fifth above the stopped pitch; "Mixed Mode" blends the two. When the sustainer is not activated the neck pickup serves as a normal humbucker. When the sustainer is activated, the neck pickup functions to sustain the strings and only the bridge pickup outputs sound. Fernandez also sells electric guitars with the sustainer built in.

Nuts, Headstocks, and Tuners

The function of the nut is to stop the strings near the headstock, thereby establishing the open string length. In addition, the nut determines the string height and spacing in the lower frets. Nuts are traditionally made from bone or ivory, but metal and synthetic materials such as plastic and tusq are being used on modern instruments. The material has an affect on tone, but of course will only be heard when open strings are sounded.

Three types of nuts are common on guitars today. The slotted nut is standard on acoustics and fixed bridge instruments, essentially made up of a block with slots cut in the top for the strings to drop into (Fig. 1.16a). When strings are bent they often slip in the nut and, once released, may not return to their original position, causing the string to go out of tune. This can be particularly problematic on guitars with vibrato bridge systems, and to address it these instruments often employ a roller or locking nut. A roller nut has tiny bearings in the slots to help the string glide smoothly through the nut without sticking (Fig. 1.16b). By contrast, a locking nut clamps the string at the nut, preventing it from slipping at all (Fig. 1.16c). Once locked down, however, the instrument can only be tuned with fine tuners positioned at the bridge.

The headstock extends from the end of the fretboard and supports the tuners. It may be made from the same piece of wood as the neck or it may be glued on, the latter typically done to increase the break angle of the strings over the nut. The break angle can affect the volume, timbre, and sustain of an instrument, but perhaps more than anything else, it impacts the feel of the strings, especially when they are bent. A sharper angle generally gives the strings a tighter feel, while a lower angle results in a looser feel. Slot-head

(a) (b) (c)

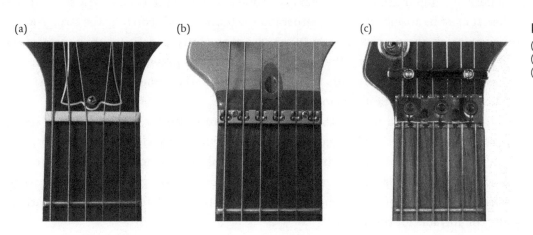

Figure 1.16
(a) A slotted nut;
(b) a roller nut;
(c) a locking nut.

Figure 1.17
(a) A classical guitar headstock; (b) a steel string 3+3 headstock; (c) a steel string 6-in-line headstock.

(a)   (b)   (c)

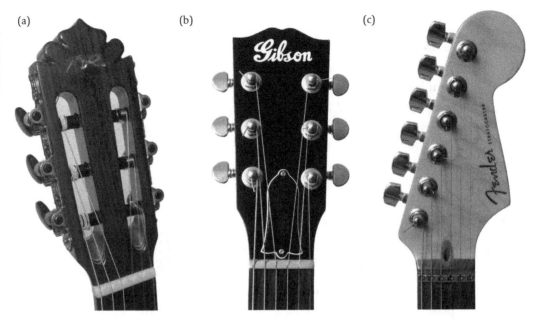

tuners, like those found on the classical guitar, wind the strings around posts embedded in cavities cut out of the headstock, which adds to the break angle (Fig. 1.17a). By contrast, steel stringed instruments typically have posts that extend outward from the face of the headstock, lessening the angle (Figs. 1.17b and 1.17c).

Modern instruments use gears, referred to as "machine heads," to turn the post and alter the tension of the string.[9] Manufacturers qualify machine heads with a ratio such as 14:1 or 18:1, which indicates the number of times the tuning knob must be turned for the post to make one full revolution. The tuners are typically distributed in either a 3+3 or 6-in-line configuration. In the 3+3 configuration, the tuners for the three bass strings are mounted on one side of the headstock, while the three treble string tuners are mounted on the other (Figs. 1.17a and 1.17b). By contrast, the 6-in-line configuration places all six tuning keys on one side (Fig. 1.17c). Note that the string lengths behind the nut vary in these two designs, which has ramifications for techniques that engage these string segments.

Necks and Fretboards

The neck of a guitar attaches to the body at one end and supports the headstock at the other. It must be strong enough to withstand the tension placed on it by the strings without warping or vibrating excessively. In the case of steel string instruments, a metal truss rod is often built in, running the length of the neck and providing additional support. Truss rods also offer adjustments to control the relief—the amount of bow or resistance in the neck—an important step in setting up a guitar.

Neck width is measured at the nut. The standard width for a classical nylon string instrument is 2 inches, while steel string acoustic guitars are closer to $1\frac{3}{4}$ inches, and the electric can be as low as $1\frac{5}{8}$ inches.[10] As a general rule, wider necks allow for greater string spacing, which is advantageous in the context of fingerstyles. Conversely, narrow necks produce a tighter sound when the strings are strummed quickly and make barring more comfortable for the left hand.[11]

The fretboard refers to the front face of the neck and supports the fret wires and any decorative inlays. Some necks use a single piece of wood for the neck and fretboard, while others are constructed with a separate fretboard, typically made of ebony, rosewood, mahogany, or cedar, which is glued to the top of the neck. There is debate as to whether the fretboard material has an effect on the sound of the instrument. In theory, one would expect it to, but given the varying opinions surrounding the issue it is probably fair to say that any effect is marginal.

Scale Length

Scale length refers to the vibrating length of open strings and is measured from the inner edge of the nut to the point on the saddle between the third and fourth strings.[12] The typical scale of a nylon string guitar is 26 inches, while that of a steel string instrument ranges from $24\frac{1}{2}$ to $25\frac{1}{2}$ inches. A longer scale length requires greater tension on the strings to bring them up to pitch. To understand this, imagine taking a guitar in E-standard tuning and placing a capo on the first fret. This shortens the scale length and also raises the pitch of the open strings by a half step. In order to get the instrument back to E-standard tuning with the capo in place, all of the strings would need to be lowered by a half step, resulting in a short-scale guitar in E-standard tuning with rather slack strings. Because scale length affects string tension, it also has an influence on the tone and feel of the instrument. Instruments with a shorter scale length have a slack feel under the fingers, making it easier to fret and bend the strings. However, they tend to produce less volume and have a slightly duller tone with less sustain.

Bridges, Saddles, and Tailpieces

Acoustic Guitar Bridge Systems

The principal function of an acoustic bridge system is to transfer vibrations from the string to the soundboard. The bridge itself is made of a hardwood such as ebony or rosewood and glued to the top. Most bridges are slotted for a saddle, which is made from a single piece of bone, ivory, or synthetic material.[13] Acting as the counterpart to the nut, the saddle serves to stop the string and transfer vibrations through the bridge to the soundboard. The saddle also determines the string height at the bridge, and along with the nut, the scale length.

Each string is anchored to the bridge and then passes over the saddle and up the neck toward the headstock. Steel string acoustic bridges typically anchor the ball-ends of the strings in holes drilled into the face of the instrument behind the saddle using tapered bridge pins made of plastic, wood, bone, or ivory.[14] By contrast, a pinless bridge has holes drilled horizontally so that that the strings can be anchored without the need to pass through the soundboard. In addition to maintaining the integrity of the soundboard, a pinless bridge reduces the break angle between the anchor point and the top of the saddle. Pinless bridges are standard on nylon string instruments but they can be found on some steel string instruments.

The archtop acoustic guitar employs an alternative "floating" bridge design that simply rests on the soundboard, held in place by the tension of the strings much like the bridge on a bowed string instrument (Fig. 1.18). The strings are anchored to a separate

Figure 1.18
A floating bridge and trapeze tailpiece on a Gibson ES175D hollow body electric.

trapeze tailpiece that attaches to the tail of the guitar. When the strings are taut they lift the tailpiece so that nothing except the bridge is touching the soundboard. Mainly used in hollow body acoustic and semi-hollow body electric instruments, the floating bridge and trapeze tailpiece design allows both the strings and soundboard to vibrate more naturally. The trapeze tailpiece also leaves long string segments behind the bridge, offering lower behind-the-bridge tones. The sound of a trapeze tailpiece might be described as "airy" when compared to a stop tail, and perhaps with less sustain. As for the bridge itself, options range from plain wood to more sophisticated designs that provide height and intonation adjustments per string.

Electric Guitar Bridge Systems

The principal function of an electric guitar bridge system is to hold the strings firmly in place while stopping them at the saddle. In addition, the bridge and saddle determine the string height and spacing, intonation, and, along with the nut, the overall scale length. Since amplification of the electric guitar occurs through pickups, the transference of energy from the strings to the soundboard is not a chief concern. This has led to a variety of designs that are quite distinct from those found on the acoustic guitar. Broadly speaking, these can be divided into two types: fixed and vibrato.

Fixed Bridges

A fixed bridge anchors the strings to a stable and immovable part of the instrument. Anchor points may be on the bridge itself or external to it, such as on a separate tailpiece or through the body of the instrument. Fixed bridges generally offer more sustain than vibrato types. More important, fixed bridge instruments are easier to tune since the tension of each string is independent of the other strings. For this reason, they are preferable when working with alternative tunings.

The wraparound bridge is perhaps the simplest of the fixed bridge designs. It is essentially a metal bar fixed to the body of the instrument that functions both to anchor the

(a)   (b)   (c)

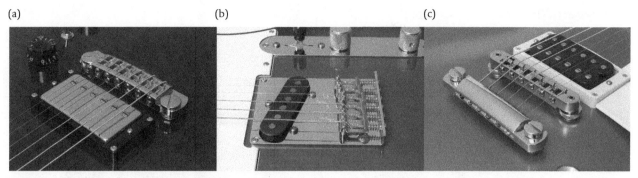

Figure 1.19
(a) A wraparound bridge; (b) a Fender-style ashtray bridge; (c) a Gibson Tune-o-matic bridge and stop tailpiece.

strings and to saddle them. The strings are inserted from the pickup side of the bridge and then wrap around from the back, over the top, and run up the neck toward the headstock. The wraparound bridge shown in Figure 1.19a has height adjustments on each end, but not for individual saddles.

The Fender-style ashtray bridge is most often associated with the Telecaster guitar and is unique in that the bridge and bridge pickup are mounted to a metal plate. This may contribute to the characteristic twang of the Telecaster. The strings pass through the back of the body, up through the tray, and over the bridge. The Telecaster in Figure 1.19b has barrel saddles for each string, providing adjustments for string height and intonation.

Gibson's Tune-o-matic system consists of a bridge and separate stop tailpiece (Fig. 1.19c). Anchoring the strings to a separate tailpiece allows the string break angle behind the bridge to be adjusted. A raised tailpiece creates a shallow angle and lessens the string tension, giving the instrument a looser feel. To the contrary, a steeper angle generally results in a tighter feel and greater sustain.[15] The Tune-o-matic system also offers height adjustments on each end, and intonation adjustments per string. In addition, the design provides behind-the-bridge string segments that can be engaged during performance.

Vibrato Bridge Systems

Vibrato bridge systems enable the tension of all six strings to be altered uniformly by way of a lever-shaped vibrato arm or "whammy bar," leading to a variety of pitch-bend and portamento effects. The terms "vibrato" and "tremolo" are both used to describe these bridges, and while vibrato effects are achievable, none produce an actual tremolo.[16] I will refer to them as vibrato bridges, except in reference to branded names.

Fender's "synchronized tremolo" system is the default on most Stratocaster-style instruments (Fig. 1.20). The bridge sits in a cavity routed in the body with springs on the underside to counter the tension of the strings. When all six strings are brought to tension the bridge "floats" in a position at which the forward tension of the strings is balanced with the backward pull of the springs.[17] A floating vibrato bridge can bend strings upward, albeit within a marginal range, and the instability of the bridge adds a slack feel to the strings. Alternatively, springs can be added or tightened so that the backward pull exceeds the forward tension from the strings, causing the bridge to press firmly against the body. Only downward bends can be achieved with this setup, but it makes the instrument easier to tune and prevents it from going out of tune when a string breaks.

Figure 1.20
A Fender
Synchronized
Tremolo System on
a Stratocaster.

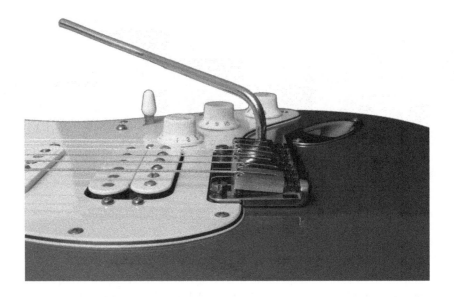

The principal gripes with vibrato bridge systems are intonational. Because the position of the bridge is dependent on the combined tension of the six strings, a change to one affects them all. Consequently, when players tune the instrument it is common for them to have to cycle through the strings a few times before the bridge settles into its point of equilibrium with all strings at pitch. Moreover, if an alternative tuning is used the spring tension in the back may need to be adjusted to account for the new combined string tension. And of course, the instrument will go out of tune when a string breaks, as this disrupts the balance of tension between the strings and springs.

Another complaint with vibrato bridge systems is that they do not stay in tune. When a vibrato bar is used, the string slips over the nut and bridge saddles. Ideally, the string should return to its original position when the tension is released, but friction can cause it to stick. This problem can be mitigated by a roller nut and roller saddles or by ensuring that these contact areas are properly lubricated. The Floyd Rose double-locking tremolo system addresses the issue by clamping the strings at the bridge and nut to prevent slippage, hence the "double-locking" appellation. Once the strings are locked at the nut end, the tuning keys do not function. For this reason, fine tuners are provided on the bridge itself. Floyd Rose systems are sought for their stable intonation, although that is relative to other vibrato systems, as none approach the stability of a fixed bridge.

Cam-operated vibrato systems provide an alternative to fulcrum-based systems without the need to rout a cavity in the body of the instrument. The Bigsby Vibrato System comprises a separate bridge and tailpiece (Fig. 1.13). The strings attach to the underside of the cylindrical tailpiece, wrap around the top, and then are sent over the saddles and down the neck. When the arm is moved the tailpiece rotates about its axis, altering the tension on the strings. The bend range on a Bigsby is limited to about a third down, less than other systems. But the Bigsby system is unique in that it provides behind-the-bridge string segments. The Kahler Tremolo System also anchors the strings to a cylinder-shaped cam that rocks back and forth when the arm is used while the saddles remain stationary. Of particular note, the Kahler system has a screw that locks the cam in place, essentially converting it into a fixed bridge.

Pickups

Acoustic Guitar Pickups

Soundboard Transducers

Soundboard transducers are small piezoelectric devices that attach to the soundboard, picking up vibrations directly from the wood. They may be attached to the underside of the soundboard in permanent installations or to the outer surface with adhesive putty, the latter allowing the pickup to be removed or repositioned with ease (Fig. 1.21). Indeed, moving the pickup to various locations on the instrument yields a range of guitar tones unattainable with fixed solutions. Soundboard transducers can be used on both steel and nylon string instruments and sound quite natural when compared to other pickup types.

Undersaddle Transducers

Undersaddle transducers are made of thin piezoelectric strips that sit between the saddle and bridge, picking up vibrations as they pass to the soundboard. These are typically permanent installations and are common on acoustic instruments sold with built-in electronics.[18] Undersaddle transducers are available in passive and active varieties and function on both nylon and steel string guitars. They tend to sound quite natural but omit the body characteristics from the overall tone, and players sometimes complain of a characteristic "quack" when attacking notes at louder dynamics.

Electromagnetic Sound Hole Pickups

Sound hole pickups attach to the opening of the sound hole and sit under the strings, similar to the pickups on an electric guitar (Fig. 1.22). Passive and active varieties are available that are easy to install and remove. They are inexpensive, durable, and fairly resistant to feedback, but they tend to sound more amplified than other designs. Further, because they are electromagnetic, their application is confined to steel string instruments.

Figure 1.21
An Ehrlund soundboard transducer and preamp.

Figure 1.22
A Fishman Rare
Earth Humbucking
sound hole pickup
(photo from
Fishman.com).

Figure 1.23
A Planet Waves
sound hole cover.

Multi-Source Blender Systems

Multi-source blender systems combine a number of diverse transducers with the ability to control the balance between the different sources. Most common is the combination of an undersaddle piezoelectric pickup with an onboard microphone, the latter positioned inside the instrument to add some of the body characteristics to the tone. In addition to mixing capabilities, most blender systems have built-in preamps and offer equalization controls.

Sound Hole Covers

Sound hole covers are employed to minimize feedback when the instrument is amplified (Fig. 1.23). Commercial products range from those that are completely covered to those with varying degrees of vents. Sound hole covers do not mute or muffle the instrument, as most sound emanates from the surface area of the soundboard and not from the sound hole. They do, however, have a subtle affect on the acoustic sound, reducing the volume and attenuating bass frequencies. In fact, a cover can reduce the booming bass of a larger-bodied guitar, giving it some of the transparency of a smaller design.

Electric Guitar Pickups

Active and Passive Pickups

The electric guitar uses electromagnetic pickups, which come in passive and active varieties. Passive pickups are far more prevalent, as they are the oldest and remain standard on most popular guitar models. The coils of a passive pickup require many turns of wire to obtain a reasonable output level, which has the effect of accentuating mid- and low-range frequencies at the expense of higher ones, as well as making the pickups susceptible to radio frequency interference. Nonetheless, many players prefer passive pickups, citing a greater dynamic range and more natural tone quality. In addition, the tone becomes duller when the volume knob is reduced on a passive pickup, which can be used as a means of timbral control.

Active pickups function similarly to passive types but have significantly fewer turns of wire in the coil, resulting in a flatter frequency response, lower output, and less susceptibility to radio frequency interference. The output is, in fact, so low that a preamp is required to boost the signal. As such, active pickups require a power source, typically provided by a 9V battery housed in the body of the instrument. Once preamped, the signal may come out of the instrument significantly hotter than that from a passive pickup. Active pickups are typically chosen for their low noise, but many guitarists feel that they compress the signal and reduce the dynamic range.

Single Coil and Humbucker Pickups

Single coil pickups contain only a single row of magnetic polepieces (Fig. 1.19b). They produce a thin and bright sound with pronounced attack, excellent for clean, twangy tones and light distortion. Their clarity also makes them well suited for instrumental preparations. The principal disadvantages of single coil pickups are that they are prone to electromagnetic interference and output a relatively low-level signal, which usually fails to push a distortion box into heavy overdrive.

Ray Butts and Seth Lover developed the humbucker pickup independently in the late 1950s, primarily to address the noise issues associated with single coil pickups. Humbuckers consist of two coils placed side by side and wound in opposite directions with their magnetic poles reversed in polarity (Figs. 1.19a and 1.19c). The signals from each coil are summed, which has the effect of canceling much of the radio frequency interference while amplifying the wanted guitar sound. The resulting signal tends to be significantly hotter and fatter than that of a single coil pickup. If heavy distortion is the goal, the humbucker pickup is the way to go.

Electric guitars can have up to three pickups, often mixing single coil and humbucker varieties on the same instrument. As a general rule, pickups near the bridge sound brighter while those closer to the neck sound more mellow. When more than one pickup is available a selector switch is provided, usually with options to isolate any one of the pickups, as well as positions that sum them in various combinations. It is not uncommon for guitarists to switch pickups during a piece as a means of timbral control.

Volume and Tone Knobs

Pickups are connected to onboard volume and tone knobs, the number and wiring of which vary from one instrument to another. There may be a volume and tone knob for each pickup, or pickups may be summed to a single knob. A gradient of timbres is available using the volume and tone controls. Too often, electric players set all knobs to maximum and never touch them, which neglects the potential of pickups for tone control. When adjusting the sound, one might instead try dialing the pickup selector, volume, and tone knobs back so that there are options to make the sound both brighter and duller.

Hexaphonic and MIDI Pickups

A hexaphonic pickup has six discrete analog outputs, one for each string. Passive, active, electromagnetic, and piezo-based solutions are available. The pickup is usually wired to a 7-pin or 13-pin connector that serves as the output jack, meaning that it must be connected to a compatible device in order to get at the signals. For this reason, instruments fitted with a hex pickup usually have conventional pickups connected to a standard mono output so that the guitar can be used normally. Hexaphonic pickups are most commonly used in the context of MIDI and guitar synthesizer systems, as the task of estimating pitch is made simpler when the signals from each string are isolated. While capabilities vary from one system to the next, an examination of Roland's guitar synthesis technology illustrates how these systems generally work.

Roland's GK-series pickup system has three principal components: the hexaphonic pickup, a controller, and a sound module. The pickup mounts non-intrusively between the bridge and bridge pickup and connects to the controller, which itself attaches to the lower bout of the guitar. In addition to the six outputs from the GK pickup, the guitar's mono output from the conventional pickups is also connected to the controller. All signals are then output via a 13-pin connector on the controller to an external sound module.

Roland's system only uses the outputs from the hexaphonic pickup to analyze the guitar performance, extracting pitch, rhythm, and dynamic information. These data are then used to drive synthesis algorithms in the sound module, the output of which can be combined with the normal guitar signal from the conventional pickup. The sound module also converts the six outputs to MIDI and provides a MIDI OUT so that the device can be connected to any MIDI sound module. It does not, however, provide access to the six analog signals from the hex pickup, although breakout boxes and cables are available through third-party vendors. Note that Roland's GK-series pickups are active and must be connected to a Roland sound module to obtain power, even if the module is not being used.

If having six analog outputs is the goal, then Paul Rubenstein seems to be on the right path. His company Ubertar sells passive hexaphonic pickups that are designed to provide six high-quality analog outputs without concern for MIDI or synthesis. These are simply conventional guitar pickups with a separate output for each string. They connect to a breakout box via a 7- or 13-pin din connector and require no power. Ubertar also sells one- and two-string mini pickups.

01341171719116

HUMBER LIBRARIES

2

Contemporary Tuning Practices

Standard Tunings

The most common guitar tuning in use today is E-standard, consisting of the open-string pitches E2-A2-D3-G3-B3-E4 and the open-string intervals P4-P4-P4-M3-P4 (Fig. 2.1).[1] Logically, all transpositions of E-standard tuning can also be considered "standard" in the sense that the pitch relationships and finger patterns on the fretboard remain the same. From this perspective, E-standard is just one of 12 theoretically possible standard tunings. Another, D-standard, can be obtained by lowering all strings a whole step to the pitches D2-G2-C3-F3-A3-D4. Transpositions of standard tuning may be employed to place the instrument in a more comfortable range for a vocalist, to facilitate playing in a particular key, or to alter the overall timbral quality of the instrument.

In practice, issues of string tension, both slack and taut, make it difficult to achieve all 12 standard tuning transpositions. With less tension on the strings, lower tunings accrue a slack quality that results in a duller sound, pitch instability, poor intonation, and an increased likelihood of fret buzz. Heavier string gauges can mitigate some of these issues. Transpositions higher than E-standard increase tension on the strings, which will eventually lead to a string breaking, or even worse, damage to the instrument. Lighter gauge strings can be raised with less tension on the neck, but a capo is usually a better solution for tunings above D-standard.

Alternative Tunings

Alternative tunings can be approached from two fundamentally different perspectives. The first focuses on non-standard ways of tuning the guitar within the 12-tone equal tempered system prevalent in Western music and from which common practice tonality is derived. A second and more radical approach to tuning abandons 12-tone equal temperament altogether, replacing it with a different collection of pitches; 19-tone equal temperament, 24-tone equal temperament, and just intonation are a few possibilities discussed later in this chapter. Such alternative tuning systems often necessitate a re-thinking of the musical language itself, as the same harmonic concerns that are present in 12-tone equal temperament may not be relevant with a different collection of pitches.

Figure 2.1
E-Standard tuning.

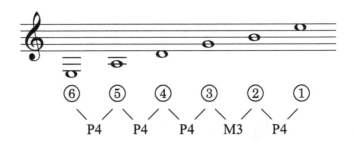

Non-Standard 12-Tone Equal Tempered Tunings

Modern guitarists and composers employ a wide variety of non-standard 12-tone equal tempered tunings; some of these have become well known while others are specialized, created for particular works. There could be numerous reasons for employing a non-standard 12-tone equal tempered tuning: (1) to extend the range of the instrument; (2) to facilitate playing in a particular key; (3) to simplify fingerings in a particular work; (4) to allow certain pitch or timbral relationships to be explored; (5) to create unusual chord voicings and sonorities; (6) to increase the resonance of the instrument through a greater use of open strings, sympathetic vibrations, or unisons sounding together; (7) to alter the distribution of pitches on the fretboard, making it easier to step outside of one's own musical tendencies and discover fresh ideas. This section progresses from alternative tunings that have become well established to those that are more esoteric. When considering any new 12-tone equal tempered tuning, one might be particularly cognizant of the open-string intervals, as these, perhaps more than anything else, affect the layout of the fretboard, disrupt familiar patterns and chord shapes, and impact the ability to easily read notation.

Drop Tunings

Drop tuning implies that the sixth string is lowered, resulting in an interval wider than the perfect fourth typically found between the lower two strings in standard tuning. Drop tunings were used in some of the earliest guitar music and became quite common in the 19th century, primarily to facilitate playing in a particular key. Today they can be found in classical, folk, blues, country, jazz, and contemporary genres and are particularly widespread in rock music, giving the electric guitar a deeper and darker sound. Common drop tunings are discussed below, with a more extensive list provided on the companion website.

Drop D Tuning

Drop D is by far the most common of the drop tunings. It is similar to E-standard, except that the sixth string is lowered a whole step, resulting in the open-string pitches D2-A2-D3-G3-B3-E4 (Fig. 2.2). The close resemblance to standard tuning makes it easy for guitarists to play and read music in drop D. Moreover, many lower drop tunings retain this same open-string interval pattern and can simply be viewed as transpositions of drop D. Once players are familiar with the fingerboard and chord shapes in drop D, adjusting to those other drop tunings is trivial. In keys of D, the low D on the open sixth string adds weight to the tonic chord as well as placing the tonic and dominant scale degrees on the two open bass strings.

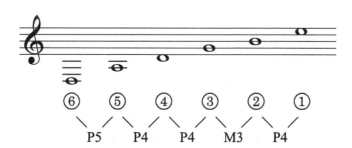

Figure 2.2
Drop-D tuning.

Figure 2.3
Excerpt from Soundgarden's "Spoonman" (1994) in drop D tuning (transcribed by the author) [▶ Media 2.1].

Today, drop D tuning finds widespread use in rock music. It not only gives the guitar a deeper sound, but the perfect fifth between strings five and six makes it possible to play power chords simply by barring the lower strings. Power chords consist of only the root and fifth of the chord. Lacking the third, they are neutral and can substitute for both major and minor harmonies in a key. Absence of the third also yields a clearer sonority, especially when distortion is used. This is a consequence of the irrational ratios used in 12-tone equal temperament, which result in spectral roughness and beating between the overtones of different pitches. Because distortion tends to accentuate the overtones of each note, this spectral roughness becomes more apparent.[2] Soundgarden's "Spoonman" (1994) makes extensive use of power chords (Fig. 2.3).

Drop C Tuning

Drop C tunings all involve lowering the sixth string a major third from E2 to C2. There are a number of options in practice for handling the remaining strings. The most common of these lowers the other strings by a whole step, resulting in the open-string pitches C2-G2-C3-F3-A3-D4—essentially a transposition of drop D (Fig. 2.4a). While not as prevalent as drop D, this version of drop C is fairly common in rock genres, employed for its heavier sonority.[3] A second possibility is to drop the sixth string from E2 down to C2 while leaving the remaining strings in standard tuning, resulting in the open-string pitches C2-A2-D3-G3-B3-E4 (Fig. 2.4b). I use this tuning on a steel-string acoustic in *Slinky* (2004), primarily to exploit the unstable slack quality of the lowered sixth string. Other works to utilize this tuning include John Mayer's "Neon" (2001) and Reginald Smith-Brindle's *Concerto de Angelis* (1973). A third variation of drop C tuning involves lowering the sixth and fifth strings while leaving the others at the E-standard pitches, resulting in the open-string pitches C2-G2-D3-G3-B3-E4 (Fig. 2.4c). This configuration has the

Figure 2.4

Three versions of
drop C tuning.

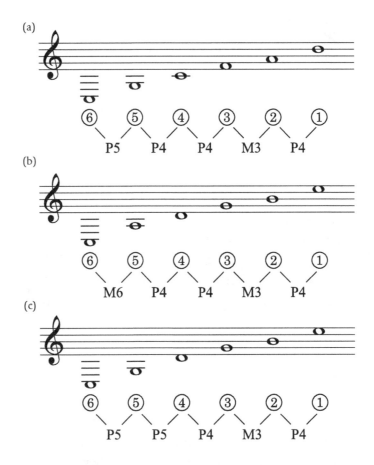

advantage of extending the range of the instrument downward while retaining the familiar perfect fifth between the lower two strings. Chet Atkins uses it on "Waiting for Susie B." (1996). It has also been employed when making guitar arrangements of works originally composed for string instruments tuned in fifths. For example, Andrew York uses it in his arrangement of Bach's Cello Suite No. 3 in C Major (2003).

Lower Drop Tunings

Craving deeper and heavier guitar sounds, modern metal bands such as Parkway Drive, Nile, and KoRn have extended drop tunings downward to B, and in some cases even drop A. Both of these lower drop tunings resemble drop D in terms of the open-string intervals, but with all strings transposed downward by their respective intervals. These lower drop tunings are viable on steel string acoustic and electric guitars, especially when heavy gauge strings are used to compensate for the slack tension. However, drop tunings beyond C are rarely employed on nylon string guitars because the slack strings lose their voice, sounding dull and no longer able to project.

Double Drop D

Double drop D is a variant of drop D tuning in which the first string is also lowered to D, resulting in the open-string pitches D2-A2-D3-G3-B3-D4 and the open-string intervals P5-P4-P4-M3-m3. With the octave doubling between the first and sixth strings reestablished, the first string could be left to ring open against the open sixth string or barred along with it to brighten the sonority of chords. As with drop D, the double drop

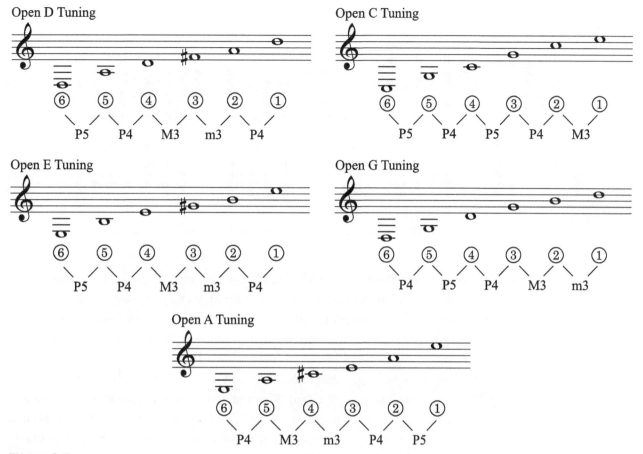

Figure 2.5
Common open "major" tunings.

configuration can theoretically be transposed to any pitch class. For example, double drop C would consist of the open-string pitches C2-G2-C3-F3-A3-C4.

Open Tunings

In an open tuning, the pitches of the six open strings form a chord. While one can imagine tuning to any chord quality, the most common open tunings are major, minor, and modal, the latter replacing the third of the chord with a fourth or second. A striking characteristic of open tunings is their rich and resounding sonority, in large part because they make greater use of open strings. In addition, chords in open tunings can more often make use of all six strings, in contrast to the many chords that omit strings in standard tunings.

Open Major Tunings

Open major tunings form major chords when all strings are sounded open.[4] The most common are open D, open E, open C, open G, and open A (Fig. 2.5). Note that with the exception of open D and open E, these tunings are not mere transpositions; they differ in their open-string interval patterns and in their arrangement of chord tones. When selecting an open tuning, one might consider the location of the root of the open chord. Some tunings place the root on the sixth string, lending weight to the tonic. Others place it on the fifth string while tuning the sixth string to the fifth of the chord—a

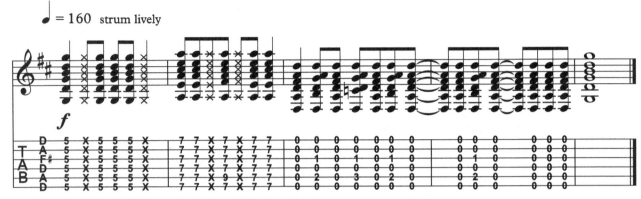

Figure 2.6

Excerpt from Joni Mitchell's "Big Yellow Taxi" (1970) in open D tuning (transcribed by the author) [▶ Media 2.2].

perfect fourth below the root—which affords the sort of I-V bass ostinato commonly found in country and folk genres. Melodic considerations may also factor into the selection of a tuning. For instance, it might be sensible to have the principal melody string tuned to the root, third, or fifth of the chord, depending on the range and starting pitch of the melody.

In an open major tuning, major chords can be formed anywhere by simply placing a vertical barré across all strings. It might be noted, however, that converting this barred chord to minor is problematic since the flattened third is behind the barré. Of course, it is possible to obtain minor chords in a major tuning by using other fingerings. Folk guitarist and songwriter Joni Mitchell uses many open tunings in her songs. A transcription of the verse from "Big Yellow Taxi" (1970) is provided in Figure 2.6, offering a good example of the resonant quality of strummed chords. Mitchell performs the work with a capo, which transposes everything upward. For clarity, it is transcribed here in open D.

Drone effects work wonderfully well in open tunings, allowing for melodies or movable chord shapes to be played over an open string harmony. Henry Worrall used this effect in his work *Sebastopol* (1860), in open D. An excerpt from the work is given in Figure 2.7, showing a fingered melody on the first string sounding over a D major harmony on the remaining open strings. This particular piece inspired many guitarists to explore open tunings, and as a result, open D is often referred to as "Sebastopol" or "Vestapol" tuning.

Slide guitarists often employ open tunings so that the straight barré of the slide creates familiar harmonies. The altered voicing of these tunings also makes a significant contribution to the delta blues sound. Figure 2.8 is taken from the introduction of Muddy Waters's "I Feel Like Going Home" (1948), with the guitar in an open G tuning.

Harmonics sound particularly resonant in open tunings. When a harmonic is sounded, any string that also has a harmonic node at the same pitch will vibrate sympathetically.[5] The predominance of doublings and closely related chord tones in an open tuning leads to considerably more sympathetic vibrations than occurs in most other tunings. Of practical import, open tunings tend to offer a reduced collection of available harmonics; but most are diatonic to the open key, and harmonic chords are obtainable using a barré in a single position.

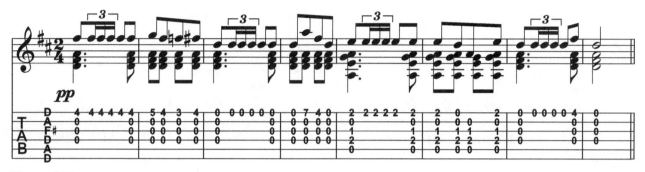

Figure 2.7

Excerpt from Henry Worrall's *Sebastopol* (1860) in open D tuning (reproduced from the original score by the author) [▶ Media 2.3].

Figure 2.8

Excerpt from Muddy Waters' "I Feel Like Going Home" (1948) in open G tuning (transcribed by the author) [▶ Media 2.4].

Open Minor Tunings

Open minor tunings—referred to as "cross-note tunings" by Mississippi delta blues guitarists—produce minor chords when all strings are played together. Bukka White and Skip James often used the open D minor and E minor tunings shown in Figure 2.9, which are identical to their open major counterparts except that the third string is lowered by a half step. A notable characteristic of these particular open minor tunings is that the upper three strings have the same intervallic configuration as in standard tuning while the lower

Open D Minor Tuning

Open E Minor Tuning

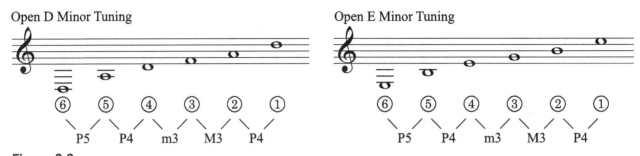

Figure 2.9
Common open minor tunings.

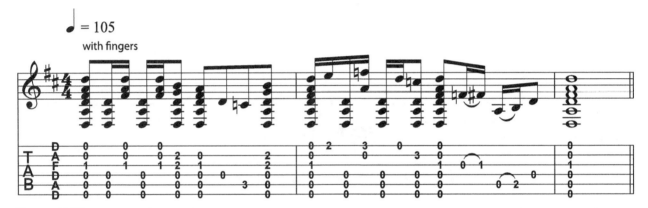

Figure 2.10
Excerpt from Bukka White's "Aberdeen Mississippi Blues" in open D minor tuning (transcribed and arranged by the author) [▶ Media 2.5].

three strings resemble drop D, which most guitarists are familiar with. Furthermore, barred chords in open minor tunings can be converted from minor to major simply by raising the third a half step. Indeed, White and James often used open minor tunings for works in major keys to exploit the flattened third, a characteristic common to the blues. Figure 2.10 provides a short excerpt from Bukka White's "Aberdeen Mississippi Blues" (1940), transcribed here in open D minor. Note the raised third (fingered) in the tonic chord that appears at the downbeat of each measure, and the flattened third (F-natural) in measure 2.

Carlo Domeniconi uses an open D minor tuning in his work *Koyunbaba* (1985) for the nylon string instrument. The score is written as if in D minor, with strings tuned to the pitches D2-A2-D3-A3-D4-F4, a variant of the more common configuration shown earlier. At the end of the score, however, the composer indicates that the instrument should be lowered a half step to the pitches C♯-G♯-C♯-G♯-C♯-E, presumably to alleviate tension on the neck caused by the raised strings. Domeniconi makes heavy use of open strings throughout the work, as can be seen in the excerpt provided in Figure 2.11. The quickly alternating hammer-ons and pull-offs on predominantly open strings result in a resonant minor drone quality of mesmerizing beauty and intensity.

Open Modal Tunings

Modal tunings omit the third of the chord, resulting in open-string harmonies that are neither major nor minor in quality. In such tunings, the third is usually replaced with a fourth to create a sus4 chord, or less often with a second, resulting in a sus2 chord. The

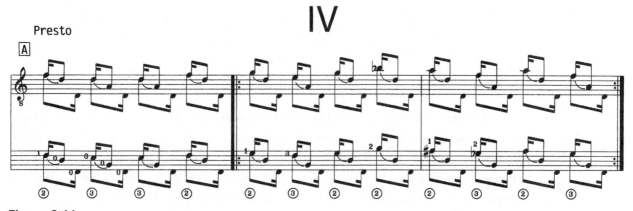

Figure 2.11

Excerpt from Carlo Domeniconi's *Koyunbaba* (1985) in open D minor tuning.

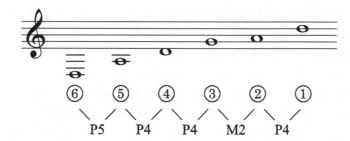

Figure 2.12

Open D modal tuning.

Figure 2.13

Excerpt from Davey Graham's "She Moved through the Fair" (transcribed by the author) [▶ Media 2.6].

most common of the modal tunings is modal D, or "DADGAD" tuning (Fig. 2.12). It is also referred to as Celtic tuning because of its prevalence in Celtic folk music. British guitarist Davy Graham popularized the tuning in the 1960s, when he used it in performances of traditional Irish folk music and music with Indian and Moroccan influences. Indeed, modal tunings that replace the third of the chord with a fourth above the root are reminiscent of sitar tuning. Graham's arrangement of the traditional Irish melody "She Moved through the Fair" (1962) had a lasting impression on many British guitarists, including Jimmy Page, whose instrumental work "White Summer" (1968), originally recorded with the Yardbirds and later as the introduction to Led Zeppelin's "Black Mountain Side" (1969), is almost identical. Figure 2.13 shows a transcription of the beginning of "She

Figure 2.14

Nashville tuning.

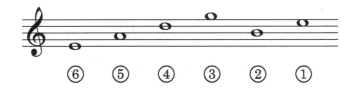

Moved through the Fair." Graham's performances of the work incorporated a fair amount of improvisation, and consequently, the transcription is intended to be indicative of the sort of thing he did. Interestingly, Graham would transpose the guitar downward and then use a capo to bring it back up to D, creating a slack quality in the strings reminiscent of many Eastern string instruments without actually altering the register.

Nashville Tuning

Nashville tuning, also referred to as high-strung tuning, is a re-entrant configuration in which all strings are tuned to the E-standard pitch classes, but strings three through six are raised one octave (Fig. 2.14). Another way to conceptualize Nashville tuning is to imagine stringing a six-string instrument with only the higher string in each pair of a 12-string set. When played together with a six-string guitar in standard tuning the result can sound similar to a 12-string instrument, with the added benefit that the two parts can also play independently. Nashville studio guitarist Ray Edenton is credited with having been the first to employ Nashville tuning. In the 1950s Edenton began tuning the third string up one octave, giving his guitar a brighter sound. He soon moved to full high-strung tuning, which can be heard on his recordings with the Everly Brothers of "Bye Bye Love" (1957) and "Wake Up Little Suzie" (1957) (Trott, 2009). Nashville tuning can also be heard on the Rolling Stones' "Wild Horses" (1971), Pink Floyd's "Hey You" (1979), and Kansas's "Dust in the Wind" (1978). A comparison of standard and Nashville tunings is available on the companion website [⊙ Media 2.7].

Setting up a guitar in Nashville tuning requires that the lower four strings be changed to lighter gauges. Consequently, guitarists who employ this tuning will often have an instrument reserved for it. It is possible to buy string sets for Nashville tuning. Alternatively, only the higher strings of a 12-string set could be used or strings can be purchased individually. The gauges for a light set might be .010, .014, .009, .012, .018, .027, and a medium set might be .012, .016, .010, .014, .020, .030. Note that the sixth string is usually wound while all others are plain steel.

Uniform Tunings

When the intervals between open strings are all the same, the tuning is described as uniform.[6] Figure 2.15 provides a number of common uniform tunings. Of these, all fourths tuning has attracted the most attention because it is closest to standard tuning, and in fact, simplifies the fretboard by removing the anomalous major third between the second and third strings. As a consequence, the same chord and scale shapes can be played across all strings without having to shift up one fret when crossing the second. Guitarists William Ackerman, Bob Bianco, and Stanley Jordan have used all fourths tuning.

Jazz guitarist Ralph Patt began using major third tuning in the mid-1960s as a means of simplifying atonal improvisation. The tuning allows access to the chromatic scale in a

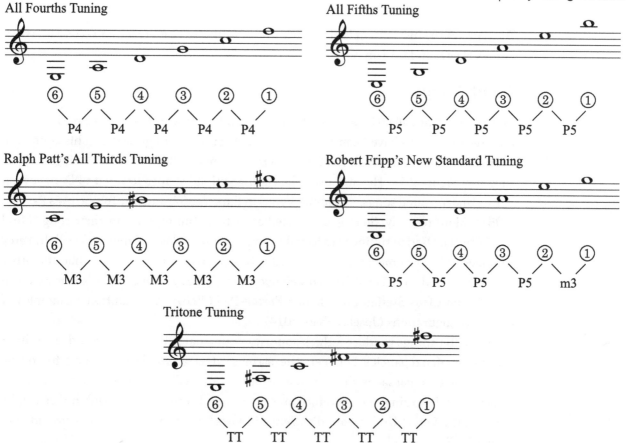

Figure 2.15
Common uniform tunings.

single position spanning four frets without the need for large stretches or hand shifts. Figure 2.15 shows Patt's major third tuning, which is rather high in register. Lower transpositions are also feasible.

All fifths tuning is sometimes referred to as "mandoguitar tuning" because the second, third, fourth, and fifth strings are tuned the same as those on the mandolin. It is true that all fifths tuning is somewhat impractical due to the high tension placed on the first string to reach B4—a fifth up from the E4 in E-standard. However, this pitch can be obtained using a very light gauge on the first string or by starting on a pitch lower than C2, although in the latter case the slack quality of the lower string may become a concern.

Robert Fripp introduced New Standard Tuning in the mid-1980s in response to the impracticality of all fifths tuning. Fripp's tuning relieves the tension on the first string by replacing the perfect fifth between the highest two strings with a minor third. New Standard Tuning is technically not a uniform tuning, nor do the open-string intervals correspond to "standard" tuning as that term has been used in this book. However, many guitarists use it in place of all fifths tuning because it is easier to achieve

Tritone tuning, also referred to as "augmented fourths tuning" or "diminished fifths tuning," has a number of unique properties worth examining. First, the interval of a tritone divides the octave in half; consequently, stacking tritones on successive strings results in the repetition of only two pitch classes, making it much easier to memorize and navigate notes on the fretboard. In addition, this tuning greatly simplifies the fingering for whole-tone scales and harmonic structures, and to a lesser extent, octatonic scales.

The range of the instrument is also expanded significantly, a mere minor second less than Fripp's New Standard Tuning.

Ostrich Tuning

In ostrich tunings all strings are set to the same pitch class, either as unisons or octaves. Lou Reed is said to have been the first to utilize such a configuration in his song "The Ostrich" (1964), from which the tuning derives its name. Reed tuned all strings to D, as shown in Figure 2.16. He later used the tuning with all strings lowered to D♭ in several Velvet Underground songs, including "Venus in Furs" (1967) and "All Tomorrow's Parties" (1967). More recently, Soundgarden used an ostrich tuning on E in their song "Mind Riot" (1991). Ostrich tunings are found in contemporary classical music as well. In Percy Grainger's *Shallow Brown* (1910) one guitar has all strings tuned to B♭, while the other has them tuned to F. Yuval Shaked's *einseitig ruhig* (1982), Klaus Huber's *Luminescenza* (1992), and Claus-Steffen Mahnkopf's *Kurtág-Duo* (2010) offer additional examples of ostrich configurations (Josel & Tsao, 2014).

Ostrich tunings produce a thick sonority with a natural chorus effect due to slight intonation discrepancies between the strings. It is a wonderful tuning for drone effects. Melodic passages that consist of notes fingered on a single string while the others are left to ring open produce an exotic sound resembling a tambura, as can be heard in the Velvet Underground's "Venus in Furs," an excerpt of which is provided in Figure 2.17.

Pure ostrich tuning is limited in terms of harmonic possibilities, as it requires large stretches for fingered intervals—seven frets to obtain a perfect fifth! Partial ostrich

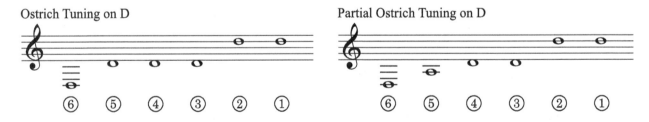

Figure 2.16
Full and partial ostrich tunings on D.

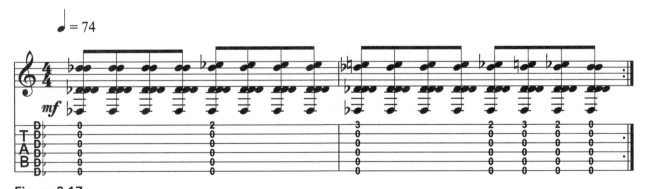

Figure 2.17
Excerpt from Velvet Underground's "Venus in Furs" (1967) in an ostrich tuning on D-flat (transcribed by the author) [▶ Media 2.8].

tunings in which many, but not all, of the strings are tuned to the same pitch class offer a remedy for such harmonic confinement. The introduction of one or two additional pitch classes is enough to enable harmonic variety. Figure 2.16 shows a partial ostrich tuning on D in which the fifth string is left at A2, resulting in a perfect fifth between the fifth and sixth strings. As such, the lower three strings resemble drop D tuning, making it easy to navigate harmonic changes with familiar fingerings while still retaining the rich, choral sonority that characterizes these tunings.

Sonic Youth makes use of partial ostrich tunings extensively. Some of these, such as A2-A2-E3-E3-A3-A4, focus on the doubling of two pitch classes and thus might be labeled "double-ostrich." Others, such as F♯2-F♯2-F♯3-F♯3-E3-B3, are re-entrant—the strings are not tuned successively from lower to higher pitches.

Specialized Tunings

Rather than employing established tunings, guitarists often create novel configurations for particular works, usually devised to meet certain musical demands. Carlo Domeniconi's *The Bridge of the Birds* (1998) employs an open pentatonic tuning with the strings tuned to the pitches C2-A2-D3-G3-A3-E4. The music pivots between A-minor pentatonic (A-C-D-E-G) and its relative C-major pentatonic (C-D-E-G-A) pitch sets. The tuning allows the player to make greater use of open strings and also to access many natural harmonics from the pentatonic pitch set. The opening section from the score is provided in Figure 2.18. In "Casida del Herido por el Agua"

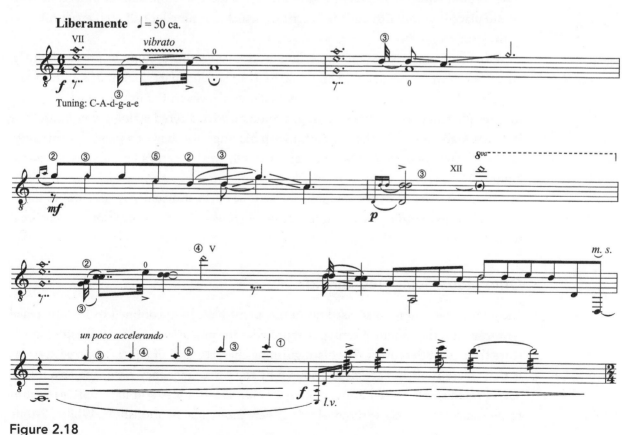

Figure 2.18

Opening section of Carlo Domeniconi's *The Bridge of the Birds* (1998) for guitar, employing a specialized pentatonic tuning (© 2010 by Edition Chanterelle im Allegra Musikverlag, Germany).

38

Figure 2.19

Excerpt from Mike Frengel's *And Then Romina* . . . , for electric guitar and electronics, using a specialized tuning to exploit unisons on different strings [▶ Media 2.9].

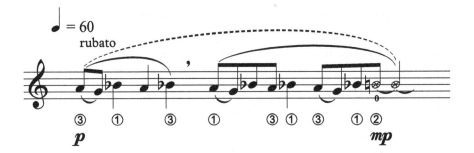

Figure 2.20

Some specialized tunings used by Pavement guitarist Stephen Malkmus.

Tuning
D2-A2-D3-A3-B3-E4
D#2-A#2-D3-F3-A#3-D4
D2-A2-D3-F3-B3-E4
C2-G2-D3-A3-B3-E4
D2-A2-C#3-G#3-B3-E4
E2-G#2-B2-E3-B3-E4
D2-E2-C3-G3-B3-E4

from George Crumb's *Songs, Drones, and Refrains of Death* (1968) the third string is raised to a G♯, which enables the G♯-natural harmonics found throughout the movement. In addition, the fifth string is lowered to a G and the sixth string is lowered to a D, which Crumb uses to create a repeated open-fourth ostinato. Finally, I use the tuning E2-F2-D3-G3-B3-G3 in my work *And Then Romina* . . . , for prepared electric guitar and electronics (2000). This configuration was motivated by an interest in exploring timbral variations between different fingerings of the same unison pitch. Sections of the work contain similar melodic materials on the unison-tuned first and third strings, an excerpt of which is shown in Figure 2.19. In a later section, similar unison materials are played on the fifth and sixth strings, which are tuned a half step apart for ease of fingering.

Pavement guitarist Stephen Malkmus uses specialized tunings predominantly, only a few of which are listed in Figure 2.20. For the most part, Malkmus's guitar writing is tonal, at times with chromatic extensions. However, the unusual chord voicing that results from the modified tuning, combined with altered string tensions and the fact that Malkmus plays electric guitar with his fingers in lieu of a pick, all contribute to the unique sonority of his style, and indeed, to the band's characteristic sound. Figure 2.21 offers an excerpt from the verse of "Stop Breathin" which uses the tuning D♯2-A♯2-D3-F3-A♯3-D4, providing an example of the unusual instrumental sonority that an alternate tuning can produce, even when used in the context of conventional tonal harmonies.

Other Equal Tempered Tunings

The alternative tunings discussed up to this point have been confined to 12-tone equal temperament, the system of tuning that provides the pitches used in most Western music since the mid-18th century. The distinguishing characteristic of equal tempered systems is that adjacent pitches are all distributed by the same frequency ratio, and as a result, sound equidistant. Such a uniform interval size allows scales and harmonic structures to be transposed freely without altering their intervallic relationships. While 12-tone

Figure 2.21
Excerpt from Pavement's "Stop Breathin," using a specialized tuning (transcribed by the author) [▶ Media 2.10].

equal temperament partitions the octave into twelve evenly spaced pitches, any number of divisions is possible. Today, 19-, 22-, 24-, 31-, 34- and 36-tone equal temperament systems have become recognized alternatives to the 12-tone standard. These tunings typically require a specialized guitar with more than twelve frets per octave, although composers have found clever ways to obtain some of them using two guitars with standard necks, each tuned differently so that their combined contributions yield the intended pitch collection.

19-Tone Equal Temperament

Joseph Yasser (1932) and Joel Mandelbaum (1961) are among the early advocates to highlight the benefits of 19-tone equal temperament. First, it contains a subset of pitches that approximate those found in 12-tone equal temperament, allowing works composed for 12-tone standard tuning to be played in the 19-tone system. Even more compelling, these 12 pitches are closer approximations to the just intonated natural intervals than they are in 12-tone equal temperament. Of course, 19-tone equal temperament also provides seven additional pitches. Finally, music in 19-tone equal temperament can be conveniently notated on a standard five-line staff using non-equivalent enharmonics where, for example, C♯ and D♭ are conceived as different pitches. The 19 distinct pitches in 19-tone equal temperament can thus be labeled as in Figure 2.22. Neil Haverstick's *Mysteries* (2006) for solo guitar utilizes 19-tone equal temperament (Fig. 2.23). The composer supplements the notation with tablature to facilitate reading, a useful practice when alternative tunings are employed.

C, C♯, D♭, D, D♯, E♭, E, E♯, F, F♯, G♭, G, G♯, A♭, A, A♯, B♭, B, B♯

Figure 2.22
One possible naming for the 19 distinct pitches in 19-tone equal temperament.

MYSTERIES
guitare frettée en tempérament égal à 19 tons
19 tone equal temperament fretted guitar

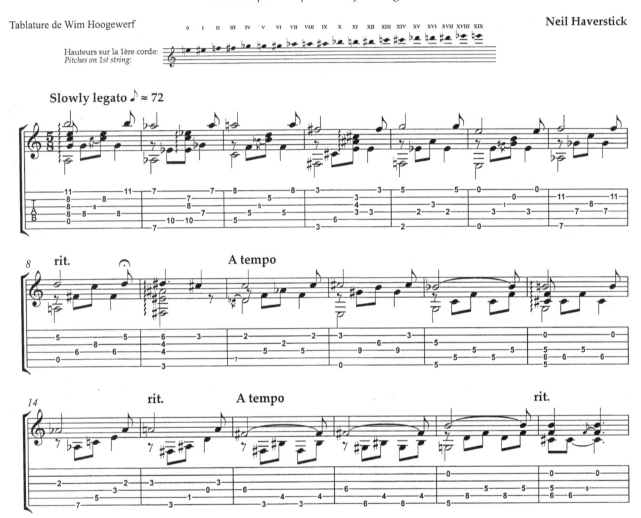

Figure 2.23
Excerpt from Neil Haverstick's *Mysteries* (2004) for solo guitar in 19-tone equal temperament
(Published by C.P.E.A., Christine Paquelet Edition Arts sarl, Paris).

24-Tone Equal Temperament

Quarter-tone tuning, or 24-tone equal temperament, is another established alternative to the standard 12 notes per octave. It contains the same 12 pitches found in 12-tone equal temperament, with additional quarter tones in between them. In *Let Newton Be* (2007), Daniel Hjorth creates an aggregate 24-tone equal tempered pitch collection by combining two instruments in standard tuning but a quarter tone apart. Hjorth reveals

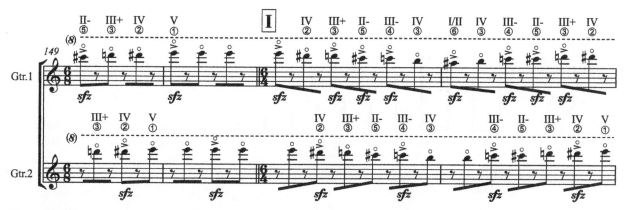

Figure 2.24

Excerpt from Daniel Hjorth's *Let Newton Be* (2007), for two guitars tuned a quarter tone apart.

Figure 2.25

Quarter-tone tuning used in Sven-David Sandström's *Surrounded* (1972).

the enlarged pitch palette in the first section of the work, with the guitars locked in a rhythmic hocket such that the individual notes on each instrument can be heard distinctly (Fig. 2.24). Through additive and subtractive processes a quarter-tone scale of ascending and descending natural harmonics gradually emerges that ultimately spans from written E6 down to B♭5. Curiously, both guitars drop the sixth string down to an E♭2, most likely to access the B♭ harmonic on that string—written as an A♯ in the score—needed to complete this chromatic descent. By contrast, the two guitars play in unison throughout the final section of the work, with their sounds fusing into a single, musically inseparable voice with an enharmonic, bell-like quality. In the notation, Hjorth writes the pitches as they would sound normally, even though one guitar is tuned a quarter tone higher.

Sven-David Sandström devised an interesting approach to quarter-tone tuning on a single guitar for his work *Surrounded* (1972). From E-standard, Sandström simply lowers the second and sixth strings by a quarter tone and raises the fourth string by a quarter tone (Fig. 2.25). The music can be easily read, due to its similarity to standard tuning, yet the quarter tones create an enharmonic quality quite distinct from that of standard tuning.

Just Intonation

Any sound comprises many frequencies that collectively make up its spectrum.[7] The spectral components in a periodic sound—that is, a sound perceived as a single tone—are arranged according to the harmonic series, whereby the frequencies progress upward in whole-number multiples of the lowest frequency, or fundamental. For instance, a tone

Figure 2.26

The first 10 harmonics of a periodic tone with a fundamental frequency of 110 Hz, corresponding to the musical pitch A2.

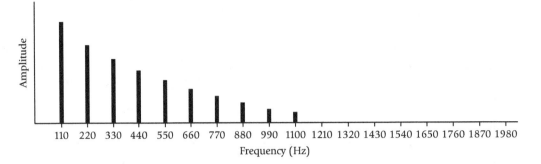

Figure 2.27

Harmonic alignment of two tones a just-intonated (3 2) fifth apart.

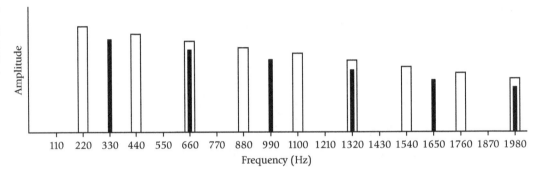

with a fundamental frequency of 110 Hz (A2) will have a second harmonic at 220 Hz, a third at 330 Hz, a fourth at 440 Hz, and so on (Fig. 2.26). The harmonic series might therefore be viewed as a series of intervals defined by the whole-number ratios 2:1, 3:2, 4:3, 5:4, 6:5, 7:6, 8:7, 9:8, 10:9, and so on. When the amplitudes of successive harmonics decline sufficiently, the spectra of a complex periodic sound fuse into a single percept at the fundamental. Put simply, the fundamental frequency represents the tone that we hear while the spectral components, along with their relative amplitudes, contribute to the timbre of that tone.[8]

Just intonated tunings are based on whole number ratios between pitches, similar to those found in the harmonic series. Such tunings can be traced back to Pythagoras (ca. 580–500 BCE), who studied musical intervals by dividing a string's length, quite logically, into whole number proportions such as halves, thirds, quarters, and so on. Just intonation is arguably the most intuitive method of tuning since it is mathematically simple and reflects the ratios found in the harmonics of the tones themselves. Indeed, the relationship between the ratios of the harmonic series and those that have been chosen in various tuning systems is curious to say the least. Gareth Loy (2006) points out that the most ubiquitous intervals used in Western tonal music—the octave, fifth, and third—are also the first three distinct pitch classes found in the harmonic series. As tunings evolved with Western music, most were based on just systems until equal temperament rose to prominence in the mid-eighteenth century.

Intervals tuned in whole number ratios sound particularly pure in comparison to their equal tempered approximations [▶ Media 2.11]. To understand why, one must consider how the spectra of the two tones interact. The harmonics of justly intonated tones often coincide perfectly, with the degree of coincidence relative to the ratio between the fundamentals. Figure 2.27 compares the lower-ordered spectra of two tones a just fifth (3:2) apart: the white bars represent the harmonics of A3 (220 Hz) and the black bars those of

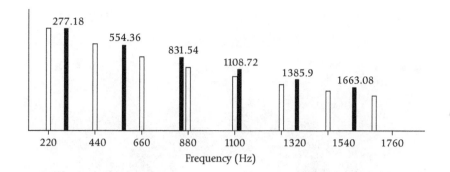

Figure 2.28
Spectral comparison of equal tempered major thirds.

Figure 2.29
The just intonated scale used in Lou Harrison's *Serenade for Guitar and Optional Percussion* (1978).

E4 (330 Hz). Notice that every other harmonic in the higher tone coincides with every third harmonic in the lower. Equally important, however, the harmonics that do not coincide are centered between components, far enough away to avoid beating.

In order to create an equal tempered system in which the intervals between successive pitches are perceived as equidistant, simple whole number ratios must be compromised. As a result, the sort of spectral coincidence seen in Figure 2.27 is lost. Figure 2.28 overlays the lower-ordered spectra of two tones forming an equal tempered major third, with the white bars representing the harmonics of A3 (220 Hz) and the black bars signifying those of C♯4 (277.18 Hz). Note that the fundamental frequencies do not form a simple whole-number ratio. Also notice that harmonics of the two tones often come close, but do not precisely coincide. This results in beating or spectral roughness, causing the equal-tempered intervals to sound less stable.

A drawback of just intonated systems is that they result in intervals of varying sizes between successive pitches. Consider the just intonated scale shown in Figure 2.29, used by Lou Harrison in his *Serenade for Guitar and Optional Percussion* (1978). This scale contains two different semitones: a larger interval (16/15) found between D-E♭ and B-C, and a smaller interval (25/24) between F-F♯. This poses problems when trying to transpose musical structures, as can be confirmed if we imagine transposing a hypothetical three-note motive D-E♭-F up to F-F♯-G♯. Although the half step-whole step pattern remains the same, the interval ratios are different. Modulation to a new key is equally problematic, as it would require retuning the instrument to the new tonic pitch, which is impractical during performance. Undoubtedly, it was the Classical era's concern for harmonic modulation that attracted composers and instrument builders to equal temperament. As concerns for modulation faded over the 20th century, many have advocated a return to the purity of intervals found in just intonation.

Fretting for Just Intonated Tunings

The fretboard on a standard guitar makes an exploration of just intonation problematic. While the open strings can be justly tuned, any fingered notes will be in equal tempered

Figure 2.30
Tolgahan
Çoğulu playing
his adjustable
microtonal guitar
with movable
fretlets (photo by
Başak Ulukőse).

proportions to others on the same string. To further complicate matters, the various interval sizes required cannot be obtained using straight frets that span the width of the neck and serve all six strings. To properly explore just intonation on the guitar requires a specially made fretboard in which the frets are positioned independently for each string. Fortunately, such fretboards exist. Luthier Walter Vogt developed his Fret-Mobile system in which every fretlet under each string could be adjusted by sliding it along a track built into the fretboard. Hervè R. Chouard's Finely Tempered guitars and Tolgahan Çoğulu's Adjustable Microtonal Guitar continue this practice today (Fig. 2.30).

Another option for exploring just intonation is to use a fretless neck or a steel guitar, both of which offer free intonation. Colored tape or chalk can be used to mark the position of pitches on the fretboard, offering a simple yet flexible visual guide for the player.

The scarcity of just intonated guitars has led some composers to devise ingenious methods of working with just, or close-to-just, systems using standard instruments. In Georg Hajdu's *RE:Guitar* (1999) the open strings of a standard guitar are tuned to the just ratios 5/4, 7/4, 9/4, 11/4, and 17/4, approximating the equal tempered pitches E-G♯-D-F♯-B♭-F. Hajdu evades the equal tempered fretboard by employing natural harmonics throughout the work, which provide additional tones in whole number ratios to the open strings. Figure 2.31 provides an excerpt from section one of the work, in which harmonics form a descending chromatic scale afforded by the initial tuning. In later passages notes are stopped on the fretboard, but always barred across a single fret to retain the just ratios between chord tones. Hadju notates the music using a separate staff for each string, leaving no doubt as to where the composer wants the notes to be played. The score also uses scordatura notation, with the pitches notated as if played in standard tuning and not at their sounding pitch. For clarity, a staff has been added to the figure using microtonal notation to show the sounding results.

Like many of James Tenney's works, the tonal content of *Septet* (1981/2000) is derived from the harmonic series. Scored for six standard electric guitars and electric bass, the composer cleverly retunes particular instruments in order to arrive at an aggregate pitch set that closely approximates the overtone series above an A fundamental, up

Figure 2.31
Excerpt from Georg
Hajdu's *RE:Guitar*
(1999), for just-
intonated guitar
(the lower staff
was added by
the author)
[▶ Media 2.12].

to the 12th harmonic. Figure 2.32 shows the first 12 harmonics of A2, along with their
cent deviations from equal temperament. In *Septet,* the bass guitar and guitars one, four,
and five are tuned to E-standard and contribute pitches A, E, and B, which represent
harmonics 1, 2, 3, 4, 6, 8, 9, and 12 within four cents of accuracy. Guitar two provides
the 5th and 10th harmonics (C♯), in the harmonic series, are 14 cents flat of an equal
tempered major third. Tenney adapts to this by downtuning the guitar by 14 cents so
that the pitches are precisely tuned to the harmonics they represent. In a similar manner, guitar three supplies the 11th harmonic (D♯) and is lowered 49 cents while guitar
six provides the seventh harmonic (G) and is lowered 31 cents. In the spirit of composer
Henry Cowell, the same harmonic series proportions govern the rhythmic organization,
with the tuplet divisions corresponding to the harmonic sounded on each instrument.
Figure 2.33 shows an excerpt from Section III of *Septet.*

Dynamic Tuning Systems

A number of composers have called for changes to the tuning of the guitar over the course
of a work, referred to here as dynamic tuning. We find examples of composers modifying
the tuning mid-piece for practical reasons, as in the case of George Crumb's *Songs, Drones,
and Refrains of Death* (1968), where the guitar is silently retuned to facilitate certain harmonics in the final movement. More extraordinary are works in which the modification
of the tuning itself constitutes a primary compositional concern.

Much of Larry Polansky's music deals with issues of intonation, and his work *II—V—I*
(1997) is a vivid example of dynamic tuning. In essence, the piece is a gradual modulation
between three harmonic series with fundamental frequencies corresponding to the scale
degrees indicated in the title. With the fundamentals always on the sixth string, the others are tuned to particular harmonics of each series. The player improvises on these notes
and, over time, slowly retunes to a different pitch set corresponding to the harmonic series
of the next fundamental. Polansky refers to the concurrent sounding of different intonations

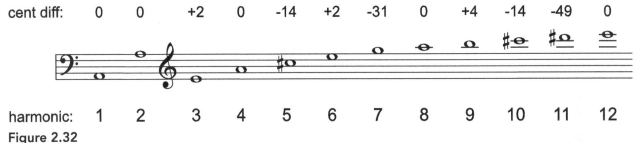

Figure 2.32
The harmonic series based on an A fundamental, which James Tenney uses as the source for the tonal content in his *Septet*.

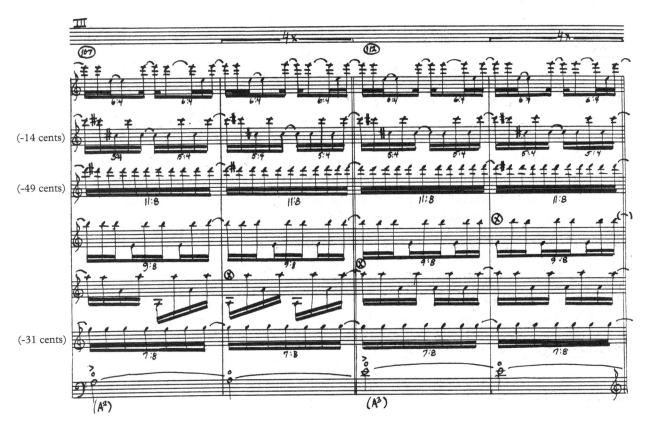

Figure 2.33
Excerpt from section III of James Tenney's *Septet* (1981/2000). The cent deviations from equal temperament on the left were added by the author (© Sonic Arts Editions. Used by permission of Smith Publications, 54 Lent Rd. Sharon, VT, 05065, USA).

as heterophonic tuning, which is heard in II—V—I when the player is in the process of modulating between two series. The composer provides multiple versions of the work: two for solo guitar and one for two guitars. The text-based score for solo guitar version B is shown in Figure 2.34. Subscripts are used to specify the harmonic number that the pitch represents and arrows indicate the direction of deviation from equal temperament. Giacomo Fiore (2013) provides a robust account of this and other just intonated works by Polansky. Figure 2.35, taken from Fiore, illustrates the progression in II—V—I for solo guitar version B in detail.

Mark Applebaum's *DNA* (2004) for solo guitar unfolds as a series of variations based on a roughly 78-second theme. Applebaum employs two variation techniques in the work. First, each of the seven variations is a distinct excerpt—roughly 53 seconds—from the main theme. Second, each variation is in a different tuning. Starting in standard tuning,

(II)	(V)	(I)	
D↓₇	E₃	F#₅	(1ˢᵗ string)
C#↓₃	C#₅	Bb↑₁₃	
G#₅	F↑₁₃	Ab↓₁₁	
Bb↓₁₁	Eb↓₁₁	C↓₇	
G#₅	G↓₇	A₃	
E₁	A₁	D₁	(6ᵗʰ string)

Figure 2.34

Score for Larry Polansky's *II—V—I* (version B). The subscript indicates the harmonic number (© Larry Polansky).

Figure 2.35

Fiore's detailed depiction of the intonation modulations in Larry Polansky's *II—V—I*, version B (Engraving by Giacomo Fiore).

each variation ends with a "tuning coda" in which one string is audibly retuned. The subsequent section is played with the same fingering—greatly simplifying performance—while the modified tuning alters the sounding result. This process continues until the strings are tuned to C2-A#2-C#3-A3-C4-D#4. Figure 2.36 shows section A from the score, which begins in E-standard and includes the tuning coda at the end.

Contrary to the previous examples of dynamic tuning, Clarence Barlow's *. . . Until . . . Version 7* (1981) for guitar seems to modulate tuning over the duration of the piece without actually making adjustments to any of the string tensions. Strings 6, 4, and 2 are tuned to A1, E3, and C4, while strings 5, 3, and 1 are tuned to those same pitches, but raised a septimal quarter tone, as indicated by the arrows in Figure 2.37. The septimal quarter tone has a ratio of 36:35 (or 48.77 cents) and, in this particular case, approximates the difference between the seventh harmonic on the A string and the third harmonic on the C string. The piece begins with a 17-note series made of natural harmonics played entirely on the strings in standard tuning, with the septimal quarter tone already presenting itself in the difference between the G on the second string and the quarter tone-raised G on the sixth string. The series is repeated, each time substituting one note of the original for the same pitch on a raised string. Harmonically, this process creates an arch trajectory that begins consonant, gradually becoming more dissonant as the weight of both tunings is felt concurrently, and then returning to consonance toward the end of the piece, but now a septimal quarter tone higher. Excerpts from the beginning, middle, and end of the score are provided in Figure 2.38. Note that the composer uses a specialized tablature system to facilitate reading of the harmonics.

Notating Music in Alternative Tunings

Ideally, a score should indicate both the actions necessary to realize the work and the sounding result of those actions. With the relocation of pitches on the fretboard caused by alternative tunings, satisfying both of these goals in notation is challenging. Transpositions of

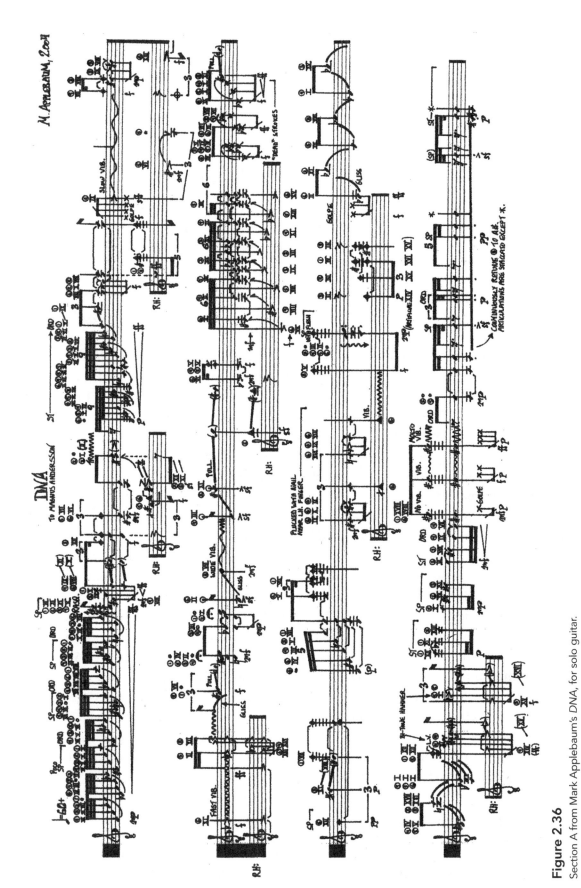

Figure 2.36

Section A from Mark Applebaum's *DNA*, for solo guitar.

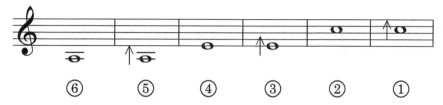

Figure 2.37
Tuning for Clarence Barlow's ... *Until* ... *Version 7* (1981). Arrows indicate that the pitch is raised a septimal quarter tone.

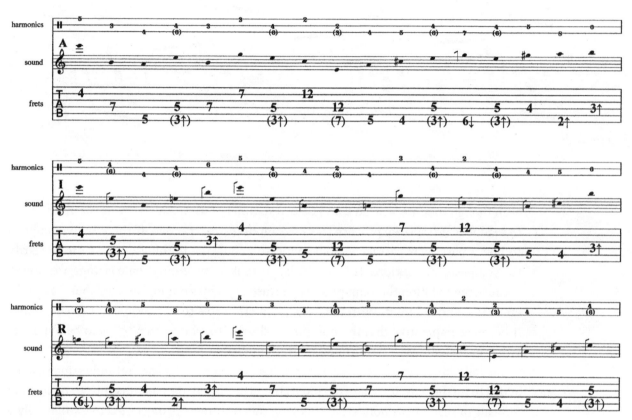

Figure 2.38
Three excerpts from Clarence Barlow's ... *Until* ... *Version 7* (1981) (© cbarlow).

standard tuning are easy enough to read because the finger patterns do not change. Even drop tunings can be fairly clear since only one or two strings deviate from the open-string intervals found in standard tunings. However, more radical tunings can leave even the best of guitarists stumbling around the fretboard in search of the correct pitches.

To facilitate readability, works in alternative tunings often employ scordatura notation, in which the tuning is indicated at the start of the score but the written pitches represent those that would sound if the instrument were tuned to E-standard. In other words, the score details the actions that must be taken to realize the music at the expense of the sounding results. Scordatura notation was used in a few of the works discussed in this chapter, including Applebaum's *DNA* (Fig. 2.36), Domeniconi's *Koyunbaba* (Fig. 2.11), Hadju's *RE:Guitar* (Fig. 2.31), and Henry Worrall's *Sebastopol*. Note that earlier score examples from *Sebastopol* were transposed to sounding pitch by the author for clarity. The excerpt in Figure 2.39 is true to the published score and uses scordatura notation. For example, in the first measure, the two notes on the first beat will sound D and F♯,

Tune the Guitar thus:  and finger as if tuned in the ordinary manner.

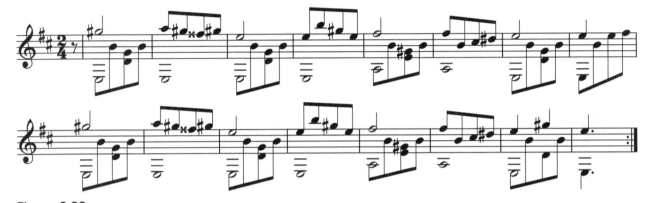

Figure 2.39
Opening measures of Henry Worrall's *Sebastopol* in open D tuning using scordatura notation (reproduced from the original score by the author).

even though they are written E and G♯. Scordatura notation makes the music much easier to read, but it is a risky practice from a composer's perspective. If there is any doubt as to how a particular passage should sound there may be nothing in the score to clarify the composer's intentions. It is particularly problematic if only some strings are altered because the notation then comprises a mixture of pitches notated as they sound and others that sound different. With the same pitch often able to be played on different strings it becomes imperative that the notation is clear as to where the pitch is to be obtained, either by including the string number, fret number, or both.

If sounding pitches are preferred in the score, then string and fret indications can be added to further specify where the pitch should be played. Because it is considerably more difficult to read music notated in this way, this technique is most effective when only a limited number of strings are modified. In such cases, fret indications only need to be given for pitches that are to be played on the alternatively tuned strings.

Carlo Domeniconi includes both "real" (i.e., sounding) and "scordatura" staves in the score for *Koyunbaba* (Fig. 2.11). This is a great option because it provides both an easily readable staff and a staff documenting the expected sounding result. It does, however, occupy a fair amount of space on the page, which ultimately increases the number of page turns required during performance. Given that today's notation software tools make it possible to produce individual parts from a main score with minimal effort, the best practice may be to have two scores: one that includes both sounding and scordatura staves and another with just the scordatura staff, the latter to be used for performance.

Similar to the two-staff model described above, the scordatura staff could be replaced with a tablature staff that indicates the fingerings. Neil Haverstick includes a tablature staff in *Mysteries* (Fig. 2.23) and I have used tablature to accompany scordatura notation in many of the examples in this chapter. While tablature may be great for indicating string and fret positions, it is limited in its ability to convey other aspects of notation. For this reason it can be difficult to reduce a score to a tab-only version for performance.

3

Notation Basics

Range

The guitar is a transposing instrument, sounding an octave lower than written. Despite its relatively low range, music for the instrument is notated on a standard five-line staff in the treble clef. It is rare to find guitar music employing any other clef.[1] Figure 3.1 shows the written and sounding ranges for 19-, 20-, and 22-fret guitars in E-standard tuning, corresponding to typical classical, steel string acoustic, and electric instruments, respectively. Figure 3.2 provides ranges per string. Both figures refer to the ranges of fretted strings. Higher pitches can certainly be obtained through techniques such as harmonics, string bends, or use of a slide above the fretboard.

Strings, Frets, and Fingerings

Notational conventions for specifying strings, frets, and fingerings can be used to clarify precisely how music written for the guitar should be performed. These details are not necessary, and opinions vary among players as to their usefulness. While they can certainly facilitate reading, they can just as easily make the music more difficult to perform if done poorly. Many players will simply ignore them if other approaches are deemed more suitable to their playing style. Composers who do not play the instrument themselves would be wise to seek advice from a guitarist before including such indications. An overall "less-is-better" approach to notation may prove more effective where strings, frets, and fingerings are concerned. Reserving such performance details for situations where it really matters adds weight to the directive and players are more likely to adhere to it.

Strings

The strings of the guitar are numbered 1 to 6 from high to low and are designated in notation by circled numbers placed above or below the staff (Fig. 3.2). The strings have overlapping ranges, and consequently, most pitches on the guitar can be obtained in more than one way. A string indication is usually all that is required to specify where a particular note should be played. After all, there will only be one option on any given string. Good reasons

Figure 3.1

Ranges for standard nylon string, steel string acoustic, and electric instruments.

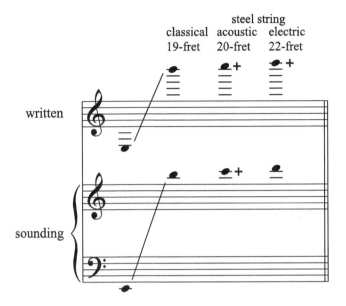

Figure 3.2

Ranges for the individual strings of the 19-, 20-, and 22-fret guitars.

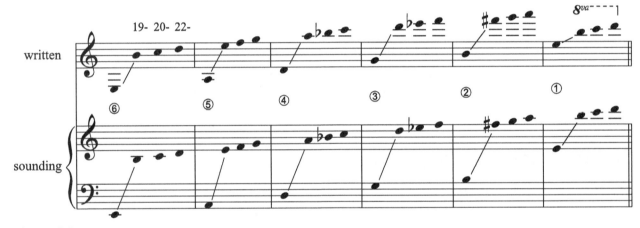

Figure 3.3

Excerpt from Peter Maxwell Davies's *Lullaby* (1978).

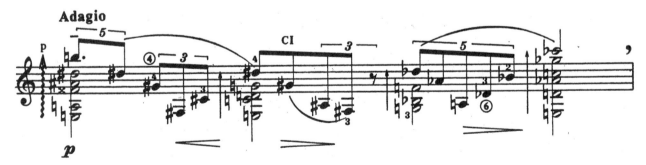

to provide them include (1) to achieve a particular timbral quality; (2) to clarify tricky passages; (3) when alternative tunings are employed, since the pitches on the fretboard are no longer where one expects them to be; (4) in the notation of harmonics; (5) when notating extended techniques or instrumental preparations. Notice how sparingly string directives are given in Figure 3.3, from Peter Maxwell Davies's *Lullaby* (1978).

Frets

Fret indications are notated using capitalized roman numerals. In most cases they are unnecessary; a string indication is both sufficient and preferable. There are, however, good reasons to provide fret indications, including (1) when alternative tunings are used, since the notes are no longer where the performer expects them to be on the fretboard; (2) in certain harmonic notations; (3) when notating barré; (4) when notating extended techniques or instrumental preparations.

Fingerings

It is standard practice to label the fingers on the left hand using the plain text numbers 1, 2, 3, and 4 for the index, middle, ring, and little fingers, respectively (Fig. 3.4). The capital letter "T" can be used for the left hand thumb in the rare instances in which it is used to stop a string. While open strings can be designated with a string indication, it is more common to use the number 0, referring to the 0th fret or "no fingers."[2] A dash before a left hand fingering, such as "-4," indicates that the player should continue holding the finger in position from a previous note or chord. Angled dashes imply that the note should be obtained by silently sliding the finger from a previous position along the string. This notation should not be confused with a glissando or portamento, in which the slide from one position to another is heard. Left hand fingerings are prevalent in guitar notation and are particularly effective when used to clarify a tricky passage or when an open string is intended. As with string indications, they are not required throughout a score, and limiting their use to instances where they are truly helpful gives the instruction greater import.

The lower case letters *p, i, m, a,* and *c* are used to refer to the digits on the right hand, derived from the Spanish words pulgar, indicio, medio, anular, and chiquito, respectively. While the chiquito finger is used on rare occasion, it is generally neglected in fingerstyles and should be avoided unless absolutely necessary. Right hand fingerings are less prevalent than those of the left hand in traditional guitar notation. When they are included, it is typically to clarify a tricky passage or for a particular timbral effect. For instance, the "*p*" in the first chord of Figure 3.3 serves to enforce a downstroke with the flesh of the thumb for a duller sound. Right hand finger indications can become more crucial in the context of unorthodox techniques.

Tablature

As an alternative to standard notation, music for the guitar can be written using tablature, a system applied to many fretted instruments that dates back to the Middle Ages. Modern guitar tablature uses a six-line staff with each line representing a different string. Numbers are placed directly on the lines to indicate the fret at which the string

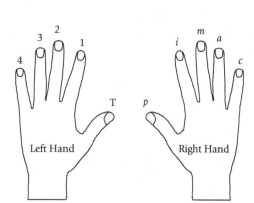

Figure 3.4

Standard labels used to indicate fingers on the left and right hands in notation.

should be stopped (Fig. 3.5). The principal advantage of tablature is that it is explicit as to what strings and frets should be used to obtain the notes—a specificity that requires additional effort using standard notation. However, tablature focuses solely on the actions involved in realizing a performance at the expense of the sounding results. It can be difficult to look at tablature and get a sense of what the music should sound like, or more important, to know if what is being produced is what the composer intended.

Tablature can be highly effective in clarifying the mechanics of a performance when used as a supplement to standard notation. This is particularly true when alternative tunings or extended techniques are employed since the sounding results are often different from those that would be expected if the instrument were tuned and played in the normal manner. Combined with standard notation, tablature can be limited to finger movements that result in audible changes to the instrument's sound, such as newly attacked pitches, slurs, taps, and glissandi. In Figure 3.5, rhythms, ties, articulation markings, and fingerings are omitted from the tablature because they are provided in the standard notation staff above. All of these elements, however, could be included in tablature if it were to stand alone, as shown in Figure 3.6.[3] Note, however, that the rhythmic system used in tablature is not as sophisticated as that found in standard notation. For instance, in the absence of note heads, quarter notes and half notes look the same, as can be seen in the lower voice in Figure 3.6.

Figure 3.5

Tablature that supplements standard notation is often limited to finger movements of the left hand that affect change in the instrument's output.

Figure 3.6

Tablature with rhythm and articulation markings.

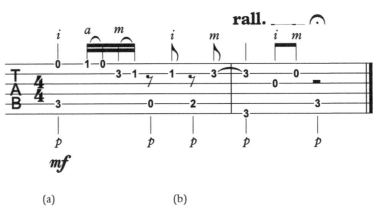

Figure 3.7

Ligado notation: (a) ascending and descending; (b) spanning several notes.

Ligado

Smoothness of a musical line can be attained through the use of ligado, also referred to as hammer-ons and pull-offs in popular music parlance. An ascending ligado is achieved by attacking a string in the normal manner and then hammering down on the same string with a left hand finger at a higher fret. A descending ligado is performed by stopping a string with the left hand and pulling the finger off in a plucking motion to sound a lower pitch. Guitarists typically blend a substantial amount of ligado into their playing, as attacking every note with the right hand runs the risk of sounding overly mechanical.

Slurs are used to denote ligado in guitar notation (Fig. 3.7a). It is not uncommon for performers to play several ligado notes in succession (Fig. 3.7b). It is important to consider that ligado techniques are restricted to pitches on the same string, and unless an open string is involved, limited to a range that the hand can span—roughly four or five frets in the lower positions. Notation absent of any slur markings will likely be played with ligado at the performer's discretion unless otherwise indicated.

Stroke Direction

Stroke direction refers to the angle at which a string is attacked. A downstroke hits the string from above in a motion toward the floor, while an upstroke engages the string in an upward direction from below. As a general rule, downstrokes sound heavier than upstrokes, making them a sensible choice for downbeats or accented events, although this tendency can be countered with playing technique. Figure 3.8a shows the standard stroke direction symbols, with downstrokes placed on the downbeats and upstrokes on the upbeats.

Pick players alternate stroke direction freely on all strings, usually for economy of hand movement more than anything else. The downstroke is customary at slower tempos, but alternate picking eventually becomes necessary as speed increases. In many situations, a careful consideration of stroke directions can minimize the motion required by the right hand. Figures 3.8b and 3.8c illustrate two such situations.

Stroke direction acquires greater significance in the context of fingerstyle techniques. When attacking individual strings with the fingers the natural tendency is to pull the digits inward toward the palm with each stroke. As a consequence, the thumb most naturally engages the strings with downstrokes while the other fingers employ upstrokes. Attacking a string in a direction contrary to the digit's natural tendency is

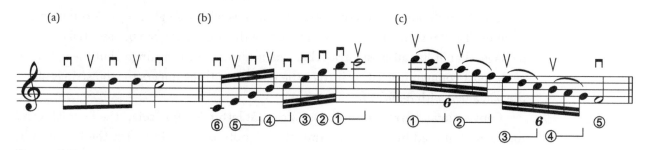

Figure 3.8
The use of particular stroke directions to minimize right hand movement in (a) scalar motion; (b) arpeggios; (c) descending ligado.

a substantially different technique, both in terms of finger movement and because the string is now struck with the topside of the nail. While this is a commonly employed method of strumming the strings, stroke directions contrary to the natural finger movements are rarely employed on individual notes as they can make the music awkward to perform. Indeed, the natural tendencies for finger movement are so strong that, in most cases, stroke direction is implied in right hand fingering and need not be notated explicitly.

Strumming and Strum Direction

A strum is executed by brushing a finger or plectrum across multiple strings in a single directed motion. Strums can be performed as downstrokes or upstrokes with considerable difference in sonority: downstrokes tend to place more emphasis on the lower strings, while upstroke strums accentuate the higher strings. When a pick is used there is no need to explain that a chord should be strummed, as that is the normal method of playing notes simultaneously.[4] Strumming indication may still be valuable to enforce particular patterns or to distinguish between an arpeggiated strum and a more brisk one. In fingerstyles, however, chords of four or fewer notes can also be plucked by attacking the individual strings with separate fingers simultaneously. Additional indications are therefore required to differentiate a strummed chord from one that is plucked.

Arrows are typically used to designate a strum. The orientation of the arrow refers to the order in which the chord tones should be attacked as they appear on the staff, which is inversely related to the direction of the hand movement across the strings. Hence, an upward arrow indicates a downstroke, while a downward arrow represents an upstroke. A wavy arrow denotes a slower, arpeggiated strum, while a straight arrow conveys that the strumming motion should be swift so that the notes of the chord sound more or less simultaneously. Downstroke strums are often played with the fingers using the topside of the nail for a crisper sound. Alternatively, they can be played with the flesh of the thumb for a duller and darker sonority. These distinctions are made in notation using a combination of stroke direction and right hand fingerings. For instance, the chord at the start of Figure 3.3 is arpeggiated in a downstroke with the thumb. The latter three chords in the same example are more briskly strummed.

Barré

Barré is the technique of stopping multiple strings with a single finger. A common element of all guitar styles, it makes efficient use of the fingers and can be essential for many passages that utilize all six strings. A bar can be formed with any finger, but the index finger is most commonly used, as it frees the remaining three fingers to stop strings above the bar, albeit with reduced facility.

Conventional barré notation uses a capital letter "C" for "ceja," the Spanish word for barré, followed by a roman numeral to denote the fret in which the bar is to be

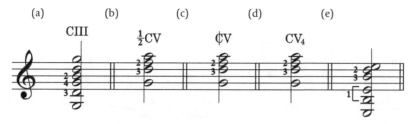

Figure 3.9

Barré notation: (a) full barré at the third fret; (b) half-barré at the fifth fret, although four strings are actually stopped; (c) alternate half-barré at the fifth fret; (d) partial barré using subscript to denote the number of strings stopped; (e) an internal barré on the fourth and fifth strings.

placed. A distinction is made between a full barré, indicated by a "C" (Fig. 3.9a), and a half barré, indicated as "$\frac{1}{2}$C" (Fig. 3.9b) or "¢" (Fig. 3.9c). The descriptors "full" and "half" should not be taken literally; a passage requiring a bar across five strings may be notated as a full barré, while a two- or four-string barré may be notated as a half barré. Strictly speaking, it would be more accurate to view any barré involving fewer than six strings as a partial barré. A more precise approach

Figure 3.10

Notation for an A-shape double bar chord.

to barré notation uses a subscript or superscript number appended to the fret indication to denote the number of strings under the bar, always starting with the first. For example, in Figure 3.9d, the "CV_4" denotes a partial bar placed at the fifth fret over strings 1 through 4 with the inner chord tones stopped at frets above the bar with fingers 2 and 3.

It is also possible to place a partial barré over consecutive inner strings while leaving the outer strings unaffected. Such an internal barré is notated with vertical brackets. In Figure 3.9e only the fourth and fifth strings are stopped with the first finger. It can be quite difficult for a performer to let the string immediately under an internal bar ring unobstructed. In the figure, notice that the B on the third string is fingered above the bar, a more reasonable request so long as the pitch is within a few frets.

Some chord shapes require that both the first and third fingers form bars across strings. The most common of these is the A-shape barré, which yields a major chord with the root on the fifth string. Figure 3.10 shows it notated on a traditional staff using an internal barré for the third finger.

Hinge Barré

Hinge barré is a technique in which the index finger is placed in the bar position but allowed to pivot on an outer string such that it can be lifted off of the others. It is typically employed to simplify an otherwise complicated fingering. Figure 3.11 provides an excerpt from Mauro Giuliani's *Sonatine* Op. 71 in which the hinge is on the tip of the finger, allowing higher strings to sound open. The technique can also be employed at the bottom of the finger. It can be denoted using standard barré

Figure 3.11

Notation for hinge barré from Mauro Giuliani's *Sonatine* Op. 71, Nr. 2 (transcribed by the author).

Figure 3.12

Cross-fret barré notation.

notation with the word "hinge" included. If more precision is needed, a dotted horizontal line could be defined as a hinged bar and a solid line as a fully depressed bar, as in Figure 3.11.

Cross-Fret Barré

A barring finger is usually confined to a single fret. However, it is possible to position the bar diagonally so that either the highest or lowest string is stopped in an adjacent fret. Christopher Parkening's fingering of J. S. Bach's "Sheep May Safely Graze" (1973) employs several cross-fret barré, always with the bottom portion of the index finger in the lower fret and the tip in the adjacent upper fret. He notates it by indicating both frets with roman numerals, similar to Figure. 3.12.

Left Hand Thumb over Neck

While technically not barré, the left hand thumb can be wrapped over the top of the fretboard so that it stops the sixth string, serving a similar function. Early blues guitarists used this technique often in place of a barré because it frees the first finger for melodic activity on the higher strings. Indeed, many fingerstyle blues songs are considerably more difficult, if not impossible, using a proper barré; take "My Creole Belle" (1963) by Mississippi John Hurt, for example (Fig. 3.13).

Polyphonic Notation

The guitar is a polyphonic instrument capable of sounding several pitches or distinct voices simultaneously. However, such capabilities are limited compared to many other polyphonic instruments such as the piano, harp, or marimba. This is because the guitar is based on a particularly economic design in which many pitches are obtained from a single string by stopping it at various locations. A wealth of articulations is afforded by this design, but it does impose limitations on the polyphonic capabilities of the instrument. For instance, there are pitches in the lowest register of the guitar's range that cannot be sounded together since they are only obtainable on a single string. Likewise, notes that share a string cannot be sustained, as each subsequent note necessarily interrupts the previous one. As polyphonic demands increase, these peculiarities can make the music awkward, if not impossible, to perform on the instrument. In his *Treatise on Modern Instrumentation and*

* (T) = L.H. thumb over the neck

Figure 3.13
Thumb over the neck in "My Creole Belle" by Mississippi John Hurt (transcribed by the author). [▶ Media 3.1].

Figure 3.14
Voices notated in Nikita Koshkin's *Da Capo 24 Easy Pieces, II. Melody* (© 2001. Editions Orphée).

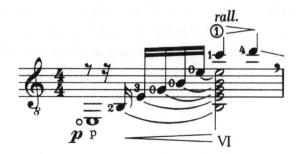

Figure 3.15
Ties used to indicate sustained notes of an arpeggiated chord in Hans Werner Henze's *Royal Winter Music, Second Sonata, I. Sir Andrew Aguecheek* (1983).

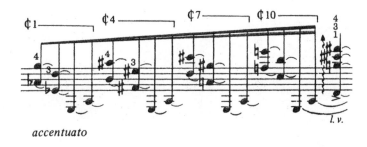

Figure 3.16
Excerpt from Alberto Ginastera's *Sonata for Guitar* (1978), showing the use of open-ended ties to signify sustained notes.

Orchestration (1855), Hector Berlioz vehemently cautions composers of the dangers of writing polyphonically for the guitar if they are not guitarists themselves. It is always advisable to consult a fingering chart or guitarist to ensure that the music is manageable.

The notation of pitches that are to be held over others can quickly lead to a highly cluttered score that appears more complex on paper than it actually is to perform. Sustained notes can be handled in a number of ways that minimize visual complexity on the page. The most suitable notational approach for a particular passage is usually to be found in the music itself. If the music contains distinct voices that are, to some degree, separated by register, then standard voicing might be applied. Figure 3.14 from Nikita Koshkin's *Da Capo: 24 Easy Pieces* (2001) offers an example.

In passages that are not voiced, ties may be used to connect note heads over extended distances irrespective of the durational value of the notes themselves, as can be seen in Figure 3.15 from Hans Werner Henze's *Royal Winter Music*'s "Sir Andrew Aguecheek" (1983). While this marks a break from standard conventions of notation, it makes clear the duration of the sustained notes, despite the absence of inner note values in the tie, and can be highly effective in simplifying the score. However, ties should not intersect other note heads or stems, and as a consequence, this notational approach is often not an option.

A final method of notating sustained notes is to use an open-ended tie extending from the note head along with the plain text "let vibrate," abbreviated "l.v." Figure 3.16 offers an example from Alberto Ginastera's *Sonata for Guitar* (1978). Although Ginastera omits the plain text, it is good practice to include the "*l.v.*" indication in the first occurrence of it in the piece. While tidy, this notation is imprecise in its specification of how long the notes should be held. Performers will typically hold them for as long as is reasonable. Jacques Charpentier writes "*L.V. al fine*" at cadential points in Etude No. 1 (1974) to convey that the strings should be allowed to vibrate until the sound dies away naturally.

Performance Techniques

Attacking the Strings

The strings of the guitar are normally set into motion with the right hand, either using the fingers or a pick. To a large extent, the choice falls along stylistic lines: fingers are the norm for classical and many folk genres while picks are more common to popular music. Instrument design factors in as well. The wide-spaced, soft nylon strings of the classical guitar are ideal for fingerstyles, whereas the closer string spacing found on most steel string guitars is well suited for strumming.[1] These are, of course, merely generalizations. In practice, right hand techniques, guitar designs, and musical genres are mixed freely. In particular, fingers are frequently employed on steel string instruments, and to a lesser extent, picks are employed on nylon string instruments.[2]

Moving beyond convention, almost any found object can be used to attack the strings. Objects that are not inherently pick-like are of particular interest because they demand reconsideration of the performance practice and often lead to novel sounding materials. This chapter explores methods of attacking the strings that range from the conventional to those that are more esoteric, including a variety of alternative plectra, some of which are manufactured for the guitar while others are adapted for musical purposes.

Fingerstyles

The guitar reaches its greatest polyphonic potential when played with the fingers, principally because non-adjacent strings can be plucked simultaneously. The ability to maintain multiple independent voices with the fingers is particularly advantageous in solo contexts, as the instrument can provide both thematic and supportive parts. It would be erroneous, however, to view fingerstyles as a single, unified approach. Quite to the contrary, there are diverse techniques within musical styles and substantially different techniques employed across genres. For instance, classical guitarists hold the hand upright so that the fingers are perpendicular to the strings and use *p, i, m,* and *a* more-or-less equally to engage the strings. By contrast, country blues players often anchor the hand to the soundboard below the strings with fingers *a* and *c*.[3] While this hand position limits the usable fingers to *p, i,* and *m,* it affords the thumb greater power and stability, which facilitates the driving bass lines that permeate the music. Moreover, it allows the side of the palm to rest against the lower strings near the bridge, a common damping technique employed on the steel string instrument. Although it is not always necessary for notation to convey the particulars of finger techniques, it is important for composers to recognize the wide-ranging variance in right hand techniques and their conventional pairing with musical styles. A player proficient in one style may not be so adept at techniques associated with another. In this regard, the importance of choosing an appropriate player for a given work cannot be overstressed.

Pluck Surfaces

Strings can be attacked using the nails or the flesh of the fingertips, resulting in distinct timbres. As a general rule, nails sound bright and crisp, while flesh produces a softer, duller tone with a less pronounced attack. The terms "nails" or "flesh" can be placed above or below the staff to indicate how the strings should be plucked. In *Las Seis Cuerdas* (1963), Alvaros Company goes further by developing a collection of symbols that describe precisely how the fingers should engage the strings. Each symbol denotes whether the nail or flesh should be used, as well as the angle and location of the finger along the string (Fig. 4.1).

Alzapua and Rasgueado

Flamenco guitar players incorporate a variety of idiosyncratic techniques that are quite distinct from those typically found in classical literature, despite the similarities of the instruments. Two such techniques that have migrated to contemporary classical music are alzapua and rasgueado, both of which are primarily employed on nylon strings.

Alzapua is a technique in which the thumb attacks the strings in alternating downstrokes and upstrokes, the latter using the topside of the nail. Single strings and groups of strings can be targeted and mixed freely to create complex rhythmic accompaniment patterns as well as melodic motion. Alzapua can be notated by combining stroke directions with a "*p*" finger indication (Fig. 4.2a).

Rasgueado is a stylized strumming technique in which the player cycles through digits in a rapid pattern to produce an aggressive, tremolo-like repetition of a chord or other sounding material. The manner of executing rasgueado involves starting with the hand

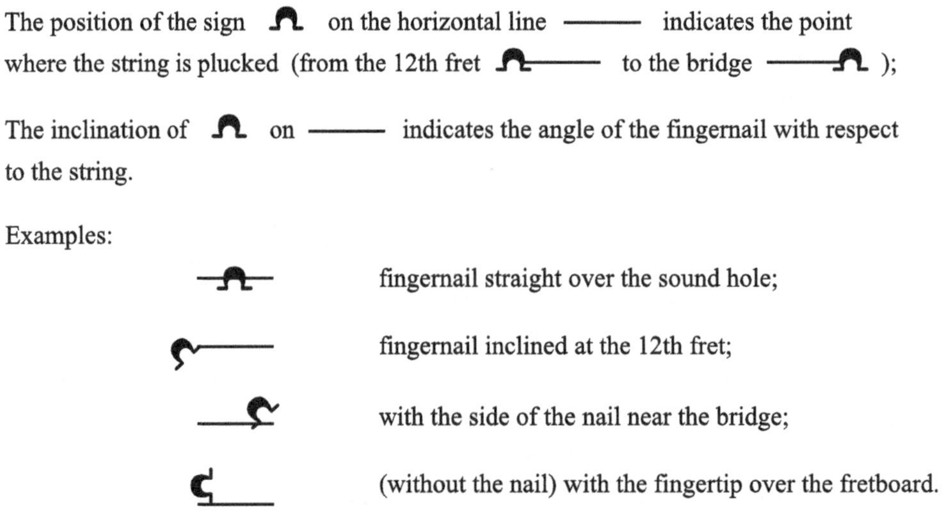

Figure 4.1
Detailed right hand finger indications in Alvaros Company's *Las Seis Cuerdas* (1963) (translated and reproduced by the author) (© Sugarmusic s.p.a., Edizioni Suvini Zerboni).

The position of the sign 🜊 on the horizontal line ——— indicates the point where the string is plucked (from the 12th fret 🜊——— to the bridge ———🜊);

The inclination of 🜊 on ——— indicates the angle of the fingernail with respect to the string.

Examples:

———🜊——— fingernail straight over the sound hole;

🜊——— fingernail inclined at the 12th fret;

———🜊 with the side of the nail near the bridge;

🜊——— (without the nail) with the fingertip over the fretboard.

closed so that each finger is slightly tucked behind the next and then flicking them, one at a time, against the strings, as if opening the hand. The technique demands that the fingers strike the strings with the topside of the nails in a downward direction contrary to their natural tendencies. The player is able to cycle through the digits repeatedly—*c, a, m,* and *i,* for example—to produce a vibrant and rhythmically charged strumming effect. Rasgueado is notated using stroke direction arrows along with the text "rasg." placed above the staff (Fig. 4.2b). Fingerings are optional. Rasgueado is a difficult technique that requires considerable practice to master. Classical guitarists with experience playing modern works may be expected to have developed the technique, but others are less likely to have it under control.

Clawhammer

Clawhammer is a banjo fingerstyle technique that can be applied to the guitar, although it differs from traditional guitar techniques in significant ways. In basic clawhammer, only the thumb and one other finger—usually *i* or *m*—are used and all strings are attacked with downstrokes. While natural for the thumb, the fingers strike the strings with the topside of the fingernail in a downward motion toward the soundboard. Rather than moving the fingers at the joints, the hand is held rigid in a claw-like position and the entire wrist and forearm are employed to strike the hand against the strings in a motion not unlike knocking on a door (Fig. 4.3). It is important to recognize that the five-string

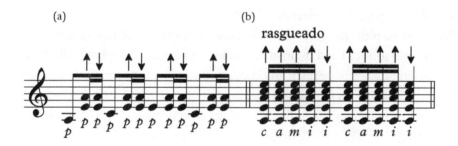

Figure 4.2
(a) Alzapua notation
[▶ Media 4.1];
(b) rasgueado
notation
[▶ Media 4.2].

Figure 4.3
The hand
position for banjo
clawhammer.

banjo uses a re-entrant tuning in which the fifth string is tuned higher than the others. As a consequence, the thumb's role in banjo clawhammer is typically confined to weaker beats since it primarily plays the higher-tuned fifth string. Nonetheless, the general claw-hammer technique offers an exciting alternative to standard fingerstyles that is certainly worth exploring on the guitar.

Plectra

Flatpicks

A pick is a rigid wafer-like object normally held between the thumb and index finger that is used to strike the strings. Plectra have been used to play guitar-like instruments since the Middle Ages. In the 16th century the practice fell out of favor as fingerstyles began to develop, but it re-emerged as the dominant playing technique in Western popular music of the 20th century. Today, picks are primarily associated with steel string instruments. They can, however, be used on nylon strings to great effect.

Compared to strings plucked with nails, picked notes sound crisp and bright with sharply defined attacks. Moreover, variations in timbre that result from attacking the string at different locations are more salient. In particular, picking very close to the bridge yields tones with a sparkling brightness difficult to match with the fingers. Picks come in a variety of materials, shapes, and gauges, all of which have some effect on the timbre. More often, however, picks are chosen because of how they feel in the hand, with shape and pliability the principal concerns.

Played with a pick, the guitar is extremely agile, capable of highly articulate melodic passages as well as rapid and defined strumming patterns. Polyphonically, however, the inability to simultaneously attack any combination of strings constrains the movement of voices significantly. As a consequence, polyphonic writing for the picked guitar tends to be limited to movement on adjacent strings or syncopated movement between non-adjacent strings.

Use of a pick can be indicated in notation simply by writing "pick" above the staff. Players may alternate between a pick and the fingers, which often requires that the pick be relinquished from the hand entirely. There are purpose-built pick holders available that attach to the guitar, a guitar strap, or a microphone stand, but the pick can just as easily be placed on a music stand or held in the mouth. Switching from fingers to a pick or vice versa can be done comfortably in the duration of a half note at 120 beats per minute.

Hybrid Picking

Hybrid picking involves use of both a pick and the fingers. The technique is primarily employed by pick players in order to expand the polyphonic potential of the guitar. The pick is held between the thumb and index finger and is mainly used for lower strings, while the *m* and *a* fingers pluck the higher strings (Fig. 4.4). It takes considerable practice to master hybrid picking. Once proficient, however, players can employ the technique with great agility while quickly alternating between hybrid and normal picking modes. Hybrid picking, or "chicken pickin," as it is playfully labeled, is a characteristic element

Figure 4.4
Right hand position used in hybrid picking.

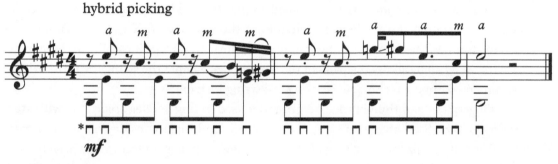

* ⊓ = downstroke with pick

Figure 4.5

Suggested notation for hybrid picking [▶ Media 4.3].

of country guitar styles. There, the fingers lift the strings as they are plucked so that they snap against the fretboard, contributing to the "twang" quality of the country guitar sound. Notable hybrid pickers include James Burton, Roy Buchanan, Glen Campbell, and Brad Paisley.

Notation for hybrid picking should include the text "hybrid picking" above the staff, along with right hand fingerings for the notes (Fig. 4.5). Use of the pick can be denoted with a downstroke symbol, although this must be defined explicitly as the symbol takes on a specialized meaning in this context. The standard finger indications *m* and *a* are used for the middle and ring fingers, respectively.

Fingerpicks and Thumbpicks

Fingerpicks and thumbpicks attach to the ends of the digits, essentially providing an individual pick for each finger. The picks are typically made of plastic or metal, the latter sounding brighter. As purchased, the picking surface can be quite large, extending well beyond the tip of the finger. Plastic picks can be filed to the size and shape desired using a standard nail file. Metal picks can be bent to shape.

Figure 4.6
Fingerpicks and thumbpicks: (a) a fingerpick oriented for upstrokes; (b) a fingerpick oriented for downstrokes; (c) a thumbpick.

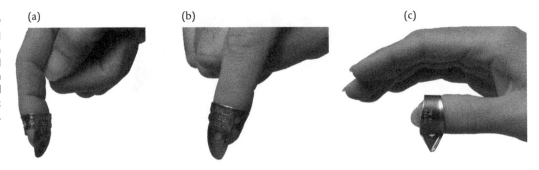

Fingerpicks are typically worn so that the striking surface is on the underside of the finger, opposite the nail (Fig. 4.6a). This orientation is suitable for upstrokes with the fingers, the norm in most fingerstyle techniques. In the case of techniques that use the fingers for downstrokes—clawhammer is one example—the picks are worn on the topside of the finger over the nail (Fig. 4.6b).

Thumbpicks, by contrast, are designed so that the picking surface extends from the side of the thumb at a 90-degree angle toward the soundboard (Fig. 4.6c). Rather than having to angle the thumb into the soundboard, the player keeps it parallel to the strings. This elevated angle allows the palm of the hand to rest against the strings near the bridge, a common damping technique used on steel string instruments.

Fingerpicks and thumbpicks are primarily used in fingerstyles associated with steel string guitars. Steel strings are rough on the nails and cause considerable wear or even breakage. This is particularly true of the wound lower strings. Indeed, some players wear only a thumbpick, preferring their natural nails for the treble strings. Conversely, fingerpicks combined with the flesh of the thumb can help to place melodic materials in the foreground against a much more somber bass.

The EBow

The EBow—short for "Electronic Bow"— is a battery-powered device held in the right hand and used to set the strings of the guitar in motion. It functions by generating an oscillating electromagnetic field that can be focused on a single string, causing it to sustain without decay. In contrast to the sharp attack of a picked or plucked string, EBowed tones have relatively long attacks, as it takes a moment for the string to begin to vibrate. The soft attack combined with infinite sustain imbues these tones with a bowed string character quite unlike normal guitar notes. While designed for use with the electric guitar, the EBow functions on most metal stringed instruments, although dynamics tend to be quite soft without amplification.

The EBow is constructed with two GuideGrooves designed to rest on non-adjacent strings while driving a third that runs between them (Fig. 4.7). As such, it can only actuate one string at a time. The GuideGrooves are beveled in order to direct the device to the optimal position with the target string centered in the DriveChannel. The player can easily feel when the device is in place without having to look at it and the GuideGrooves help to maintain this position as the device is moved horizontally along the fretboard. Clearly, the GuideGrooves are most effective when both can be used to straddle the target

Figure 4.7
An EBow with GuideGrooves resting on the fourth and sixth strings while the device drives the fifth string; (inset) the two beveled GuideGrooves on the underside of an EBow.

string. This, however, is only possible when targeting strings two through five. It is possible to EBow the first or sixth strings, but without the aid of the second GuideGroove the player must take care to keep the device positioned properly. Given the added performance complexity, it is sensible to confine melodic passages for the EBow to the inner strings where possible.

Standard and Harmonic Modes of Operation

There are two EBow models on the market: the original EBow, which functions in Standard mode, and the PlusEBow, which can be switched between Standard and Harmonic modes of operation.[4] When the EBow is in Standard Mode the pitch that sounds is usually the fundamental of the vibrating string length—that is, the pitch that would be expected given the fingering. At times, the sounding pitch may shift to a higher harmonic. These harmonic shifts can be encouraged by stopping the string in a lower fret, bending the string slightly while it is being driven, or by holding the EBow over a harmonic node. Conversely, lightly damping the string with the palm near the bridge can help to suppress harmonic shifts. Because harmonic shifts can be controlled, Standard Mode is a sensible choice whenever notated pitches are intended.

In Harmonic Mode the EBow accentuates harmonic shifts to the extent that one can no longer expect the fundamental pitch to sound. Moreover, when harmonic shifts occur, the overtone that sounds is not necessarily the one expected given the position of the EBow along the string, but will more often be the next higher harmonic. For instance, when an open string is played with the EBow positioned over the second harmonic node—the 12th fret—the third harmonic tends to sound. Shifts to other harmonics are encouraged by moving the EBow horizontally along the string or by slightly bending a stopped note. Harmonic shifts are highly characteristic of the EBow and are certainly worth exploring, but they are difficult to control and somewhat unpredictable in Harmonic Mode, making it a challenge to play even a simple melody and have it sound as written. A demonstration of the contrast between Standard and Harmonic modes of operation is available on the companion website [▶ Media 4.6].

Intensity

Dynamics and timbre can be controlled skillfully and expressively with an EBow. In most cases these two dimensions are linked as expected: The louder the sound becomes, the brighter its timbre tends to be. For the sake of brevity, the term "intensity" is used here to encapsulate this dynamic-timbre alliance when describing the quality of sound produced by an EBow.

The EBow is effective on the entire length of the string from the bridge to the nut, and movement of the device along the string is a central means of regulating intensity. On an electric guitar the pickups create "hot spots" above the coils where the sound is most intense, charged with a distinctive buzz-like quality. In order to explore the full range of EBow techniques the performer must be able to apply the device without reservation over the hot spot, which can sound excessively loud under normal playing conditions. To counter this, many players turn the volume on the instrument down before applying an EBow.[5] To a large extent, control over intensity can be thought of in terms of the EBow's position along the string in relation to the hot spots. A demonstration can be found on the companion website [▶ Media 4.4]. Keep in mind that activating more than one pickup yields multiple hot spots near the bridge. It is not uncommon to use only the neck pickup, as that provides a sufficient segment of string between the bridge and hot spot along which intensity can be controlled. Of course, the EBow functions equally well on the fretboard side of the pickup.

The intensity of an EBow can also be controlled by varying the proximity of the device to the target string (Fig. 4.8). Applying slight pressure to push the device closer to the string increases intensity, while lifting it away diminishes intensity. Rather than lifting the EBow completely off the strings, a player can tilt it forward so that the back end rises off the strings while the GuideGrooves remain planted at the front end to maintain stability.

Figure 4.8
Tilting the EBow off the strings to control intensity [▶ Media 4.5].

EBow Melodies

Wonderfully legato melodies are obtained with an EBow, which are smoothest when played on one string with a single left hand finger moving quickly to different positions. This one-finger playing technique is particular to the EBow and therefore the notation should provide string and fingering indications whenever it is intended. Figure 4.9 offers an example of a legato EBowed melody written to minimize string and finger changes. Slur lines are used to emphasize that the notes are to be played on a single string without lifting the EBow. Also notice that the slides from one pitch to the next captured in the left hand fingering are silent, suggesting that the string should not be depressed during the motion. They could just as well be glissandi.

EBow Arpeggios

While the EBow can only drive one string at a time, the beveling of the GuideGrooves allows the player to shift the device to different strings without having to lift it away from the instrument. Arpeggiated harmonies can be achieved by fingering a chord with the left hand and moving the device from string to string [▶ Media 4.7]. With the EBow near the hot spot these arpeggios can sound surprisingly like a bowed string instrument. Note, however, that the soft attacks of the EBow limit the speed at which string switching can occur.

EBow Buzzing

A buzzing component can be added to an EBowed note by applying a small amount of pressure focused on a single edge of the device, just until the vibrating string begins to make light contact with it [▶ Media 4.8]. Too much pressure will stop the string from vibrating entirely. Applied subtly, the result is an irregular and aggressive buzzing or rattling sound coupled with the continuous drive of the EBow. Under normal circumstances such interference to a plucked string would hasten the decay of the note. The continuous sustain of the EBow evades this expectation by driving the tone through the collisions, adding to the charged quality of the device. The buzzing can be controlled to a considerable extent through changes in pressure, but this requires a very steady and concentrated touch. To some extent one must be willing to except what emerges when working with EBow buzz, but results are generally satisfying.

EBow Slide

The EBow can function simultaneously as a slide by reversing it, tilting it forward, and applying pressure until the front edge of the device firmly stops the string (Fig. 4.10). At the proper angle the EBow continues to drive the target string and can be moved

Figure 4.9

A legato EBow melody with string and finger changes minimized for smoothness [▶ Media 4.6].

Figure 4.10
EBow slide
technique above
the fretboard.

Figure 4.11
EBow slide used
in Mike Frengel's
*And Then,
Romina . . .* (2001)
[▶ Media 4.9].

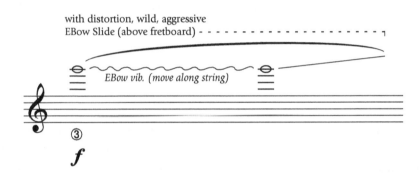

horizontally to create smooth changes in pitch. I employ this technique in my work *And Then, Romina . . .* (2001) to obtain a variety of wailing vibrato and portamento effects over the pickups (Fig. 4.11). EBow slides are confined to string regions near the bridge, as the GuideGrooves tend to hit the wood when applied over the fretboard, preventing the EBow from being depressed far enough to firmly stop the string.

String Bows

Quite a few notable rock guitarists have explored the use of string bows on the electric guitar, including Jimmy Page (Led Zeppelin), Lee Ranaldo (Sonic Youth), Jonny Greenwood (Radiohead), and Jón Þór Birgisson (Sigur Rós), the latter making it a regular part of his playing style. Individual bowed tones acquire a string-like morphology that is quite distinct from the attack-decay envelope of a typical plucked note. However, agility on the instrument is severely compromised. Applied to the guitar, a string bow is typically held above the fretboard so that it dangles down over the strings. Unlike the arched bridge on a bowed string instrument, the guitar has a flat bridge that places all strings at a relatively even level and makes it impractical to target inner strings individually. In addition, bowing toward the bridge can be problematic because the bow tends to hit the body of the instrument. It is easiest to target individual outer strings with the bow positioned over the fretboard.

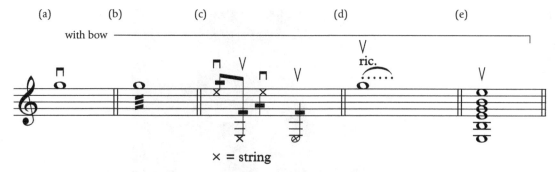

Figure 4.12

String bow notation: (a) an individual note bowed with a downstroke [▶ Media 4.10]; (b) a bowed repeat tremolo [▶ Media 4.11]; (c) bowing the strings behind the nut [▶ Media 4.12]; (d) a ricochet upstroke [▶ Media 4.13]; (e) a bowed chord [▶ Media 4.14].

Long, drawn-out notes on a single outer string tend to be the norm when a bow is used. However, other intriguing effects include (1) bowed tremolo; (2) screeching sounds bowed near or behind the bridge or nut; (3) ricochet articulations achieved by allowing the bow to bounce freely on the strings; (4) chords obtained by bowing all six strings, although these tend to sound murky. Figure 4.12 offers notation adopted from string literature for each of these techniques. In all cases, it is necessary to write "with bow" above the staff, which can be canceled with "pick" or "fingers."[6] Note that stroke directions seem to be reversed when the bow is held from above the strings. A proper downstroke should draw the bow over the string from the frog (the handle) to the tip, which will require raising the arm in the guitar technique.

Fausto Romitelli calls for the guitar to be played col lengo (with the wood of the bow) in *Trash TV Trance* (2002). The pitch heard is determined by the location of the bow along the string, with the wood essentially acting like a slide, both stopping the string and causing it to vibrate. In *Trash TV Trance* the bowing locations along the string are notated to produce a cyclic pitch pattern that serves as accompaniment for thematic material played using the left hand alone [▶ Media 4.15].

The Piranha Guitar Bow

The Piranha Guitar Bow has been created specifically for use with the steel string guitar. It is a small device held in the hand or worn on a single right hand finger with an arched bowing surface so that the inner strings can be targeted (Fig. 4.13). The short bow length prevents long, drawn out notes like those typical of a standard string bow. Instead, the Piranha Bow adds a bowed quality to the attacks of notes, relying on string resonance for sustain. The Piranha Bow is a relatively new device, and as such, it has not been widely adopted in practice. It is, however, more flexible than a standard bow, and players interested in bowed effects might consider this option. Note that it does not work well on nylon strings.

Slides as Plectra

A slide is typically worn on a left hand finger and used to stop the strings. However, slides, steels, or similarly cylindrical objects can be used to attack the strings, serving simultaneously to establish the vibrating string length and to set the string in motion. Strings

Figure 4.13
The Piranha Guitar
Bow, sold by
Hello Mfg
[▶ Media 4.16].

can be attacked with the slide held in either the left or right hand, the latter making it easier to target locations near the bridge. As with any unorthodox plectrum, experimentation yields a wealth of interesting possibilities, three of which are discussed below.

Slide Taps

A string can be set into motion by tapping it with a slide. A light touch is all that is required to produce a clear tone. When a slide strikes a string, energy is distributed in both directions from the attack location, resulting in two distinct tones: a front tone that extends from the attack location to the instrument's bridge and a back tone extending from the attack location to the nut. These two tones, collectively referred to as a bi-tone, are locked in a reciprocal relationship; as the attack location shifts toward the bridge, the front tone rises in pitch while the back tone is lowered, and vice versa. It is possible to dampen the front or back string segments in order to isolate the other, although the back tones lack amplification and are naturally quite soft. With the strings dampened, articulate staccato taps can be obtained by immediately lifting the slide away from the string after each attack. Figure 4.14a offers notation for staccato slide taps in which the back tones are dampened to isolate the front tones. Applying this same basic technique without string dampening produces a trill tremolo between the pitch corresponding to the tap location and the pitch produced by the string length when the slide is not stopping it (Fig. 4.14b). Alternatively, the slide can remain pressed against the string after the attack for greater sustain, making it possible to obtain short vibrato and portamento gestures (Fig. 4.14c).

Slide Texture with Indeterminate Tones

A distinctive wobbly texture comprised of unstable and indeterminate pitches can be produced by holding a slide lengthwise between two adjacent strings and rotating it back and forth by small degrees about its center (Fig. 4.15a). The pitch range corresponds to the string segments that the slide spans, which can be expanded by combining the rotational motion of the slide with horizontal movement along the strings or by shifting to different pairs of strings. Figure 4.15a provides a suggested notation for a slide texture using a graphic symbol. The pitches are parenthesized, indicative of strings rather than sounding tones. Given that pitch is treated indeterminately, a tablature-based solution might be clearer. Figure 4.15b offers a vivid depiction of exactly what the player does.

Slide Bowing

Holding a slide perpendicular to the strings and "bowing" in quick alternation produces a smooth chordal resonance combined with the subtle agitation of tremolo. Chord tones are a result of the slide's location along the strings, which is confined to barred configurations. Figure 4.16 provides an excerpt from my own work *And Then, Romina . . .* (2001)

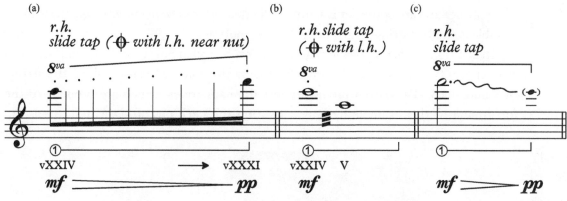

Figure 4.14

Various effects using a slide as a plectrum: (a) a slide tap staccato gesture [▶ Media 4.17]; (b) trill tremolo using slide taps for the higher note [▶ Media 4.18]; (c) a descending portamento gesture [▶ Media 4.19].

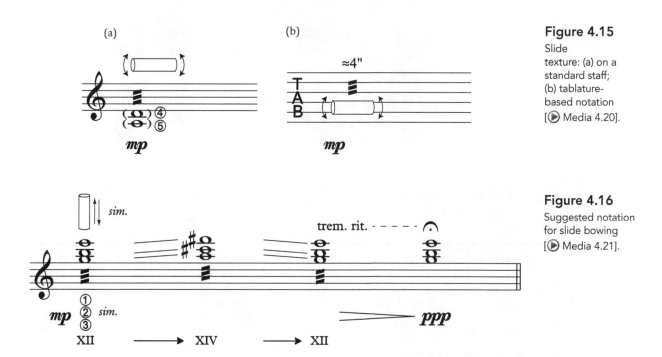

Figure 4.15

Slide texture: (a) on a standard staff; (b) tablature-based notation [▶ Media 4.20].

Figure 4.16

Suggested notation for slide bowing [▶ Media 4.21].

in which the player oscillates the bowing location between the 12th and 14th frets, causing the intonation to waver. Strikingly, harmonics can rise to the foreground of the sonority as the bow moves over the harmonic node at the 12th fret, ringing out at times like feedback.

Threaded Bows

A variety of tense and abrasive sounds can be obtained by "bowing" a string with a threaded bolt or screw so that the thread ridges iteratively snag it (Fig. 4.17). Using slow strokes it is possible to isolate individual attacks, which creates substantial tension that is then released when the string gives way over the ridge. With faster strokes, tension is created and released by changes in the stroke velocity. There is considerable variation in the threading of bolts and screws. Attributes that tend to be most important are thread spacing and thread height. As a general rule, coarse threads offer more control on the lower strings and are better for isolating individual attacks, while finer threading is more suitable for higher strings and quicker bowing motions.

In addition to their abrasive characteristics, threaded bow sounds are imbued with a tonal quality made up of a bi-tone defined by the object's position along the string. In Figure 4.18, the written pitches reflect the back tones, which are brought to the foreground in this example by only activating the neck pickup. Fret indications are

Figure 4.17
A suggested technique for holding a bolt or screw in the right hand.

with bolt, as if bowing
slow, pulse uneven, with neck pickup only

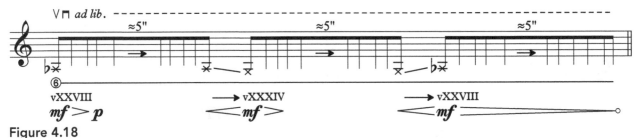

Figure 4.18
Suggested notation for a threaded bow on the strings [▶ Media 4.22].

provided that correspond to the bowing location. The fret numbers are virtual, denoting positions if the fretboard were to continue toward the bridge. Without actual frets as guides, such indications merely give an approximate bowing location. More likely, the player will rely on the notated pitch to ensure proper intonation. Optionally, these locations could be marked on the string with chalk or a guide can be attached to the body beneath the strings.

Two-String Dowel Tremolo

A soft, irregular trill tremolo effect can be obtained by jiggling a thin dowel-shaped object between any two adjacent strings. A conducting baton works particularly well for this, as the bulb handle provides a counterweight behind the hand that yields greater control. With the dowel held in the right hand, the left is free to engage the instrument as normal. Standard trill tremolo notation can be used for dowel tremolo, although a symbol or text is needed to specify that a dowel should be used. Figure 4.19 offers a graphic solution with bracketed strings to imply that the action occurs between them.

Mini Hand Fans

The blades of a battery operated mini hand fan (Fig. 4.20) can be used to attack the strings of the guitar, producing a mechanical repeat tremolo. Single-string tremolos tend to be limited to the outer strings, as the fan blades are usually too large to target individual inner strings. It is possible, however, to strike any two or three adjacent strings for chordal effects. Daniel Hjorth employs mini fans for chordal tremolo in *Let Newton Be* (2007), adapting drum roll notation to denote the effect (Fig. 4.21). Standard unmeasured tremolo notation would work equally well, as long as the text "with fan" is included. Dynamics can be controlled by altering the proximity of the device to the string. The angle at which the blades strike the string is also significant; a sharper angle yields more articulate attacks, but if increased too far eventually leads to a rough and uneven tremolo. Fans can be applied to all guitar types, but on electric instruments the fan motor is amplified through the pickups when held near them. Fausto Romitelli employs a mini fan only for this noise in *Trash TV Trance* (2002), using proximity to the pickups to control dynamics.

Figure 4.19
Dowel tremolo using a conducting baton between two adjacent strings [▶ Media 4.23].

Figure 4.20
A handheld, battery-operated mini fan.

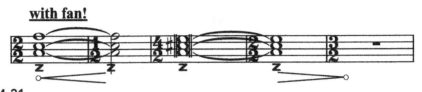

with fan!

Figure 4.21
A mini fan used in one of the guitar parts from Daniel Hjorth's *Let Newton Be* (2007) [▶ Media 4.24].

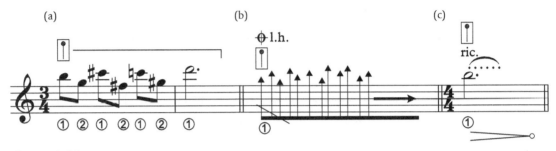

(a)   (b)   (c)

Figure 4.22
Beater notation: (a) an unmuted passage played with a beater [▶ Media 4.25]; (b) indeterminate pitches attacked near the bridge on a muted string [▶ Media 4.26]; (c) a ricochet, bouncing effect [▶ Media 4.27].

Percussive Beaters

Strings can be struck with a beater to create a particularly percussive attack. Purpose-built percussion beaters are often large and cumbersome when applied to the guitar. Found objects such as chopsticks, wooden pencils, or dowels generally offer more suitable alternatives. Any single string can be attacked given an appropriate beater and a little practice. However, the close string spacing on the guitar makes it considerably more difficult to target individual inner strings. Switching to adjacent strings at a moderate tempo is perfectly reasonable, but rhythmically complex passages are best avoided.

There are two pitches to be considered when striking a string with a beater: one corresponding to the overall vibrating string length and the other determined by the location where the beater hits the string. If the string is not dampened, the prominent pitch is that corresponding to the string length (Fig. 4.22a). Damping the string with the left hand yields a staccato tone corresponding to the distance from the bridge to the attack location. Precise intonation generally cannot be expected here, as it is difficult to hit the string with enough accuracy to play even a simple melodic passage well. The technique is more suitable for an indeterminate treatment of pitch (Fig. 4.22b).

An effect reminiscent of ricochet bowing on a bowed string instrument can be obtained by allowing the beater to fall loosely on the string such that it bounces until coming to rest (Fig. 4.22c). The rate and number of bounces can be controlled to some extent by altering the angle of the beater as it falls on the string or by exerting slight pressure on it from the hand to suppress the bounces. Dampening the strings with the left hand yields a considerably more articulate bounce while highlighting the pitch associated with the attack location.

Figure 4.23
A suggested method for holding a beater in the right hand with the guitar in the normal playing position.

With the guitar held in a normal playing position use of a beater is typically confined to the right hand, leaving the left to stop the strings on the fretboard. The beater can be held between the thumb and index finger above the strings so that it dangles downward in front of them (Fig. 4.23). A fulcrum should be established so that the beater swings freely, bouncing off the strings. From this position, varying degrees of control can be obtained by subtle movements of the thumb and index fingers that are holding the beater, the use of fingers *m* or *a* to propel the beater against the strings, or movements of the entire hand. The charm of the technique rests in the particular rubato quality it creates at the event level, which seems to follow physics rather than musical tendencies. This is obtained by relinquishing control to some extent so that the object can swing freely.

Beaters can be employed with greater rhythmic vitality on a tabletop guitar. In this position the beater can be held like a drumstick and the instrument played in a manner resembling the hammered dulcimer. With a beater in only the right hand, the left is capable of simple string stopping from above the fretboard. More rhythmically vibrant materials are possible with a beater in each hand, although pitches are then limited to open strings. Use of a third bridge preparation pairs well with two-handed beater techniques because the bridge divides the strings in two, essentially creating 12 open string segments [▶ Media 4.28] (see Third Bridges in Chapter 6). In addition, a third bridge elevates the strings, which makes it easier to strike them over the fretboard. Taking the preparation a step further, some strings might be removed to provide ample space between those remaining so that they can be targeted more easily.

Attack Location

Attacking a string at different locations is one of the principal means by which timbre is modified on the guitar. The timbre gradually shifts from being thin and bright near the

Figure 4.24

Attack locations defined in Gilbert Biberian's *Prisms II* (1970).

Fo.	Flautando; strike the note at the half way nodal point (R.H.)
To.	Sul Tasto; R.H. placed between XIIth and XIXth frets, irrespective of pitch
Bo.	Sul Boca; R.H. placed over sound hole
No.	Normale; R.H. between sound hole and bridge, nearer the sound hole
Po.	Ponticello; play as near the bridge as possible

bridge to hollow and somber at the midpoint of the vibrating string's length, a transformation that is then mirrored as the attack location moves from the midpoint to the nut or stopping position [▶ Media 4.29]. In solo contexts, timbral contrasts might be used to distinguish voices, define structure, or for special effect. In ensemble settings, especially when playing with other guitars, timbral distinctions can be highly effective in segregating one part from another and balancing the instrument with the rest of the group.

Attack location is most often instructed in general terms, leaving the performer a degree of interpretative freedom. "Sul ponticello" signifies that the string should be attacked near the bridge and results in a thin, bright timbre that can easily cut through the musical surface. By contrast, "sul tasto" means that the string should be attacked over the fretboard, usually between the 12th and 15th frets, producing a more somber tone. These techniques are indicated with plain text above or below the staff and can be canceled with the terms "ordinary" or "normal."

Sul ponticello and sul tasto represent two ends of a continuum over which a gradual transformation of timbre occurs. It may be desirable to define intermediary positions between these poles. Elliott Carter requests "$\frac{1}{2}$ pont." in *Changes* (1983). Reginald Smith Brindle writes "12°" in "The Harp of David" from *Guitarcosmos 3* (1979) to denote sul tasto at the 12th fret, but any fret number could be given. In *Prisms II* (1969), Gilbert Biberian defines five attack locations between the bridge and the string's midpoint, reproduced in Figure 4.24. The flautando effect, achieved by attacking at the midpoint of the vibrating string's length, produces a particularly dull and hollow tone quality. Since the string length changes as the string is stopped at different positions, the midpoint also shifts. Accordingly, playing a passage flautando usually requires that the right hand shift attack location in a coordinated effort with the left hand fretting [▶ Media 4.30]. To this end, Biberian appends a fret number to his flautando indications, such as "Fo. XII."

Attack locations need not be stationary. Timbral shifts can be obtained by gradually moving the attack location over a number of notes, as in the excerpt from Elliott Carter's *Changes* (Fig. 4.25).

Attacking Behind the Nut or Bridge

Most guitars have short segments of string between the nut and tuners that can be attacked directly (Fig. 1.17) [▶ Media 4.31]. In addition, some electric and steel-string acoustic instruments have a tailpiece that is separate from the bridge, providing similar string segments behind the bridge (Fig. 1.19c). Attacking the strings behind the nut

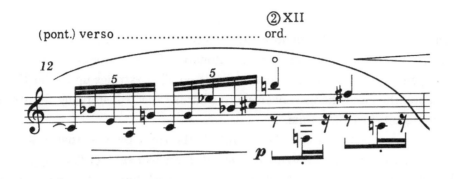

Figure 4.25
Excerpt from Elliott Carter's *Changes* (1986), showing a gradual shift from sul ponticello to an ordinary attack location.

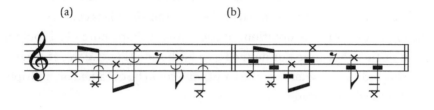

Figure 4.26
(a) Notation for attacking behind the bridge; (b) notation for attacking behind the nut.

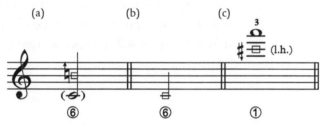

Figure 4.27
Back tone notation: (a) the front tone is given a normal parenthesized note head and the sounding pitch of the back tone is indicated with a square note head; (b) only the front tone is given, but with a square note head to indicate that the back tone should be plucked; (c) a plucked multiphonic.

or bridge produces bright, high-pitched tones that are relatively soft yet tend to pierce through the musical surface due to their sharp timbre and high register. As a general rule, shorter string segments produce higher pitches. However, the exact pitches vary from one instrument to the next and therefore must be treated as indeterminate. It is worth recognizing that the two most common headstock designs—the 3+3 and the 6-inline—differ in regard to the string segments available behind the nut. On a 6-inline headstock the string lengths get progressively longer from the sixth string to the first string, whereas the three treble string segments are mirrored by the bass strings on a 3+3-style headstock. Figure 4.26a offers notation for attacking behind the bridge, taken from bowed string literature. Figure 4.26b uses an adaptation of this same basic approach for behind-the-nut attacks. Observe that "x" note heads are used to denote that the pitches are indeterminate, with their placement on the staff indicative of the string and not the sounding pitch.

Attacking Back Tones

The segment of string between a stopping finger and the nut is referred to as a back tone and can be attacked for a distinctively soft and delicate effect. Back tones are easily masked by other activity, even at softer dynamics. In solo settings, however, the dynamic contrast between back tones and normally plucked tones can be exploited to great effect. It is important to keep in mind that the intonation for back tones is not equal tempered (Appendix II shows the bi-tones available on all six strings up to the 17th fret). Furthermore, the pitch changes inversely to what is expected; stopping the string at a higher fret results in a lower tone.

Any notation for back tones should include the front tone, as that is the clearest means of conveying where the string is stopped. John Schneider (1985) suggests notating the front tone with a normal note head and the back tone with a square note head (Fig. 4.27a).[7] The front tone might be placed in parentheses if it does not sound. On the other hand, if the precise sounding pitch of the back tone is of less concern then it may be acceptable to omit it from the notation. In such cases a shape note head could be placed on the pitch of the front tone but defined as a back tone (Fig. 4.27b). It is necessary to include a string indication whenever the front tone could be obtained on multiple strings, as the back tones will be different.

At the end of "No. 2" of Heitor Villa-Lobos's *Douze Etudes,* the composer asks for a plucked multiphonic. Using the third finger to stop the string, the front tone is plucked normally with the right hand while the back tone is simultaneously plucked with the first or second finger of the left hand. Figure 4.27c provides notation for a plucked multiphonic.[8]

5

Performance Techniques
The Left Hand and More

Pitched Materials

Pizzicato

Pizzicato is obtained on the guitar by lightly damping the strings so that the resulting tones have a darker timbre and diminished sustain [⯈ Media 5.1]. Damping can be accomplished in a variety of ways. With the right hand, it can be achieved by resting the heel of the palm over the bridge so that a small amount of flesh touches the vibrating strings. The degree of damping can be controlled with considerable subtlety by altering both the amount of contact with the strings or the pressure placed on them. Palm muting is the principal damping technique used on steel string instruments but proves problematic with nylon string fingerstyles due to the upright position of the hand. Damping can also be achieved with the little finger on the right hand rested against the bridge and strings, functioning much like a palm mute while allowing the hand to remain in an upright position. Last, the string can be attacked normally and, only after the attack, dampened with the palm or finger. The result is a full-spectrum attack that then decays more rapidly than a normal tone [⯈ Media 5.2]. Using the left hand, pizzicato can be achieved by stopping a string directly on the fret wire, causing some flesh from the finger to extend over the fret and damp the string [⯈ Media 5.3]. Alternatively, a left hand finger can be placed near any stopped note or near the nut to lightly dampen the string [⯈ Media 5.4].

Pizzicato is indicated in notation with plain text, often abbreviated "pizz," and canceled with the terms "normal" or "ordinary." In Figure 5.1, the text is placed below the staff with a dashed line to indicate that it should be applied only to the lower voice, providing timbral contrast and foregrounding the melody. The directive is made clear by using stem direction to separate the voices. In "Las Seis Cuerdas" (1963), Alvaros Company indicates pizzicato on a note-by-note basis by placing an "x" over the note stems, an effective strategy when normal and pizzicato materials are combined (Fig. 5.2).

Figure 5.1

Pizzicato applied to only the lower voice [▶ Media 5.5].

Figure 5.2

Pizzicato treatment of individual notes in Alvaros Company's *Las Seis Cuerdas* (© Sugarmusic s.p.a., Edizioni Suvini Zerboni).

Figure 5.3

Carlevaro's notation for étouffé resonance [▶ Media 5.6].

Étouffé Resonance

A specialized pizzicato effect, known as étouffé resonance, is produced by attacking a dampened string and immediately removing the damping finger or palm. As a result, the note sounds muffled and dull, but decays at a rate closer to that of a normal guitar tone. Carlevaro (1978) offers the simple notation in Figure 5.3 for étouffé resonance.

Pizzicato above the Fretboard

Stopping a string above the fretboard results in a sharp pizzicato effect with subtle yet discernible pitch. Damping comes naturally to these tones since the string is stopped with the flesh of the finger as opposed to a fret wire. Closer toward the bridge the tones become very high, taking on an almost woodblock character. Downward pressure can be applied to the strings above the fretboard, bending them toward the soundboard and raising the pitch. While the bend range is marginal, the sound becomes tighter and more percussive when tension is increased.

In *Sonata for Guitar* (1978), Alberto Ginastera uses upward arrows to signify indeterminate pitches above the fretboard in an irregular rhythm (Fig. 5.4). If precise pitches are intended, virtual fret indications can be given that denote the position on the string if the fretboard continued toward the bridge (Fig. 5.5). Chalk can also be used to mark the correct locations on the strings.

Figure 5.4
Notation for indeterminate pizzicato played above the fretboard in Alberto Ginastera's *Sonata for Guitar* (1978).

Surface Pizzicato

A dampened tone can be obtained anywhere on the fretboard by lightly touching and holding a finger against a string without depressing it to the fret wire. With just the right amount of pressure applied, the pitch corresponding to the finger's location can be heard faintly and muffled [▶ Media 5.8]. Gilbert Biberian refers to this technique as surface pizzicato and uses it extensively in *Prisms II* (1969), where he notates it with triangle shape note heads. It can just as well be notated like pizzicato above the fretboard (Fig. 5.5).

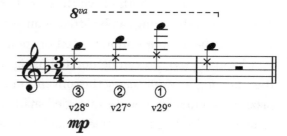

Figure 5.5
Notation for precise pitches above the fretboard using virtual fret indications [▶ Media 5.7].

Figure 5.6
Suggested notation for dynamic damping [▶ Media 5.9].

Dynamic Damping

Many pizzicato techniques offer the performer the possibility of altering the degree of damping over time. Dynamic modifications such as this can be expressed in notation by placing an arrow between two defined states. In Figure 5.6, a standard damp symbol is contrasted with an open circle to differentiate between dampened and ordinary states, while a dashed arrow is used to denote a progression from one to the other.

Snap Pizzicato

Snap pizzicato is obtained by lifting the string away from the fretboard and then releasing it so that it strikes against the fret wires, adding a sharp percussive attack to the tone.[1] The effect produced is technically not a pizzicato, but the actions resemble that of pizzicato on a bowed string, from which the technique derives its name. Snap pizzicato can be performed at all dynamic levels, although the characteristic percussive attack is most prominent at levels ranging from mezzo forte to fortissimo. The attack is also more pronounced when the string is lifted perpendicular to the fretboard, a technique that requires pinching the string between the thumb and another finger or getting

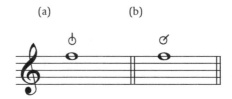

Figure 5.7
Snap pizzicato notation: (a) snap pizzicato with the string lifted perpendicular to the fretboard [▶ Media 5.10]; (b) angled snap pizzicato, with the string lifted away from the fretboard and toward the floor [▶ Media 5.11].

a nail underneath it, both of which restrict the speed that passages can be played at. Alternatively, the string can be lifted at an angle with only the thumb or a single finger, which may be a better option for fast or complex passages, albeit with less pronounced attack. Snap pizzicato can be notated using the plain text "snap pizz" above or below the staff, or graphically using the conventional symbol in Figure 5.7a. Rotating the snap pizzicato symbol can denote an angled snap pizzicato, with clockwise rotations defined as downward string displacements and counter-clockwise rotations defined as upward displacements (Fig. 5.7b).

Vibrato

Vibrato describes an oscillating variation in pitch and is implemented in two principal ways on the guitar. Axial vibrato is achieved by rocking the stopping finger on its tip parallel to the string, similar to the technique used on bowed strings. While the preferred method on nylon strings, it is considerably less common on steel string instruments and not very effective in the lowest frets. In contrast to axial vibrato, radial vibrato involves bending the string in an oscillatory motion parallel to the fret wires. Radial vibrato is the default approach on steel string instruments, allowing for significantly greater vibrato depth than its axial counterpart. Needless to say, both axial and radial vibrato methods require that the string be stopped with a finger. Vibrato can also be applied to an open string by bending the segment behind the bridge or nut or through the use of a vibrato bar on electric instruments equipped with one.

Vibrato can be indicated in notation by writing "vibrato" above or below the passage where it is to be employed. It is canceled by indicating "no vib." or "secco," the Italian word for "dry." Alternatively, vibrato can be notated symbolically with a wavy line that extends for the duration of the effect. In the absence of vibrato indications, guitarists are likely to add the effect as an inherent part of their playing technique. If secco is intended it should be stated explicitly in the score.

Time-Varying Vibrato

Textual indications for vibrato leave the rate and depth of the wavering pitch to the performer's discretion, both of which may be kept consistent over the duration of the note. It is also possible to alter these parameters over time. In *Las Seis Cuerdas* (1963), Alvaro Company defines various vibrato morphologies that are then contrasted in the music (Fig. 5.8). Nikita Koshkin offers a highly precise vibrato notation in "The Big Toy's Parade"

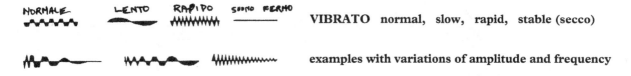

VIBRATO normal, slow, rapid, stable (secco)

examples with variations of amplitude and frequency

Figure 5.8
Vibrato morphologies defined by Alvaro Company in *Las Seis Cuerdas* (1963) (translated by the author) (© Sugarmusic s.p.a., Edizioni Suvini Zerboni).

Figure 5.9
Time-varying vibrato notation in Nikita Koshkin's *The Prince's Toys* (1992).

from *The Prince's Toys* (1992), capturing the exact pitches and rhythms that should be obtained (Fig. 5.9).

Glissando and Portamento

The terms "glissando" and "portamento" both refer to a slide from one pitch to another, the difference being that the intermediary chromatic steps are heard in a glissando while the pitch change is smooth and continuous in portamento. Sliding the finger along a string on a standard guitar neck results in glissando, as the frets impose a step-wise change in pitch. While a quick glissando performed with a light touch can certainly approach a continuous effect, true portamento requires the use of a slide-like device, a vibrato bar, string bends, altering the string tension at the tuning key, or an instrument with a fretless neck.

The distinction between glissando and portamento is reflected in notation by the type of line that connects the starting and ending pitches. A straight line between the note heads denotes portamento (Fig. 5.10a) while a wavy line denotes glissando (Fig. 5.10b). If space permits, the text "port." or "gliss." can be added just above the line and angled with it, although this is unnecessary if line types are defined and strictly adhered to. In guitar literature, it is common to find a straight line used to represent glissando, a practice that presents no issue unless techniques are used elsewhere in the work that produce true portamento. In such cases, the line distinction can become central.

The proper use of slurs is an important, and often neglected, element of portamento and glissando notation. The slur in Figure 5.10a suggests that only the first note is attacked, whereas the absence of a slur in Figure 5.10b implies that the second note should also be attacked upon arrival, adding accent and separating it from the sliding

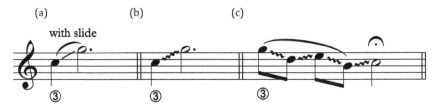

Figure 5.10

Portamento and glissando notation: (a) portamento using a slide in which only the first note is attacked [▶ Media 5.12]; (b) glissando in which the second note is also attacked [▶ Media 5.13]; (c) a glissando over several pitches, with only the first and last notes attacked [▶ Media 5.14].

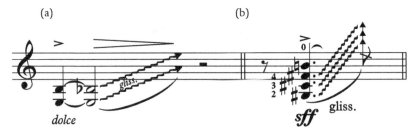

Figure 5.11

Indeterminate glissandi notation: (a) Jacques Charpentier's *Etude No. 1* (1974); (b) chordal glissando to the highest notes possible in Alberto Ginastera's *Sonata for Guitar* (1978) (examples transcribed by the author).

motion from which it emerges. Figure 5.10c shows a glissando over several pitches, with only the first and last notes attacked.

It may be desirable to leave the ending note of a glissando or portamento indeterminate. This can be conveyed with an arrow, suggesting that the slide may continue past the end of the line. Figure 5.11a provides an example from Jacques Charpentier's *Etude No. 1* (1974) in which the alignment of the arrowheads with the end of the dynamic marking implies that the glissandi are still in motion as the sound fades away.[2] Also notice in this example that the lower note of the glissando begins on an open string. In *Sonata for Guitar* (1978), Alberto Ginastera uses vertical up arrows at the end of glissandi lines to indicate that the slide should be to the highest notes possible (Fig. 5.11b).

Since glissandi can only be executed along a single string, their ranges are limited. Composers should ensure that both the starting and ending pitches of written glissandi are indeed available on the same string. It is also worth noting that glissandi on wound strings contain a noise component or "string whistle" as the finger sweeps over the ridged winding.

String Bends

Bending a string with the stopping finger increases its tension and subsequently, raises the pitch in a smooth and continuous portamento. String bends are an integral component of steel string guitar styles, and in the 20th century the technique also began to appear in music written for the classical instrument. Bends can be highly expressive, especially on the electric guitar where the range is expanded. Players are capable of bending to specific pitches with accuracy, and a continuum of microtones is available that can ornament a fretted note.

Conservatively speaking, a string can be bent a whole step in most positions on any guitar, although this may be reduced to a half step or less in the lower three frets. Beyond this rough generalization, ranges differ depending on the type of instrument and string gauges used. On an electric guitar, bends as much as a major third or more may be obtainable in the middle of the fretboard, while acoustic instruments are generally limited in comparison. Tuning the strings lower than their normal tensions or using lighter string gauges can expand the bend range significantly on any guitar.

Bends are most often upward in pitch; the player first attacks a normal stopped note and then displaces the string to raise the pitch. It is equally possible to achieve a downward pitch bend, sometimes referred to as a ghost bend, by silently displacing the string, attacking it, and then releasing the tension back to normal (Figs. 5.12b and 5.12e). Because it takes a moment to displace the string before it is attacked, a succession of ghost bends at even a moderate tempo could prove problematic.

Players will typically bend strings one through three up toward the sixth string, while strings four through six are pulled down toward the first string. This is not only more comfortable for the left hand but it also keeps the string on the fretboard. The direction of string displacement has no effect on the sound but is significant because the bent string and fingers tend to crowd the adjacent string's space and prevent it from sounding. Indeed, a bend on the first string will prevent the second, and possibly even the third and fourth strings from being used.

Various notation methods are employed in the literature for string bends. The simplest of these merely indicates the direction and interval of the bend (Figs. 5.12a-b). By convention, the intervals are expressed as "$\frac{1}{2}$" or "full," corresponding to a half step or whole step, respectively. However, microtonal bends and bends greater than a whole step could be denoted using other numerals, such as "$\frac{1}{4}$" or "3" (Fig. 5.12c). While concise, this notation leaves the rhythmic profile of the bend undefined. For example, in Figure 5.12a a performer could bend quickly to the destination pitch and hold it for the remainder of the two beats or bend the note slowly over two beats, or any number of interpretations in between. Figure 5.12c adopts the same notation for a bend and release but subdivides the half note into shorter values in order to convey the intended rhythm.

Figure 5.12

String bend notation: (a) a half-step bend upward [▶ Media 5.15]; (b) a whole-step "ghost" bend downward [▶ Media 5.16]; (c) a bend and release, up a minor third and then back to the starting pitch [▶ Media 5.17]; (d) a rhythm-specific whole step bend upward [▶ Media 5.18]; (e) a rhythm-specific whole-step "ghost" bend downward [▶ Media 5.19]; (f) a bend in which the string is re-attacked at various pitches along the way [▶ Media 5.20]; (g) a curved line used to indicate an indeterminate bend contour [▶ Media 5.21].

A more precise means of notating string bends uses a crooked bend line to connect the starting and ending pitches (Figs. 5.12d-f). This method has the advantage of capturing both the bend rhythm and the sounding pitches. Slurs can be used to regulate attacks in a manner similar to that used with glissando and portamento. In Figures 5.12d and 5.12e only the first note is attacked, whereas the absence of a slur in Figure 5.12f suggests that the string is to be attacked at each of the four notated pitches as the string is increasingly displaced.

Bends offer tremendous expressive potential when the player is given the freedom to shape the contour ad libitum. Virtuosity lies in the subtlest of pitch and rhythmic alterations that often defy notational representation, yet feel perfectly natural to a performer at the moment of execution. Indeed, one might argue that attempts to quantify the pitch and rhythmic profiles of a bend compromise the expressive potential of the technique. Greater freedom can be afforded to the performer by simply providing a general outline for a bend using a curved line (Fig. 5.12g).

Specialized Bend Effects

Unison Bends

A unison bend involves playing two notes on adjacent strings and bending the lower string upward until the pitch matches that of the higher string. The resulting effect is an audible convergence of the two tones on a single unison pitch, characterized by beating that gradually slows as the pitches merge. The rate of beating can be controlled expressively through subtle changes in pitch and is often a coveted attribute of this technique. Figure 5.13a offers notation for a unison bend.

Multi-Stop Bends

More than one string can be bent at a time. Double stop bends are fairly common, but triple and quadruple stop bends are also attainable. While bend contours are typically the same for all strings involved, it is possible to bend one string more than another. In Figure 5.13b the lower of the two strings bends up a whole step, while the higher string only bends a half step.

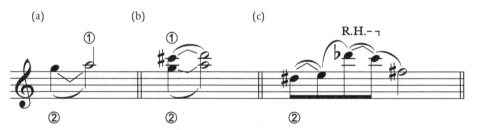

Figure 5.13

Notation for specialized bends: (a) a unison bend [▶ Media 5.22]; (b) a double stop bend [▶ Media 5.23]; (c) bend and touch technique [▶ Media 5.24].

Bend and Touch

Bends can be combined with right hand touch technique to create unusual intervallic inflections. The basic idea is to bend a string in the normal manner with the left hand and, while displaced, use a right hand finger to stop it at a higher fret. Holding the higher pitch with the right hand, the string tension can then be released to settle on the pitch of the higher fret, or the right hand can pluck the string, returning the pitch to the left hand (Fig. 5.13c).

Behind-the-Nut String Bends

Any note can be raised in pitch by depressing the segment of string between the nut and tuning key. The principal attraction of behind-the-nut bends, however, is that they can be applied to open strings and harmonics. Jimmy Page employs the technique using the right hand in Led Zeppelin's "Heartbreaker" (1969), although time is required to reach over the instrument, making it difficult to perform with agility. In a refined and considerably more difficult application of the technique the left hand is used to both stop notes in the lower frets and simultaneously depress one or more strings behind the nut. Country guitarists such as Roy Buchanan, Jerry Donahue, Danny Gatton, and Doyle Dykes incorporate this latter approach into their playing styles seamlessly, creating oblique motion that resembles a pedal steel instrument. Figure 5.14a offers an example of a country-style cadence employing a behind-the-nut bend with the left hand. Figure 5.14b applies the technique to harmonics, again with a country music nuance.

Behind-the-nut bends can be employed with greatest ease on an instrument with a 6-inline headstock (Fig. 1.17), as this design provides a relatively long segment of string between the nut and each tuning key. Bending up a half step is fairly easy, but whole step bends require a substantial amount of pressure placed on the string, which can be painful to the finger if heavy gauge strings are used.

An effect analogous to a behind-the-nut bend can be achieved on guitars that have a separate bridge and tailpiece (Fig. 1.18) by depressing the segment of string behind the bridge. Behind-the-bridge bends are most effective when the string segments are relatively long, a design that is typically found on instruments with a trapeze tailpiece.

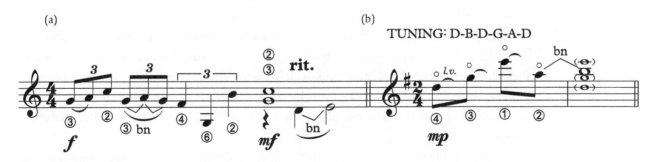

Figure 5.14

Notion for behind-the-nut bends: (a) a behind-the-nut bend with the left hand while simultaneously stopping notes in the lower frets [▶ Media 5.25]; (b) a behind-the-nut bend using harmonics in an open tuning [▶ Media 5.26].

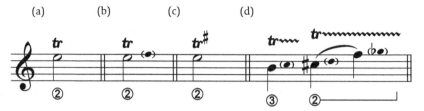

Figure 5.15
Trill notation: (a) an unspecified upper note will be interpreted as the adjacent scale degree; (b) the upper note is specified in parentheses; (c) an accidental indicates that the adjacent scale degree should be sharp; (d) wavy trill lines used to reinforce ligado and tied notes [▶ Media 5.27].

Trill and Tremolo

Trills

A trill is a rapid alternation between a written note and another that is a half or whole step above. On the guitar, these two notes are played ligado on the same string. Trills are notated with the abbreviation "tr" placed above the principal note. If the upper note is not provided then it is assumed to be the adjacent diatonic scale degree (Fig. 5.15a). The upper note can be stated explicitly, either with a parenthesized note head (Fig. 5.15b) or an accidental placed near the trill abbreviation (Fig. 5.15c), the latter always referring to the adjacent pitch class. A wavy line is used for trills that occur over tied notes, or to reinforce a ligado interpretation. Conversely, a separate wavy line on each note suggests that the attacks should be clearly articulated (Fig. 5.15d).[3]

Tremolo

The term "tremolo," literally meaning "trembling" in Italian, is applied to two different techniques that result in quite distinct effects. Kurt Stone (1980) distinguishes these as repeat tremolo and trill tremolo, nomenclature that is adopted throughout this book. Although both produce a trembling effect, repeat tremolo achieves this through rapid fluctuations in loudness, while trill tremolo relies primarily on pitch alternation.

Repeat Tremolo
Repeat tremolo refers to the fast repetition of a note, although the effect can be applied to any musical element capable of being re-attacked with accuracy. The articulated attacks produce a trembling quality brought about by a rapid fluctuation in loudness. In fingerstyles, tremolo is executed by attacking the string with multiple digits in a cyclic pattern, for example, using *a, m, i,* and *p* repeatedly in that order. Pick players will re-attack the string in alternating stroke directions. Specifics of tremolo execution such as these need not be indicated in notation, but should be considered because these techniques place limitations on the ability to play other materials concurrently.

Repeat tremolo can be notated verbatim, although this demands considerable space on the written page. In lieu of a literal transcription, tremolo is often denoted using slanted tremolo beams placed through the stem or centered above or below the note head when no stem is available, serving as a sort of notational shorthand

Figure 5.16
Repeat tremolo notation: (a) a measured tremolo played as repeated 16th notes [(▶) Media 5.28]; (b) an unmeasured tremolo, assuming a moderate to fast tempo [(▶) Media 5.29].

(Fig. 5.16). The number of tremolo beams is indicative of the rate of repetition while the note head defines the duration that the effect is to be maintained on that pitch. For example, in the first measure of Figure 5.16a the notes are repeated at a rate of a 1/16 note, with each lasting two beats. Naturally, ties can be used in the normal manner to extend the effect.

An important distinction is made between measured and unmeasured tremolo. In the measured instance the repetitions coincide with a subdivision of the pulse, whereas an unmeasured tremolo is played as fast as possible and results in an indefinite number of attacks per beat. While that may seem clear enough conceptually, the notational distinction is not explicit. As convention dictates, tremolo will be measured whenever the subdivision can be played with accuracy at the given tempo. An unmeasured tremolo is denoted by a subdivision that is just beyond that which is possible at the given tempo, resulting in a trembling effect of magnified intensity as the player labors to keep up. Indeed, it is the unmeasured tremolo that best characterizes the trembling effect. As one might imagine, the number of tremolo beams required for an unmeasured tremolo is dependent on the tempo, and to some extent, the performer. As a general rule, three tremolo beams will be interpreted as an unmeasured tremolo at moderate to fast tempi (Fig. 5.16b), while four beams may be required at a slower tempo. The matter can be put beyond doubt by clearly stating the expectation in instructions accompanying the score.

Trill Tremolo

Trill tremolo is essentially played like a trill, except that the interval between the two notes is greater than a whole step. Trill tremolos are typically played ligado on a single string with only the first note attacked, as the trembling effect is brought about primarily through variation in pitch. The intervallic range between the two notes is limited to that which the fingers can span on the fretboard and will be greater in higher positions where the frets are more closely spaced. However, if the lower note is an open string then the trill range is essentially that of the string itself.

Trill tremolos are rarely notated verbatim. More often a shorthand notation similar to that used for a repeat tremolo is adopted, although with some peculiarities. In a trill tremolo both pitches are notated side by side, with each note head reflecting the total duration of the effect. Tremolo beams are positioned between the two notes to denote the effect. The first measure of Figure 5.17 shows two unmeasured tremolos, each held for a half note. It is good practice to add slurs to emphasize that the tremolo is to be played ligado.

Figure 5.17
Unmeasured trill
tremolos, each
lasting a half note
[▶ Media 5.30].

Figure 5.18
Oscillatory
patterns and
harmonic nodes
for the first 10
harmonics of a
vibrating string.

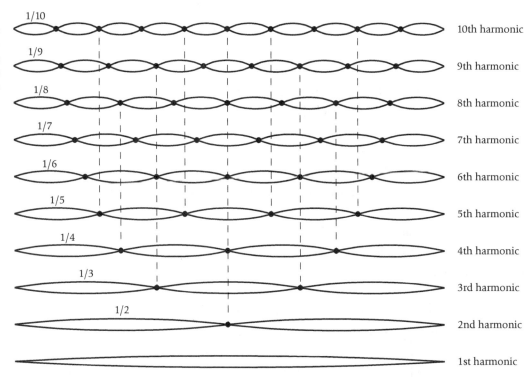

Harmonics

A harmonic is produced on the guitar by lightly touching a string at a harmonic node, a point that divides the total string length into segments of whole number proportion. Figure 5.18 illustrates the oscillatory patterns for the first 10 harmonics of a hypothetical vibrating string with nodes marked by solid dots. Resting a finger lightly against a string at one of these nodal points damps all harmonics that do not share a node at the same location, resulting in a perceived pitch at the lowest remaining harmonic. As can be seen in Figure 5.19, harmonic nodes are mirrored around the midpoint of the vibrating string's length. For example, the third harmonic of an open string can be produced by touching the string at either fret VII or fret XIX, with both resulting in the same pitch and timbre.

Intonation

In Chapter 2 attention was given to the relationship between the frequencies found in a harmonic series and those used in the 12-tone equal tempered system of tuning.[4] To summarize, harmonics are justly intonated with respect to a fundamental pitch, while the fretting on a standard guitar produces pitches that are equal tempered. Equal tempered pitches are close approximations to their harmonic counterparts, but they are not perfectly intonated with them. Figure 5.20 shows the equal tempered equivalents of the first 10 harmonics above a fundamental pitch of E2, along with their cent deviations from standard tuning (100 cents = a half step). If we compare, for example, the fifth harmonic (G-sharp)

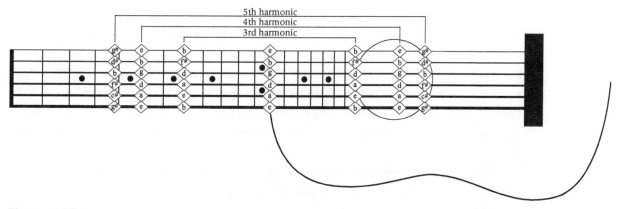

Figure 5.19
Harmonics mirrored around the midpoint of a vibrating string.

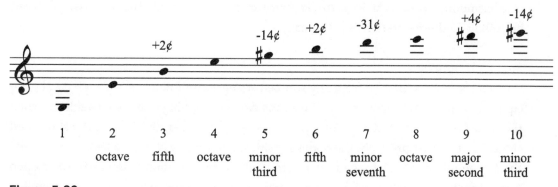

Figure 5.20
Equal-tempered equivalents for the first 10 harmonics of an E fundamental.

on an open E string with an equal tempered G-sharp the harmonic will sound 14 cents flat. Knowing the intervallic relations and intonational discrepancies between harmonics and their corresponding tempered pitches is invaluable if harmonics are to play a deliberate role in the musical harmony. Observe that harmonics corresponding to intervals of a third and seventh fall particularly flat of their equal tempered equivalent: –14 cents and –31 cents, respectively. While these discrepancies in intonation can sometimes cause harmonics to sound out of tune in the context of equal temperament, they can also be exploited to create interesting beating effects when sounded against their tempered approximations.

Harmonic Types: Open (Natural) and Stopped (Artificial)

Harmonics are considered natural or artificial depending on whether the string that they are sounded on is open or stopped. To label any harmonic artificial is somewhat of a mis-nomer since all harmonics are governed by the same physical principles. In actuality, the distinction between natural and artificial harmonics has more to do with differences in technique than with the harmonic itself. The execution of a harmonic on a stopped string requires a substantially different strategy since the left hand has the additional task of fretting the fundamental. Because some of the techniques of harmonic production discussed in this chapter can be employed on both open and stopped strings, I refrain from using the terms "natural" and "artificial," substituting instead the terms "open" and "stopped."

Open Harmonics

An open harmonic is obtained by lightly touching an open string at one of its harmonic nodes. The finger is usually removed immediately to allow the tone to sustain. Open harmonics up to the sixth are reliable on any string, and on some guitars it may be possible to reach the tenth. The second (fret XII), third (fret VII), and fourth (fret V) open harmonics speak easily with a resonance comparable to that of an open string. Higher harmonics become increasingly difficult to produce and much of their tonal purity and sustain is diminished.

Given a choice, open harmonics are preferred in most contexts, principally due to their resonant quality, but also because they require the least amount of effort to produce. Moreover, once an open harmonic sounds and the finger is lifted off the string the hand is free to engage the instrument in other ways. However, the collection of distinct pitch classes available on open strings is fairly limited, even when considering the available harmonics on all six strings. Alternative tunings can diversify the collective pitch set, but rarely do these lead to a full chromatic scale.

Stopped Harmonics

Harmonics can be obtained from any stopped string according to the same physical principles that apply to an open string. If we consider the stopping finger a movable nut then the nodes are to be found at points that mark whole number divisions of the shortened string length. More precisely, the nodes are shifted upward by N frets, where N represents the fret number of the stopped pitch. Stopped harmonics sound similar to their open counterparts, although usually with less resonance due to the involvement of a stopping finger.[5] Furthermore, higher harmonics become even harder to produce clearly since the fundamental string length is shorter. The principal advantage of the stopped harmonic technique is that any pitch can be sounded as a harmonic.

Despite their physical similarities, the additional requirement that the string be stopped demands a considerably different performance technique. Three crucial elements are involved in the production of a stopped harmonic: (1) The string must be stopped at some fret with a left hand finger; (2) the harmonic node must be touched, either using the right or left hand; (3) the string must be attacked with the right hand. In fingerstyles, the typical method of producing a stopped harmonic is to touch the node with the right hand index finger while plucking it with the middle or ring finger (Fig. 5.21a). A similar approach can be adopted with a pick held between the thumb and middle finger (Fig. 5.21b). While not as common, higher-order harmonics can be obtained by stopping the string with the first finger of the left hand while touching the node with the fourth [⯈ Media 5.35].

Harmonic Notation

Harmonic notation is notoriously inconsistent in practice, often leading to confusion as to what is intended. Three crucial details would ensure the accurate execution of harmonics: (1) the fundamental of the harmonic series, which is the pitch corresponding to the vibrating string length upon which the harmonic is isolated; (2) the node along the string's length at which the string should be lightly touched; (3) the resultant sounding pitch. Much of the confusion surrounding harmonic notation occurs because these details are presented differently depending on whether the harmonic is open or stopped and whether

(a)   (b)

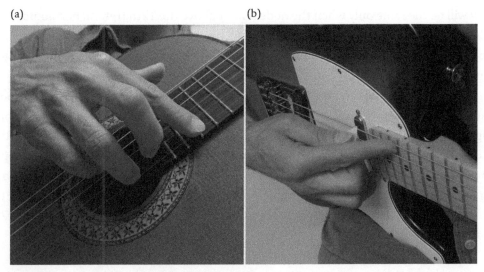

Figure 5.21

Stopped harmonic techniques: (a) the left hand stops the string while the right hand touches the node and plucks the string; (b) the left hand stops the string while the right hand touches the node and picks the string.

(a)   (b)   (c)   (d)   (e)

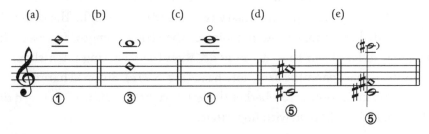

Figure 5.22

Harmonic notation: (a) an open harmonic with unison nodal and sounding pitches [▶ Media 5.31]; (b) an open harmonic with different nodal and sounding pitches [▶ Media 5.32]; (c) an open harmonic with unison nodal and sounding pitches [▶ Media 5.33]; (d) a stopped harmonic with unison nodal and sounding pitches [▶ Media 5.34]; (e) a stopped harmonic with different nodal and sounding pitches [▶ Media 5.35].

the sounding pitch is the same or different from the pitch that would be produced if the string were fully depressed at the node. Adherence to the simple guidelines below can greatly demystify written harmonics and remove ambiguity. In any case, the strategy employed for the notation of harmonics should always be explained clearly in the score.

Open Harmonic Notation

The notation for open harmonics should omit the pitch of the fundamental as it requires no action by the performer. Moreover, the presence or absence of a written fundamental provides a quick and clear means for a performer to differentiate between an open and stopped harmonic. A string indication should always be included, which indirectly conveys the fundamental to the performer and eliminates ambiguity. Beyond the question of the fundamental, there are a couple of options for handling the notation of nodes and sounding pitches. The most consistent approach is always to use a diamond shaped note head to represent the node, placed at the pitch that would sound if the string were fully depressed. In cases where the sounding pitch is the same as that referencing the node, no other indications are needed; the diamond note head reflects both the node and the sounding pitch (Fig. 5.22a). Observe, however, that the nodal pitch and the sounding pitch will be the same only when the node is at or above the 12th fret. All harmonic nodes in lower frets produce a pitch that is different from the one representing the node and should therefore include a small parenthesized note head to denote the sounding pitch (Fig. 5.22b).

An open harmonic can also be notated by placing a small circle off the staff above a normal note head, indicating that the written pitch should be heard as a harmonic (Fig. 5.22c). This notation should be reserved for situations where the sounding pitch is the same as that referencing the node. The use of harmonic circles is sensible when all open harmonics in the piece can be notated in this way. In works involving some harmonics that sound pitches other than those referencing the node it is more consistent to use diamond note heads for all, as illustrated in Figures 5.22a and 5.22b).

Stopped Harmonic Notation

The notation for a stopped harmonic must include the pitch of the stopped string, as an action is required of the performer. A diamond note head is used to indicate the node at which the string is touched. If the sounding pitch is the same as that referenced by the node then no further notation is necessary (Fig. 5.21d). This will be the case only when the node is located at or above the midpoint of the string's length. In cases where the sounding pitch differs from that at the node, then the sounding pitch should also be provided using a small, parenthesized note head (Fig. 5.21e). Stopped harmonic notation typically gives no indication as to whether the left or right hand is used to touch the node, although this could be clarified with fingerings.

Other Harmonic Techniques

Tap Harmonics

Tapping a string with a fingertip at a harmonic node produces a percussive attack with a tonal component comprising both the harmonic and fundamental pitches. Tap harmonics are effective on all types of guitars and the technique can be used on both open and stopped strings. They can be notated using the same methods adopted for open and stopped harmonics described above, with the addition of a "T.H." above or below the staff and defined in the score (Fig. 5.23a). It is possible to tap multiple adjacent strings at a harmonic node (Fig. 5.23b). The taps are limited to straight bars, but common chord types can be obtained using an open tuning. Guitarist Vicki Genfan makes extensive use of tap harmonics in her music, combined with thumb slapping

Figure 5.23
Tap harmonic
notation: (a) a single
tap harmonic
[▶ Media 5.36];
(b) a harmonic chord
[▶ Media 5.37].

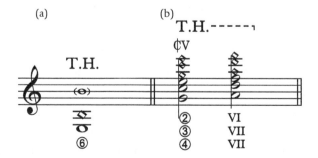

and percussive strikes on the body of her acoustic guitar, which she collectively refers to as "slap-tap" technique.

Touch Harmonics

Touch harmonics are produced by first attacking a string normally, and while it is vibrating, touching it lightly at a harmonic node. The effect is characterized by a shift from the fundamental to the harmonic. Paolo Cavallone refers to this technique as "smorzato" in *Au réveil il était midi* (2008), a term that suggests a dying away of the sound. In Figure 5.24, Cavallone uses a "T" to indicate tambora and an "S" to denote smorzato, the touch harmonic (Fig. 5.24). Of course, any unique symbol would suffice.

Pinch Harmonics

Pinch harmonics are most often associated with the electric guitar, as the technique typically involves the use of a pick and is significantly enhanced with distortion. The effect is produced by attacking a string with a pick in a downstroke, and in the same right-hand motion, lightly brushing the thumb against the string at a harmonic node. The technique can also be employed with the fingers alone by pinching the thumb and index finger together as if they were holding a pick, striking the string first with the topside of the index fingernail in a downstroke and lightly touching the thumb against the string in the same motion. Both techniques are typically performed at nodes above the fretboard. Pinch harmonics require virtually no repositioning of the hand, making it possible to switch between harmonics and normal notes nearly as quickly as if the passage were written without harmonics. The resulting harmonic is piercing and lively, often blending a hint of the fundamental with the harmonic tone. While obtainable on open strings, pinch harmonics are more often played on stopped strings where they can be intensified with vibrato or a string bend.

Pinch harmonics can be notated using the same methods described for open and stopped harmonics above, with the addition of a "P.H." above or below the staff and defined in the score (Fig. 5.25). A virtual fret indication could be included to guide the player above the fretboard.

Pizzicato Harmonics

Instead of removing the finger from the node once the string is attacked, the player can let it rest lightly against the string, producing a dampened pizzicato harmonic [▶ Media 5.39]. The technique is essentially the same as surface pizzicato, discussed earlier, but with the finger over a harmonic node. Open, stopped, and touch harmonics can be played pizzicato in this way with relative ease. Alternatively, harmonics can be dampened with a palm mute. A pizzicato harmonic can be indicated using the relevant notation method presented above with "pizz" added over the staff.

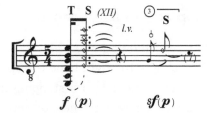

Figure 5.24

Touch harmonics, denoted by "S," in Paolo Cavallone's *Au réveil il était midi* (2008).

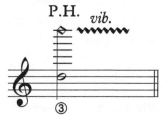

Figure 5.25

Notation for a pinch harmonic with vibrato [▶ Media 5.38].

Figure 5.26
Figure 5.26
A G major arpeggio
played as stopped
harmonics
[▶ Media 5.40].

Figure 5.27
Notation for palm
harmonics
[▶ Media 5.41].

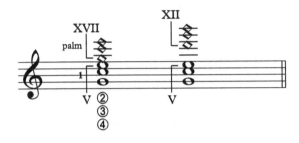

Harmonic Arpeggios

The common method of playing harmonic arpeggios is to finger a chord with the left hand and then use the stopped harmonic technique to isolate the second harmonic on each string, 12 frets above the fundamental notes of the chord. When played as second harmonics the resultant harmony is the same as that which is fingered, but an octave higher. Playing arpeggios on higher-order harmonics results in the same chord quality, but transposed upward by the harmonic interval. In any case, the right hand will have to shift to various frets so as to hit the appropriate nodes on each string. Figure 5.26 shows a G major arpeggio played as stopped harmonics.

Palm Harmonics

The palm of the right hand can be used to touch harmonic nodes above the fretboard as the string is attacked. This technique is typically employed to obtain harmonic chords on stopped strings, although it is limited to straight and diagonal chord shapes. Moving the palm to account for shifting nodes is considerably more challenging. Suggested notation is offered in Figure 5.27.

Tap and Touch Techniques

In conventional guitar styles there is a division of labor between the left and right hands. Put simply, the right hand is responsible for setting the strings in motion while the left hand is responsible for stopping them at various positions on the fretboard in order to achieve different pitches. By contrast, tapping and touch techniques are based on the principle that the string is both stopped and attacked using the same finger in a single, forceful hammering action. These techniques can be implemented with both the left and right hands independently, offering polyphonic possibilities otherwise unattainable on the instrument.

Multiphonics

When a string is tapped, energy is distributed to both sides of the finger, causing both front and back tones to sound together, an effect commonly referred to as a

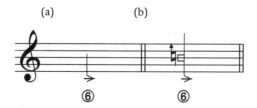

Figure 5.28

Multiphonic notation: (a) incomplete notation, showing only the front tone; (b) complete notation showing the front tone with a wedge note head and the back tone with a square note head [▶ Media 5.42].

Figure 5.29

Left hand solo passage in the Toccata from Giles Swayne's *Suite for Guitar* (© Copyright 1976 Novello & Company Ltd. All Rights Reserved. International Copyright Secured. Reprinted by permission of Novello & Company Ltd.).

multiphonic.[6] Back tones are naturally quite soft without amplification. However, on acoustic instruments or electric guitars at low volumes they can be roughly balanced with the front tones when tapped above the 12th fret, diminishing in loudness at positions closer to the nut. John Schneider (1985) suggests notating multiphonics with a wedge note head placed at the pitch corresponding to the front tone. If both front and back tones are to be represented, then a square note head could be used for the back tone (Fig. 5.28).

Left Hand Solo

Left hand solo is a technique found in contemporary classical literature that involves playing materials with the left hand alone. Unlike a multiphonic, however, the focus is on the front tones, which can be more clearly isolated by damping the string behind the stopping finger. Notes attacked with the left hand sound soft and delicate, providing an interesting contrast to normally plucked or picked materials [▶ Media 5.43]. Giles Swayne employs left hand solo for timbral contrast in the Toccata movement of his *Suite for Guitar* (1979). Material played sul ponticello is then echoed with the left hand alone, and finally echoed once more pizzicato (Fig. 5.29). Swayne uses standard notation and simply indicates the technique with the text "L.H. only." In "The Tin Soldiers" from *The Prince's Toys* (1992), Nikita Koshkin uses left hand solo in the service of polyphony; while the left hand taps dyads the right hand strums the strings behind the nut, the latter indicated graphically on the lower staff (Fig. 5.30).

Finger Tapping

Perhaps no other artist has brought more attention to finger tapping techniques than rock guitarist Eddie Van Halen, who made it a hallmark of his style. In the quintessential

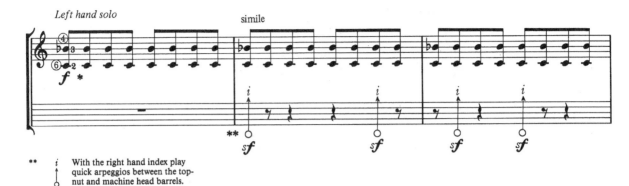

**   *i*   With the right hand index play
       ↑   quick arpeggios between the top-
       ○   nut and machine head barrels.

Figure 5.30
Left hand solo passage (upper staff) in "The Tin Soldiers" from Nikita Koshkin's *The Prince's Toys* (1992).

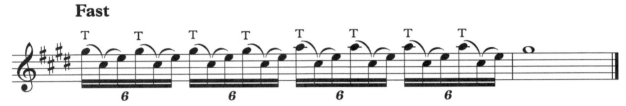

Figure 5.31
Finger tapping technique used in Van Halen's "Eruption" (1978) (transcribed by the author) [▶ Media 5.44].

Van Halen technique the right hand taps a single note, usually with finger *i* or *m,* and then pulls off to the left hand, which plays two or three additional notes ligado. This three or four note pattern is repeated to produce a sustained barrage of rapid pitches. The short and cyclic nature of the patterns is suggestive of arpeggios rather than scalar runs, precisely how Van Halen tends to use the technique. Figure 5.31 provides an excerpt from Van Halen's "Eruption" (1978), using a "T" to designate notes that are tapped.

Free Hand Touch Technique

Harry DeArmond invented the first attachable guitar pickup in the 1930s, and at that time he pioneered the touch technique to demonstrate its sensitivity. DeArmond would often play two guitars simultaneously, tapping out accompaniment on one instrument while playing melodies on the other. Jimmy Webster, a former student of DeArmond, wrote *The Touch System for Electric and Amplified Spanish Guitar* (1952), the first formal instruction book on the technique. The polyphonic potential of touch techniques was immediately apparent and led to the invention of instruments designed specifically for it. In 1974, Emmett Chapman developed the Chapman Stick, an instrument that combines bass and treble strings on a single neck. Notable contemporary players that utilize free hand touch technique on guitars include Stanley Jordan (electric guitar) and Dominic Frasca (nylon string guitar).

Free hand touch technique differs from finger tapping in that the fingers work independently of one another to tap each note, rather than relying on ligado. A competent

Figure 5.32
Notation for free hand touch technique in Leo Brouwer's *Paisaje Cubano Con Campanas* (1986).

touch player can attack notes with all four fingers on both hands independently, significantly expanding the polyphonic potential of the instrument.[7] Touch technique requires considerable practice to master, and while simple passages may be reasonable, it should not be assumed that any guitarist is capable of executing the technique with agility. Composers looking for proficiency with the technique might turn to Chapman Stick players.

Touch techniques can be indicated in standard notation by simply defining a symbol as a tap; a "+" above the note head or an "x" through the stem suffice. Leo Brouwer's *Paisaje Cubano Con Campanas* (1986) employs two-hand touch technique using a separate staff for each hand (Fig. 5.32). If fingerings are included they should follow the standard practice of using numbers for the left hand and letters for the right hand.

Bottleneck Slides

A bottleneck slide is a tube-shaped object, typically worn on a left hand finger and used to stop the strings. Rather than depressing a string to the fret wires, a slide rests lightly against the string with just enough pressure to stop it directly, essentially acting like a movable fret wire and enabling smooth portamento along the entire string length. Purpose-built slides can be purchased in a variety of materials, including steel, brass, glass, and ceramic. The material has an effect on the sound produced: metal slides sound louder and brighter; glass and ceramic sound softer and duller; bronze sounds darker than steel. Slides can also be devised from practically any found object with a smooth and hard surface. Common items include a pocket-knife, a zippo lighter, or a beer bottle. Such objects typically need to be held between two fingers, making it difficult to use the left hand for anything but maneuvering the slide.

A bottleneck slide can be worn on any of the four left hand fingers. While largely a player preference, the finger used does impact the player's ability to engage the instrument. With a slide on the fourth finger, the three dominant fingers are free to stop notes normally. However, some players claim to obtain more control over the slide when it is worn on the third, or less often, the second finger. It is not so common to place a slide on the first finger, as that leaves no available fingers to dampen the back tones behind the device, an integral component of the technique. In addition to damping behind the slide, players often use the fingers and thumb of the right hand to mute individual strings when switching from one to another.

Slides are used both melodically and harmonically, although the latter is considerably restricted with the instrument in standard tuning since the device forms a straight barré that stops the strings in a single position. Because chord shapes are confined to barré configurations, players often employ open tunings to obtain basic chord types. Slide players also make ample use of vibrato, which not only ornaments a note but also prolongs sustain. Slide vibrato typically only alters the pitch downward; otherwise the note tends to sound sharp.

Slide techniques can be notated using straight portamento lines (Fig. 5.33). These can be mixed with wavy glissando lines to distinguish the use of a slide from a fingered glissando. If greater clarity is desired an "(s)" could be added to the portamento line to emphasize that a slide is to be used. As usual, string and fret indications should be included whenever alternative tunings are employed.

Specialized Slide Techniques

Above-the-Fretboard Slide Tones
Very high pitches can be obtained by stopping a string with a slide between the end of the fretboard and the bridge [▶ Media 5.46]. In contrast to using the fingers, slide tones above the fretboard sound with the same clarity and sustain as notes stopped over the fretboard. Of course, there are no frets to offer visual guidance for intonation. For accuracy, colored chalk can be used to mark these locations on the strings. Panayiotis Kokoras makes ample use of this region of the strings in his work *Slide* (2002), In this score excerpt in Figure 5.34, the performer slowly and continuously moves the slide from the 39th to the 37th virtual fret while plucking specific strings to pull out a melody along the way.

Indeterminate Portamento Gestures
A slide circumvents the frets and allows for an endless variety of smooth portamento gestures. While it is possible to notate such contours with precision, it may be sensible to treat them indeterminately, allowing the player to focus primarily on the articulation

Figure 5.33
Standard slide notation [▶ Media 5.45].

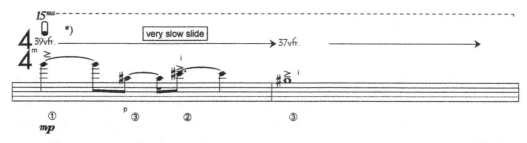

Figure 5.34
Score excerpt from Panayiotis Kokoras's *Slide* (2002).

*) The noted pithes are not neccsary to be played exactly on pitch. The slide should not stop its slow and smooth downwards motion up to bar 100 and then from bar 101 to 114.

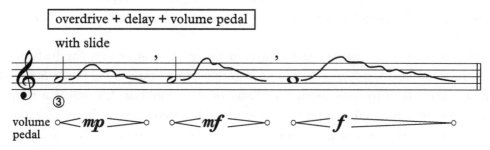

Figure 5.35
Notation for indeterminate portamento gestures using a slide in conjunction with a volume pedal, overdrive, and delay [▶ Media 5.47].

Figure 5.36
Sympathetic resonance in Peter Maxwell Davies *Sonata* (1984).

and expression of the gesture without having to worry about targeting specific notes and rhythms. Trajectories can simply be outlined using a curved line on the staff, with the line's relative height providing an approximation of the pitch contour. Figure 5.35 shows slide gestures paired with a volume pedal.

Sympathetic Resonance

An unmuted string will vibrate sympathetically when tuned in a harmonic ratio to another string that is attacked. For instance, with a guitar in E-standard tuning, playing an E3 staccato on the fourth string causes the sixth to also ring [▶ Media 5.48]. The effect is most resonant on open strings but occurs on stopped strings as well. Composers and performers can use these sympathetic vibrations to add resonance to a passage. Figure 5.36 provides an example from Peter Maxwell Davies Sonata (1984) in which the open second string is intended to vibrate sympathetically with a fretted B on the fourth string.

Non-Pitched Sounds

Body Percussion

A variety of timbrally distinct percussive sounds can be obtained by striking the body of an acoustic instrument. Made using either hand, these sounds can be syncopated with normally plucked or strummed materials to add rhythmic vitality to the music. Such integrated percussive materials are a distinctive feature of flamenco music and not uncommon to contemporary classical works. More recently, they have become characteristic of a growing number of acoustic fingerstyle players, including Mike Dawes, Antoine Dufour, Vikki Genfan, Michael Hedges, and Don Ross, who often use both hands to "slap-tap" nearly everything, including individual notes, chords, and harmonics.

Percussive sounds change significantly at different locations on the instrument, with the soundboard, sides, neck, and headstock common targets [▶ Media 5.49]. The fullest sounds tend to come from the center of the soundboard, whereas a thinner, knock-like effect is obtained near the edges. The sides produce an even thinner, tighter sound. Striking the neck or headstock causes the strings to ring and is often done for that reason.

Notation for body percussion may be as simple as using an "x" note head, defined ahead of time and integrated into the main staff. However, if percussion techniques are used extensively, then it often makes sense to employ a percussion staff. In Hans Werner Henze's *Royal Winter Music—First Sonata on Shakespearean Characters* (1976) the composer identifies three distinct locations in which the performer can strike the soundboard. He then uses a separate percussion staff to integrate the taps into the music (Fig. 5.37).

In addition to striking different parts of the instrument, the percussive quality can be affected by the part of the hand used, with the fingertip, fingernail, thumb, knuckle, side of the palm, or open palm all viable options. In *Jongo* (1993), Paulo Bellinati specifies

Figure 5.37

Excerpt from Hans Werner Henze's *Royal Winter Music – First Sonata on Shakespearean Characters* (1976), showing a separate staff used for percussive body taps.

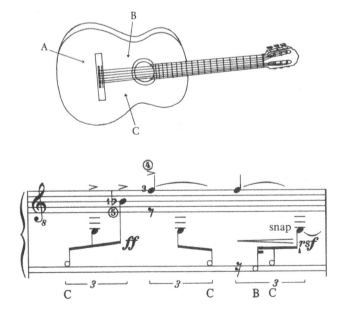

both the locations and the manner of hitting the instrument using a five-line percussion staff for both left and right hands (5.38).

Instead of striking the body, it can be rubbed, scratched, or brushed to produce a variety of softer non-pitched sounds [▶ Media 5.50]. Andre Bartetzki requests a brush in circular motions on the soundboard of an acoustic instrument in *Traces* (2007). Figure 5.39 shows an excerpt from a particularly striking passage where the brush is swirled on the soundboard with the right hand while the left hand plays solo on the fretboard.

Golpe

Golpe is a technique originating in flamenco music in which the right hand digits strike the soundboard in rhythmic unison or syncopation with plucked strings. The particulars of golpe technique vary according to whether the soundboard is hit above or below the strings. For golpe below the highest string, the strings are attacked with the thumb and the ring finger is used to tap the soundboard. For golpe above the lowest string, the thumb and middle finger are held together and in a single flicking motion the middle

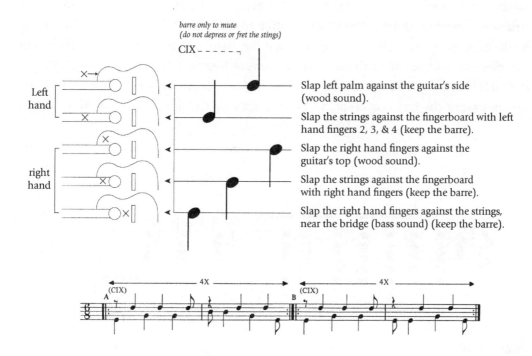

Figure 5.38

Score excerpt from Paulo Bellinati's *Jongo* (1993), showing locations where the performer should strike the body of the instrument.

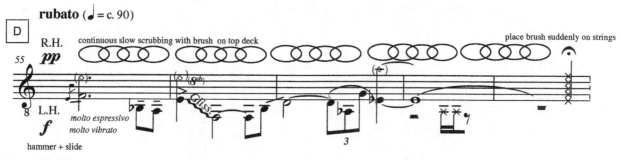

Figure 5.39

The use of a brush in Andre Bartetzki's *Traces* (2007) for acoustic guitar and live electronics.

finger strikes the strings while the thumb strikes the soundboard. Proper golpe techniques require practice to master and it cannot be assumed that any guitarist will be proficient at them. Nonetheless, simple passages that integrate taps on the soundboard with normally plucked or picked materials are not unreasonable, even if the above methods of execution are not adhered to.

Golpe is typically notated using an "x" note head placed off the staff, above or below, depending on where the soundboard is tapped (Fig. 5.40). Importantly, the note head should not sit on a ledger line. The plain text "golpe" should be included in the first instance of the technique in a score. Details regarding fingering and strum directions are optional.

Tambour

Tambour refers to a technique in which the player strikes the strings near the bridge with a flat part of the right hand, usually the side of the thumb, the side of the palm, or any combination of extended fingers.[8] It is most often applied to chords and there are two sonic components to the resulting sound: a drum-like thud produced when the hand hits the bridge and a harmonic resonance from the strings [▶ Media 5.53]. Classic tambour is played close to the bridge so that bridge and string components are roughly balanced. However, shifting the attack location toward the bridge minimizes the strings, while shifts away from the bridge emphasize the strings at the expensive of the drum-like element. At the end of the third movement of Reginald Smith Brindle's *El Polifemo de Oro* (1981) the performer is instructed to gradually move the strike location from the bridge toward the fretboard (Fig. 5.41). In *Sonata for Guitar* (1978), Alberto Ginastera

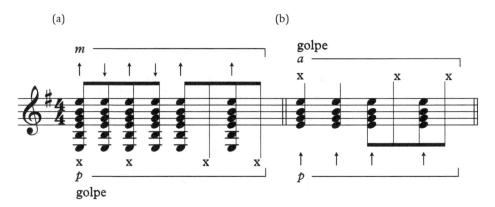

Figure 5.40

Golpe notation: (a) using the thumb on the soundboard above the strings [▶ Media 5.51]; (b) using the ring finger on the soundboard below the strings [▶ Media 5.52].

Figure 5.41

Tambour notation in Reginald Smith Brindle's *El Polifemo de Oro* (1956, revised edition 1981).

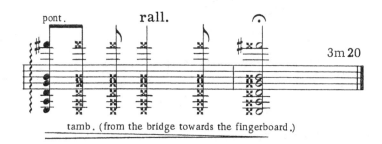

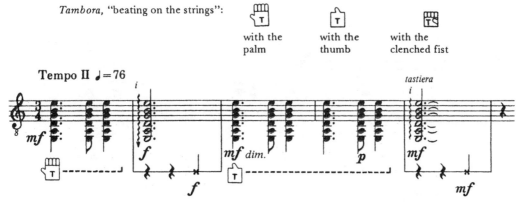

Figure 5.42
Contrasting tambour methods in Alberto Ginastera's *Sonata for Guitar* (1978).

uses graphic hand icons to distinguish three methods of striking the strings: with an open palm, with the thumb, and with a clenched first (Fig. 5.42).

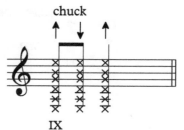

Figure 5.43
Suggested notation for a string chuck [▶ Media 5.54].

String Chucks

A string chuck is a percussive effect achieved by briskly strumming damped strings with a pick. The resulting sound should suppress pitches, leaving only the percussive attack of the pick against the strings. To this end, chucking at positions over harmonic nodes is generally avoided. Chucks are used frequently in blues, country, funk, and rock styles to add rhythmic vivacity between harmonic elements. For instance, they may be alternated with bass notes and chordal strums in a "boom-chuck" rhythmic pattern, adding a strong backbeat feel to the music. Damping can be done with either the left or right hands, the latter achieved by strumming with a downstroke and letting the palm hit the strings just before the pick strikes them. Chucks can be notated with "x" note heads placed on the staff to represent the open strings that are engaged, along with a fret indication and the text "chuck" written above or below the staff (Fig. 5.43). Stroke directions are optional but do alter the sonority of the effect; downstrokes favor the lower strings while upstrokes accentuate the higher.

String Scrapes

Wound strings can be scraped with the fingernails, the edge of a plectrum, or any other hard-edged object to produce an abrasive, scratch-like sound.[9] The effect is most pronounced when the object is held perpendicular to the string and can be subdued by reducing the angle in the direction of the scraping motion. Fast scrapes sound aggressive, but at slower speeds individual pulsations can be heard as the scraper crosses the striated ridges of the winding. While the scratch quality is predominant, there are also pitched components of front and back tones that continuously change in contrary motion according to the scratch location. The individual portamento trajectories can best be heard when scraping the string near the bridge or nut, as the tones are separated in register. Alternatively, either tone can be isolated by damping the string segments on the opposite side of the scraper. Of course, front tones tend to be louder unless the back tone is in some way amplified.

Figure 5.44

Notation for string scrapes in Reginald Smith Brindle's *Guitarcosmos 3* [▶ Media 5.55].

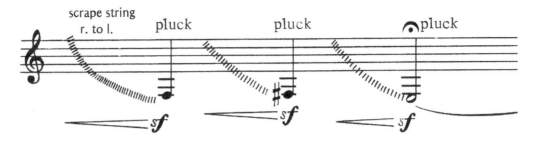

Figure 5.45

Suggest notation for a scrape tremolo [▶ Media 5.56].

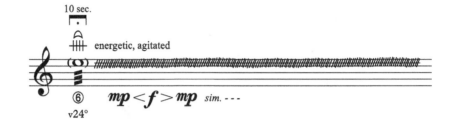

Figure 5.46

Notation for a string scrape with a varying striation rate [▶ Media 5.57].

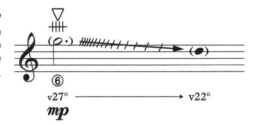

Directional Gestures

One of more stereotypical heavy metal musical gestures involves a downward pick scrape on the lower strings that leads into a power chord on the downbeat. Reginald Smith Brindle employs scrapes similarly on a nylon string instrument in "Percussion Piece" from *Guitarcosmos 3* (1979), using a striated graphic notation to represent the technique (Fig. 5.44). For a fuller sound, two adjacent strings can be scraped together.

Agitated Gestures and Scrape Tremolo

Wonderfully energetic and agitated gestures can be produced by rapidly scraping a string in short alternating motions. Confining scrapes to a narrow region of the string minimizes the portamento quality, instead producing a more focused pitch. Figure 5.45 offers notation for a scrape tremolo adapted from harp literature. Virtual fret indications are used to denote the location on the string above the fretboard. The note head approximates the tonality that should sound; in practice it will vary slightly with the scrape location. A nail symbol is used to indicate that the nail should be used; a pick symbol could just as well be presented, as in Figure 5.46.

Striation Rate

When wound strings are scraped slowly the scraper can be heard crossing the individual ridges of the winding. At steady rates the striations add a pulsating quality to the effect. Individual striations can also be isolated by increasing pressure on the string to prevent the scraper from moving past more than one ridge at a time. The result is a remarkable sense of pent-up tension that is released each time the scraper crosses the ridge. It is also worth noting that the tonal components of a string scrape are much more prominent when

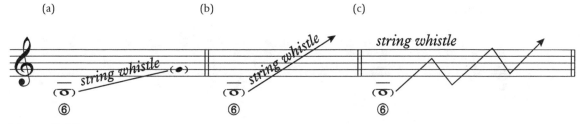

Figure 5.47
Notation for string whistle (a) with a specified ending pitch [▶ Media 5.58]; (b) with an indeterminate ending pitch [▶ Media 5.59]; (c) a more complex, indeterminate trajectory [▶ Media 5.60].

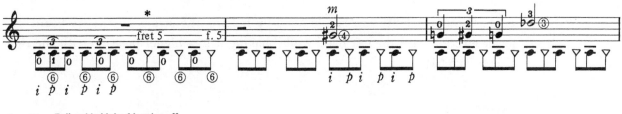

* ⅄ Pull and hold the 6th string off the side of the finger-board. An imitation of the buzzing sound of a zither.

Figure 5.48
Off-the-fretboard string bend in "The Doll with Blinking Eyes" from Nikita Koshkin's *The Prince's Toys* (1992).

striations are isolated because the tones can be heard ringing between movements of the pick. A similar effect can be achieved by turning a triangular pick between two strings. Figure 5.46 offers a notation for a string scrape characterized by a descending portamento and varying striation rate.

String Whistle

String whistle occurs when sliding the flesh of a finger along a wound string. The effect is similar to a string scrape, but softer and much more subdued. String whistle occurs incidentally when changing positions along the fretboard, and guitarists normally strive to minimize it. However, it can be played deliberately and in isolation using the left or right hand fingers, either by sliding them lightly over the strings or by pinching a string between the thumb and index finger. Glissando notation can be adopted for string whistle, allowing the duration as well as the start and ending pitches to be precisely specified (Fig. 5.47). Because of the similarity to glissando notation, text distinguishing the effect must be included in each instance.

Off-the-Fretboard String Bends

The outer strings can be bent so that they slip off of the edge of the fretboard, producing a buzzing sound when attacked in this displaced position. Nikita Koshkin employs off-the-fretboard string bends in "The Doll with Blinking Eyes" from *The Prince's Toys* (1992) to imitate the buzzing quality of a zither (Fig. 5.48). Once displaced, the string naturally wants to return to its normal position. This retracting force can be countered with the finger to shake the string, creating an unstable, wobbly effect with indeterminate

Figure 5.49
String crossing in "The Tin Soldiers" from Nikita Koshkin's *The Prince's Toys* (1992).

* An imitation of a drum. With the help of the right hand pull the 2nd string over the 1st one.

pitch. Greater stability can be obtained by holding the string off the fretboard in a lower position with the left hand while shaking it in a higher position with the right [▶ Media 5.61]

String Crossing

String crossing is a technique borrowed from the Chinese pipa that involves pulling one string across the fretboard with the right hand until it crosses an adjacent string. The player then applies a finger or barré to the strings at the crossing point to hold them in place. The sounding result has a buzz-like percussive quality mixed with tones from the two strings, although the sounding pitches are higher than those fingered and somewhat unpredictable [▶ Media 5.62]. Nikita Koshkin employs this technique in "The Tin Soldiers" from *The Prince's Toys* (1992), where the second string is crossed over the first to emulate the sound of a snare drum (Fig. 5.49). The strings are then stopped at different frets to alter the sound.

Pickup Pops and Electric Buzzes

Touching a metal object such as a bolt to the poles of a magnetic pickup can cause a loud, plosive pop that is quite distinct from most other guitar sounds [▶ Media 5.63]. The effect can pack quite a punch at high volumes. Pickup pops can be notated using a shape note head or graphic symbol defined in the instructions accompanying the score.

In *Trash TV Trance* (2002), Fausto Romitelli has the guitarist remove the $\frac{1}{4}$-inch cable from the instrument and touch it against the metal hardware to create a Morse code-like pattern of long and short buzzes [▶ Media 5.64]. The composer notates the effect using an "x" note head, but any shape note would suffice.

6

Instrumental Preparations

A prepared instrument is one that has been temporarily altered, most often by attaching foreign objects to expand its timbral and/or performance capabilities.[1] Composer John Cage is often credited as being the first to have explored the prepared instrument in depth, although he cited Henry Cowell as a source of inspiration. Starting with *Bacchanale* (1940), Cage began to wedge objects between the strings of the piano to obtain a more percussive sound collection. He composed numerous works for prepared piano, with *Sonatas and Interludes* (1948) serving as a notable example. Composers and performers since Cage have experimented with preparations on most common practice instruments, the guitar not withstanding.

The prepared guitar offers a sound palette quite distinct from the standard lexicon—one in which the attack-decay morphologies and clear tones typically associated with a plucked string are exchanged for inharmonic timbres, buzzing ornamentations, or non-pitched materials. Many preparations result in sounds with complex behaviors as the object bounces or rattles against the strings. Others suggest new methods for engaging the instrument, or even the preparation object directly. This detachment from, and in some cases resistance to, conventional musical materials and performance practice can be a great source of inspiration, inviting us to think of the organization of sounds in different terms. Yet, the fact that it is still a guitar, as opposed to an entirely new interface, allows a player to bring skills refined over years of training to a performance.

Almost any found object can be attached to the guitar in a way that produces an interesting and musically useful sound. With such an infinite array of possibilities, a comprehensive catalog of preparations is not feasible. Instead, this chapter aims to define a typology of preparations, which includes mutes, third bridges, suspended string attachments, suspended string couplers, buzzes, rattles, bouncers, snarled and crossed strings, percussive sounds, and body attachments. Specific implementations using commonly available materials will be given as examples within each category but with the broader aim of developing a general understanding of the sonic qualities and mutable nature of each type of preparation. Equipped with this foundation, guitarists and composers will be better able to get the most out of the objects at hand.

Mutes

A mute is made of a soft or spongy material and fixed to the instrument so that it muffles the vibrating strings. Set near the bridge, it produces a pizzicato effect in which pitches sound clear but with reduced sustain and a duller timbre. Moving the mute toward the center of the string increases the muffling effect and diminishes the sense of pitch [▶ Media 6.1]. Placed in the middle of a string's length, results can be surprisingly percussive. Mutes produce effects not unfamiliar to the guitar; similar sounds are routinely achieved using the palm of the right hand—a palm mute—or by damping the strings with the fingers of the left hand over the fretboard—a chuck. Of course, the advantage that a mute preparation has over these performance techniques is that it relinquishes the hands of any damping responsibility, freeing them to engage the instrument in other ways.

The use of a mute on the guitar is not common practice. The few commercial products that are available, such as the MusicBar® by Innovative Product Designs LTD (Fig. 6.1a) and the TremoloMute by Rosette Guitar Products (Fig. 6.1b), are sold primarily to reduce the volume of the instrument while practicing. A few electric guitar models, including the Fender Jaguar, have mutes fixed to the bridge that can be applied or removed simply by depressing a lever. Most instruments, however, do not have such built-in devices. Fortunately, mutes can easily be fashioned from materials found at home or in a craft store.

General Considerations

Muffling

The degree to which a mute acts to muffle the strings is determined by several factors, the first of which is the width of the mute, or more precisely, the amount of string that it touches. Wider mutes make more contact with the strings and have a greater damping effect. The amount of pressure that the mute exerts on the string also impacts the damping characteristics. For instance, spongy foam tightly squeezed between the strings and body of the instrument places more upward pressure on the strings as the foam expands than if it were loosely fitted, and as a result, will have a greater muffling effect. Third is the location at which the mute is placed along the string's length. Mutes set near the

(a)　　　　　　　　　　　　　　(b)

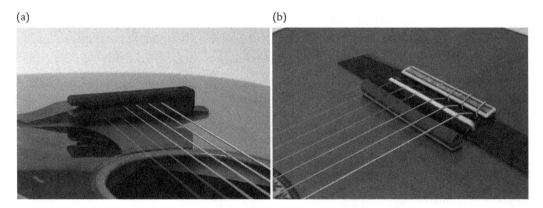

Figure 6.1
Commercially available mutes: (a) MusicBar® mute by Innovative Product Designs LTD (photo from Innovative Product Designs LTD); (b) TremoloMute by Rosette Guitar Products.

bridge or nut produce a minimal effect, with the degree of muffling increasing as the mute is moved toward the center of the string. Finally, the material that the mute is made from affects the degree of muffling. Soft materials such as foam or felt cloth are generally needed to achieve a characteristic muffled sound, but semi-soft materials such as rubber may also be used to produce a more subtle effect with greater sustain [▶ Media 6.2].

Bridge-End and Nut-End Installation Positions

The position of the mute along the string's length is central in determining which of the instrument's range of playable sounds is affected. For instance, a mute set near the bridge will muffle any note stopped on the fretboard, as it will always act on the vibrating portion of the string. By contrast, a mute positioned at the nut will only muffle open strings since any notes stopped above the preparation will place the mute outside the active string segment. Mutes placed in the middle of the string split the fretboard into prepared and unprepared regions; open strings and anything played behind the preparation will sound muffled while stopped notes above the preparation are unaffected.[2]

Implementations

Foam Rubber

Foam rubber is an excellent material for a mute as it has a strong damping effect, is readily available, and can be easily cut to the desired shape. Foam mutes can be bottom-mounted by inserting the foam between the strings and body of the guitar so that it expands upward against the strings, both holding it in place and adding the desired degree of damping. Bart Hopkin and Yuri Landman (2012) suggest cutting a bottom-mounted foam mute in a triangular shape so that it is wider for the lower strings in order to achieve a uniformly muffled result (Fig. 6.2a). Foam mutes can also be attached to the strings from above by cutting slots in the foam for the strings to slip into (Fig. 6.2b). The principal advantage of a top-mounted mute is that it can be installed and removed quickly.

(a)   (b)   (c)

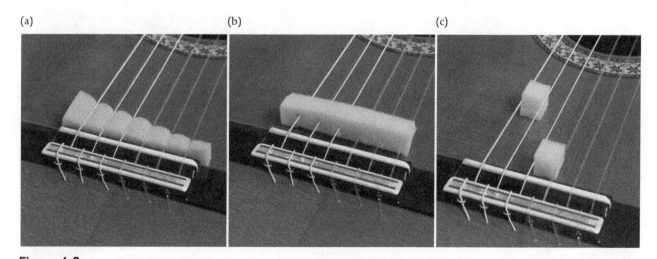

Figure 6.2

Foam rubber mutes: (a) a bottom-mounted foam mute set near the bridge [▶ Media 6.3]; (b) a top-mounted foam mute with slots cut for the six strings; (c) foam mutes wedged between pairs of adjacent strings.

114

Alternatively, foam squares can be wedged between adjacent strings, which allows for mutes to be placed at different locations or on only some of the strings (Fig. 6.2c). Wedge mutes hold their position best near the bridge; they become dislodged more easily when placed over the fretboard.

Felt Cloth Weaves

Felt cloth strips can be woven through the strings to produce a mute effect comparable to that of foam. A simple under-over weave pattern is likely to produce inconsistent results, particularly where the outer strings are concerned. More uniform damping can be obtained by weaving the felt through the strings a second time in an inverted pattern (Fig. 6.3a). The principal advantage that felt has over foam is that it can more easily be set over the fretboard, where inserting foam under the strings can be difficult and wedges and top-mounted mutes tend to become dislodged.

Twine/Yarn

The utility of twine or yarn is that it can be tied around individual strings, allowing maximal flexibility in terms of which strings are muted and where those mutes are positioned (Fig. 6.3b). The muffling effect is subtler than that of foam or felt, allowing harmonics to resonate with considerable sustain when the mutes are positioned accordingly.

Figure 6.3
(a) A felt weave mute set over the fretboard [▶ Media 6.4]; (b) twine mutes on individual strings [▶ Media 6.5].

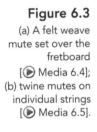
(a)

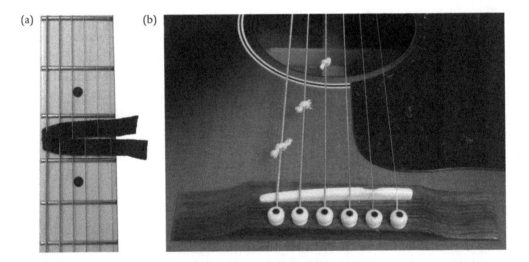
(b)

Figure 6.4
Suggested mute notation with "x" note heads used to distinguish muffled pitches from those that sound normal.

Notation

The plain text "with mute" and "without mute" can be used to indicate that a mute should be installed or removed. Graphically, the symbols ⊓ and ⊔ might be used. Because it is not common practice for guitarists to use mutes, the object and installation details must be accurately described in instructions accompanying the score. If the mute affects all strings so that everything played sounds muffled, then it may be enough to simply indicate that the mute should be used. However, in passages that mix muffled and normal materials the distinction between these sounds should be captured on the staff using distinct note heads or by placing an "x" through the stem of the muffled events. Figure 6.4 offers notation for a musical passage with a mute set at the first fret so that only the open strings are muffled.

Third Bridges

A third bridge can be devised by inserting a rigid preparation object between the strings and the body or neck of the instrument, effectively dividing the strings into distinct vibrating segments (Fig. 6.5). The bridge object must be taller than the string height so that the strings are stretched taut over it, holding it in place against the instrument while simultaneously stopping the strings. For examples of third bridges used in practice, the reader might look to Glenn Branca, Fred Frith, Kaki King, Keith Rowe, or Sonic Youth's Thurston Moore and Lee Rinaldo.

General Considerations

Bridge Materials and Shape

The material of a third bridge has a predictable effect on timbre. Metal bridges offer the brightest sound, with glass performing nearly as well. Wood bridges are warmer with less sustain. Softer materials such as cork or rubber are even duller and result in considerable damping.

(a) (b)

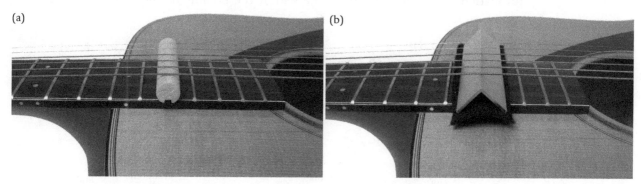

Figure 6.5
Third bridges: (a) a wooden dowel with a slot cut on the underside so that it can sit over a fret wire; (b) a metal L-shaped bracket.

The shape of the bridge, or more precisely, the amount of contact it makes with the strings as they pass over it, affects both sustain and cross-bridge resonance. Figure 6.6 provides a cut-view comparison of three potential third bridge objects: a common six-sided pencil, a round dowel, and an L-shaped bracket. In the case of the pencil, the string touches the object over the entirety of one of its flat sides, an area roughly 4 mm in width, which has a damping effect and also prevents energy from transferring across the bridge to the opposing string segment. By contrast, a round dowel touches the string in a much more focused point, resulting in greater sustain and cross-string resonance. An L-shaped bridge set in a triangular position offers even more sustain than a dowel.

Bi-Tone Components and Intonation

A third bridge divides the string into two vibrating segments: a front tone that extends from the instrument's bridge to the third bridge and a back tone extending from the third bridge to the nut (Fig. 6.7). These two tones, collectively referred to as a *bi-tone*, are locked in a reciprocal relationship; as the preparation is moved toward the bridge the front tone rises in pitch while the back tone is lowered, and vice versa. Unlike a fretted bi-tone, the intonation is not confined to the fretboard tuning and can be intonated freely with slight adjustments to the preparation's position along the string.

When a third bridge is securely wedged between the strings and instrument the front and back tones will be nearly isolated and can be treated as independent pitches. Back tones are naturally softer since they have no amplification mechanism. The front and back tones can be balanced when the third bridge is set close enough to the bridge end of the string to utilize the sound hole or pickups for the back tones. When positioned between two pickups on an electric guitar the pickup selection switch and volume knobs can be used to accentuate one of the tones while attenuating the other. Specifically, the bridge pickup will emphasize the front tone while the neck pickup will emphasize the back tone [▶ Media 6.6]. Of course, the front tones will be much higher in pitch than the back tones when the preparation is set so close to the bridge.

It is reasonable to want to set a third bridge in a position that results in specific intervals between the front and back tones. Figure 6.8 provides a list of approximate preparation locations that produce common intervals between front and back tones. The precise intonation can be found somewhere within the bounds of the listed fret. Achieving

Figure 6.6
Cut-view comparison of a string's contact with a third bridge using (a) a common six-sided pencil; (b) a round dowel; (c) an L-shaped bracket.

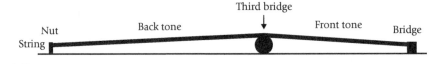

Figure 6.7
Basic principle behind a third bridge preparation.

8th fret	The back tone is one octave higher than the front tone;
9th fret	The back tone is a fifth higher than the front tone;
10th fret	The back tone is a major third higher than the front tone;
12th fret	The back and front tones are in unison;
14th fret	The front tone is a major third higher than the back tone;
16th fret	The front tone is a fifth higher than the back tone;
19th fret	The front tone is an octave higher than the back tone.

Figure 6.8
Approximate preparation locations that produce common equal tempered intervals between the front and back bi-tone components.

Figure 6.9
Single string third bridges: (left) metal woodruff key; (right) flat-head wood peg.

accurate intonation for common equal tempered intervals often requires that the third bridge be placed directly over a fret wire. In the case of wooden bridges, a groove can be cut in the underside that is large enough for the bridge to sit over the fret (Fig. 6.5a). A metal L-shaped bracket can also be positioned so that it straddles the fret wire (Fig. 6.5b).[3]

Single String Third Bridges

Smaller objects can serve as third bridges for individual strings, offering independent control over the bi-tone intonation per string (Fig. 6.9). Suitable objects include corks, rubber stoppers, flat-head wood pegs, woodruff keys, and square keys, all of which can be found at hardware stores. Objects that have been slotted for the string from the top, such as the cork in Figure 6.9, tend to hold their position best.

Performance Techniques

Attacking the Strings

The most common manner of playing a guitar prepared with a third bridge is to use both hands to attack the open strings on either side of the preparation, offering up to 12 distinct pitches: six front tones and six back tones. This manner of performance is most easily accomplished with the guitar laid flat on its back either in the lap or on a table. Kaki King employs a third bridge on a tabletop guitar in her piece "Nails" (2004). King sets the bridge over the 16th fret, creating a perfect fifth relationship between the front and back tones. The piece works entirely with the open strings on both sides of the bridge, which generates a nice amount of cross-bridge string resonance due to the harmonic relationship. A rough transcription of "Nails" is provided in Figure 6.10, intended merely to illustrate the sort of thing that King does.

Koto-Style Bends

Attacking a string on one side of the preparation while depressing it on the other side results in an upward pitch bend that is reminiscent, both in terms of sound and technique, of the string bends employed on a Japanese koto. The bend range is proportional to the string height, while the bend sensitivity increases as the depressing finger moves closer to the preparation. A string is at its maximal height near the third bridge and slopes downward closer to the fretboard as it approaches the nut and bridge (Fig. 6.7). This gradually declining string height can be leveraged to limit to the bend range and obtain consistency in the intonation of koto-style bends. For instance, given a third bridge set at the 12th fret, it may be that depressing a string all the way to the fret wire over the third fret while attacking the front tone bends the pitch upward by a minor third, while depressing the same string over the fourth fret bends it up a major third.

Preparation Instructions:

1) Insert a wooden dowel, roughly 1/2-inch in diameter, between the strings and fretboard over the 16th fret to act as a third bridge;

2) With the third bridge in place, tune the guitar as follows:

Symbol Directory

Front tones are notated using a normal note head; string indications are placed above the staff.

Back tones are notated using a shape note head; string indications are placed below the staff.

Bend and release the pitch by depressing the string on the side opposite that in which it was attacked.

♩ = **125**

All string open (front and back tones)

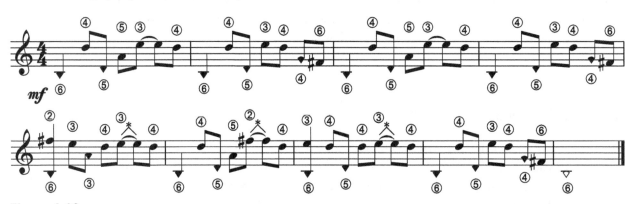

Figure 6.10
An excerpt from Kaki King's "Nails" (2004), utilizing a third bridge (transcription by the author) [▶ Media 6.7].

Standard bend lines can be used in the notation of koto-style bends, although they should be differentiated from normal bends since the technique is not the same. In the King excerpt shown in Figure 6.10 an asterisk is added to standard bend notation and defined as a koto-style bend in the instructions.

Third Bridge Modulation

Third bridges are fairly easy to reposition, which may be done to "modulate" to a new collection of front and back tones, or for the sake of the glissando effect that is produced as the bridge is moved. A screwdriver serves well as a movable third bridge, as the handle gives the player something to grab when the preparation is repositioned and also prevents the preparation from slipping through the strings when the instrument is held upright (Fig. 6.11). On fretted instruments it can be difficult to avoid hitting the fret wires as the bridge is moved, but smooth glissandi can be achieved on fretless instruments.

Third Bridge Bending

Third bridges that extend beyond the width of the neck can be teetered during performance to bend the strings. Assuming a normal playing position, this is most easily done by taking hold of the preparation above the neck and either pulling it back so that it primarily bends the treble strings or pushing it forward so that it raises the bass strings (Fig. 6.11). The ability to anchor pitches on one side of the neck while bending those on the other side creates oblique motion between the bass and treble strings that distinguishes this effect from many other slide techniques. Lee Ranaldo employs the technique in Sonic Youth's "Confusion Is Next" (1983), which can be heard clearly at the start of the song. With the guitar tuned to E2-A2-D3-E3-C4-D4, Ranaldo pulls the bridge back to bend the higher string up while anchoring the bass. He then strums the front tones and slowly brings the bridge back to its normal resting position as the strings decay.

(a) (b)

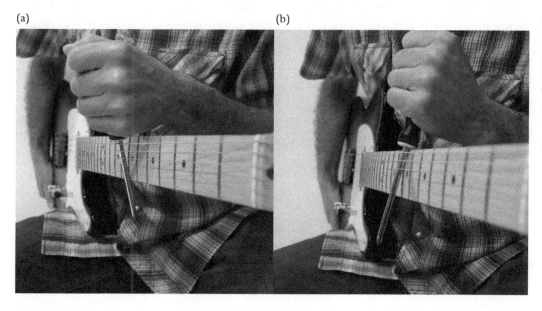

Figure 6.11
Third bridge bending: (a) bending the lower strings; (b) bending the higher strings [▶ Media 6.8].

119

Damping the Cross-Bridge Resonance

Although front and back tones are nearly isolated in a third bridge preparation, there is some degree of cross bridge resonance, which tends to be most pronounced when the back tones are attacked since the front tones are naturally amplified. While attacking notes on one side of the bridge it is possible to damp the cross-bridge resonance on the other side. Bart Hopkin and Yuri Landman (2012) offer a technique in which notes are attacked with the cross-bridge resonance initially dampened. As the note sustains, the damping mechanism—most likely the palm—is slowly removed to gradually introducing the resonance. This effect works best when the back tones are attacked and the front tones provide the resonance, as it is louder. On electric instruments the amplified front tone resonance can be very pronounced, leading to a variety of swelling effects [▶ Media 6.9].

Suspended String Attachments

Inharmonic timbres can be obtained by attaching a tight-gripping object to a string so that it is suspended without touching any other part of the instrument (Fig. 6.12). Split shot fishing sinkers and alligator clips are good candidates, but many other objects suffice, including cotter pins, slotted cork, or bolts and nuts. Results have a percussive, bell-like quality comprised of several superimposed tones, and as such, often lack a focused pitch. Moreover, the expected pitch given the fingering on the fretboard is rarely present in the composite sound. Nonetheless, the inharmonic spectral components of a suspended string attachment are, to a large extent, predictable and controllable.

General Considerations

Tonal Components

The inharmonic spectrum that results from a suspended string attachment is typically a composite of three tones—a front tone, a back tone, and a sub-tone—each with its own harmonic series. It is the superimposition of these three harmonic series that produces

Figure 6.12
Suspended string attachments: a smooth-jaw alligator clip and removable split shot fishing sinker attached to the third and fourth strings, respectively.

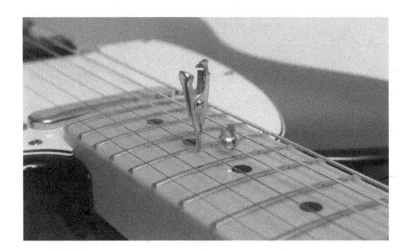

the characteristic bell-like quality of suspended string attachments. With an understanding of how these spectra are derived it is possible to gain considerable control over the composite sound.

Attaching a tight-gripping object to a string divides it into two vibrating segments in much the same way that a third bridge does, producing bi-tones that are locked in a reciprocal relationship: as the front tone is shortened the back tone is lengthened, and vice versa (Fig. 6.13). Unlike a third bridge, however, a suspended string attachment is not anchored to the body or neck of the instrument but instead touches only the string that it grips. As a result, both front and back tones are present in the composite spectrum, regardless of where the string is attacked.

In addition to bi-tones there is a sub-tone added to the spectrum of a string attachment that is usually lower than the expected pitch given the fretboard fingering. This tone is in fact the fundamental of the overall string length, but lowered in pitch due to the extra weight added to the string by the object. Accordingly, heavier attachments yield lower sub-tones. The pitch also changes depending on the location of the preparation along the string, dropping as the attachment is moved toward the center of the string.

Needless to say, suspended string attachments can be employed without concern for the actual notes in the composite spectrum. Experimenting empirically with different preparation locations yields a variety of spectral distributions: some are dissonant and inharmonic while others suggest more consonant, harmonic relationships between components; some are clear and transparent while others are more clustered and muddy; some are smooth while others produce beating between components.

Attack Location and Tonal Balance

Attacking a string at different locations alters the balance between tones in the composite spectrum of a suspended string attachment. Broadly speaking, attacking above the preparation will give emphasis to the front bi-tone while attacking behind the preparation gives emphasis to the back tone. More precisely, the balance between the front, back, and sub-tones gradually changes as the attack location is moved along the string. Figure 6.13 offers

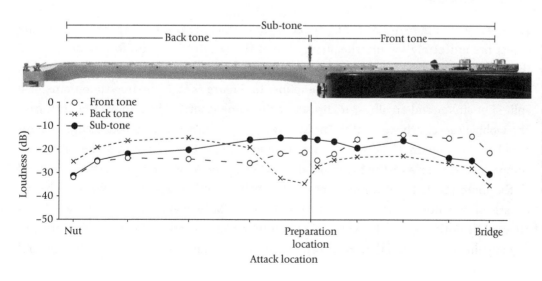

Figure 6.13

Active string segments of a suspended string attachment, along with an approximation of the relative balance between tones in the composite spectrum as the string is attacked at different locations.

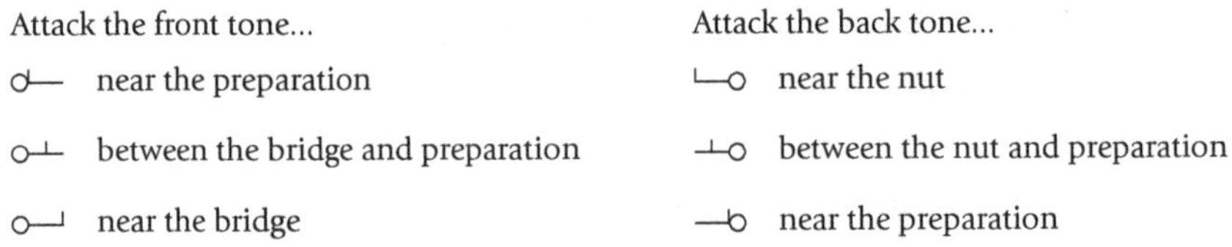

Figure 6.14

Suggested symbols
to denote attack
location relative to a
preparation object.

Attack the front tone...

o—   near the preparation

o⊥   between the bridge and preparation

o⌐   near the bridge

Attack the back tone...

└o   near the nut

⊥o   between the nut and preparation

—o   near the preparation

an account of the relative loudness of each tonal component at attack locations along the string. In most cases all three tones are present to some degree.[4] However, each of the three tones can be nearly isolated: Attacking the string very close to the bridge yields the front tone; attacking near the nut gives prominence to the back tone; attacking near the preparation, or in some cases attacking the preparation directly, exposes the sub-tone. The changes in timbre that result from altering the attack location are striking and provide an interesting compositional dimension to be explored when suspended string attachments are employed. The companion website offers a demonstration of the effect of attack location on the timbre of a suspended string attachment [⊙ Media 6.10]. Figure 6.14 offers symbols that can be used in notation to denote the attack location relative to a preparation object.

Stopping Pitches on the Fretboard

Stopping a string behind the preparation shortens the overall string length, which has the effect of raising the back tone and sub-tone. The front tone, however, remains the same since its length from the bridge to the object is unaltered. This ability to vary the back tone string length without changing the front tone provides an additional means of controlling the intervals in the composite spectra. Moreover, it can lead to some interesting effects. Attacking a string in front of a preparation while fingering notes on the fretboard behind it results in oblique motion between a dominant and unchanging front tone and sub- and back tones that move in parallel motion [⊙ Media 6.11]. Attacking behind the preparation while stopping notes exposes the parallel motion of the back and sub-tones, creating an effect reminiscent of a harmonizer pedal [⊙ Media 6.12].

Spectral Wobble

The spectral components of a suspended string attachment are most stable when the object fits uniformly around the string. When the weight is not uniformly distributed the object tends to sway back and forth as the string vibrates, adding a tremolo, and in some case vibrato, to the spectral components. Figure 6.15 compares sonograms of a split shot sinker and an alligator clip set at the same location, just above the 16th fret. The wobble can clearly be seen in the striated components of the alligator clip, as compared to the smoother and more stable components of the split shot sinker. An aural comparison reveals a distinct tremolo quality when the alligator clip is used, compared to the more stable tonal components of the fishing sinker. Spectral wobble is characteristic of alligator clips, cotter pins, and other similarly shaped objects. The wobble is affected by both the attack location and the time that the string is attacked relative to any ongoing wobble, and therefore, somewhat unpredictable. Nonetheless, a few general

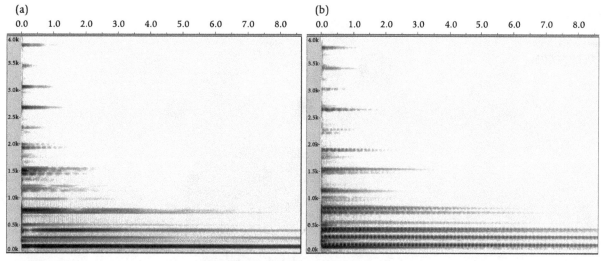

Figure 6.15

Sonograms of suspended string attachments: (a) a split shot sinker [▶ Media 6.13]; (b) an alligator clip [▶ Media 6.14].

rules apply: (1) Larger objects wobble at slower rates; (2) the wobble rate decreases with string length; (3) the wobble is more pronounced when the object is attached near the middle of the string.

Pickup Selections

When a suspended string attachment is positioned between two pickups on an electric guitar the pickup selection switch and/or separate pickup volume knobs can be used to foreground one of the bi-tones in the composite spectrum while attenuating the other. For instance, the bridge pickup will emphasize the front tone while the neck pickup will emphasize the back tone. Through a combination of pickup selection and attack location, the front and back tones can be nearly isolated [▶ Media 6.15].

Implementations

Split Shot Sinkers

Split shot sinkers are a common type of fishing weight that can be bought at sporting goods stores. Made of lead or tin and spherical in shape, they are sliced with a crevice or "split" through which a guitar string can pass (Fig. 6.16). The ball is then pinched so that it grips the string and is secured in place (Fig. 6.12).[5] Fishing sinkers are sold in round and removable varieties. Round sinkers are perfectly ball-shaped and produce minimal wobble, although they can be difficult to remove without deforming the weight. By contrast, removable split shot sinkers have "ears" that are used to open the sinker once pinched so that it can be reused. The ears add slight wobble to the spectrum, albeit marginal if compared to the wobble introduced by an alligator clip. Both round and removable sinkers are available in various sizes, which might be chosen to obtain different sub-tones. Generally speaking, a split shot sinker produces a clear and stable composite spectrum and is a good candidate when intonation of the spectral components is a concern [▶ Media 6.13].

Figure 6.16
Various sized round
and removable split
shot fishing sinkers.

Figure 6.17
Various alligator
clips: (left) a small,
smooth-jawed clip;
(middle) a large clip
with teeth; (right) a
small clip with teeth.

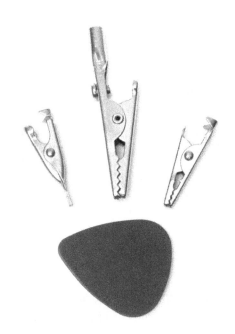

Alligator Clips

Alligator clips can be purchased from do-it-yourself electronics retailers. They are typically made of metal and come in various sizes, but all have the same general shape (Fig. 6.17). Some clips have teeth on the connecting end that help to grip the string and keep the object in place, but the teeth often add noise and a general loss of clarity to the sound. Clips with smooth jaws yield a more transparent, bell-like quality. In most instances, clips contain a fair amount of spectral wobble as the object sways back and forth with the vibrating string ⊙ Media 6.14]. Alligator clips are most successfully applied as suspended string attachments on a tabletop guitar where they can stand upright, as in Figure 6.12.

When the guitar is held in a normal playing position the clips tend to fall against adjacent strings or become dislodged altogether. On a practice note, alligator clips are ideal for experimenting with the location of a preparation, as they can be repositioned easily. Once the proper location is chosen the alligator clip can be replaced with a spit shot sinker or other more secure preparation.

Notation

When notating a suspended string attachment it is important to adequately describe the preparation object in the score, along with a detailed account of how to install it on the instrument. The instructions page from Matthew Elgart's *Snack Shop* (1981) offers a fine example, including an itemized list of objects, their measurements, and a graphic illustration of their placement on the two guitars (Fig. 6.18). A description of the expected sound can also be helpful, especially when particular sonic attributes are intended. For instance, the location of the object could be described in terms of the bi-tone components that should sound on an open string (Fig. 6.19).

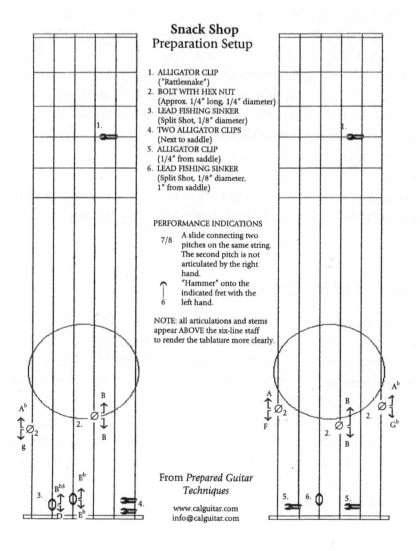

Snack Shop
Preparation Setup

1. ALLIGATOR CLIP
   ("Rattlesnake")
2. BOLT WITH HEX NUT
   (Approx. 1/4" long, 1/4" diameter)
3. LEAD FISHING SINKER
   (Split Shot, 1/8" diameter)
4. TWO ALLIGATOR CLIPS
   (Next to saddle)
5. ALLIGATOR CLIP
   (1/4" from saddle)
6. LEAD FISHING SINKER
   (Split Shot, 1/8" diameter,
   1" from saddle)

PERFORMANCE INDICATIONS

7/8 — A slide connecting two pitches on the same string. The second pitch is not articulated by the right hand.

6 — "Hammer" onto the indicated fret with the left hand.

NOTE: all articulations and stems appear ABOVE the six-line staff to render the tablature more clearly.

From *Prepared Guitar Techniques*

www.calguitar.com
info@calguitar.com

Figure 6.18

Preparation instructions from the score for Matthew Elgart's *Snack Shop* (1981).

Figure 6.19

Possible notation for a single string preparation: (a) complete notation showing all three composite tones; (b) reduced notation focused on the back tone.

Preparation Instructions

Attach a small split shot sinker to the fourth string above the fretboard to produce the following bi-tones on the open string:

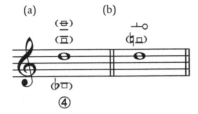

(a)   (b)

In the absence of a convention, a notational strategy must be devised and explained clearly in the instructions. If the intonation of the three tones in the composite spectrum is important, then some representation of those pitches should be included in the notation. The method for notating bi-tones introduced in Chapter 5 can be adapted: regular note heads are used to indicate the fingering while square-shaped parenthesized note heads are used to denote the sounding bi-tones and sub-tone (Fig. 6.19a). If attack location is used to bring one of the tones in the composite spectrum to the foreground, then the notation might be reduced to just the fingered pitch and that one component (Fig. 6.19b). One the other hand, if precise intonation is not the intent, then tablature may be sufficient, as used by Elgart in *Snack Shop*. Alternatively, scordatura notation can be used, in which the pitches on the staff reflect those that would sound if the instrument were not prepared. Tablature and scordatura notation are similar in that they both focus solely on the actions required to realize the work and give no indication of how it should actually sound. In cases where the tonal makeup of a preparation's resultant sound is not of concern, it might be argued that it is to the credit of tablature that it makes no attempt to document the sound, since scordatura notation is, if anything, misleading.

Suspended String-Coupling

When a preparation object is installed such that it engages two or more strings we can say that those strings are coupled (Fig. 6.20). Coupling is significant because vibrations on one string are transferred through the object to the other interconnected strings, causing them to also resonate. In fact, the bridge of a guitar acts as coupling device, transferring energy from the vibrating strings to the soundboard. However, there are minimal forced vibrations to the adjoining strings because the bridge rests firmly against the body of the instrument. Coupling preparations that are suspended in the strings and free from the body of the instrument force the vibrations primarily to the adjoining strings, adding a much more prominent resonance to the guitar's sound.

Figure 6.20
A metal dowel
string-coupling
preparation
[▶ Media 6.16].

(a)   (b)   (c)

Figure 6.21
Useful weave patterns: (a) a tight weave that alternates per string; (b) a weave that places the four inner strings at the same height; (c) a partial weave.

General Considerations

Weaves

A coupling preparation can be installed by weaving an object through the strings so that it passes under some and over others. A tight weave pattern that alternates per string tends to provide the most uniform results as well as holding the preparation firmly in place (Fig. 6.21a). Note, however, that weaves tend to create a discrepancy in the height of strings that pass over the object and those that travel under it, which can be especially pronounced when large diameter, rigid objects are used. The varying string height not only makes playing the instrument awkward, but it can also press the under-woven strings against the fret wires, preventing them from being stopped in lower positions. Indeed, weaves placed over the fretboard must be very thin if the strings passing under the object are to not touch the frets. The situation is more forgiving in the region between the end of the fretboard and the bridge, although even here, larger diameter objects will eventually cause the under-woven strings to touch the highest fret. Generally speaking, acoustic guitars are less prone to these problems.

Any weave pattern will need to have at least one or two strings passing under the object to hold it in place. With that proviso, however, various patterns may be employed. The weave pattern shown in Figure 6.21b places the four inner strings at the same height. Partial weaves can also be employed that only engage a subset of contiguous strings, although such preparations tend to become dislodged more easily (Fig. 6.21c). Note that each weave pattern in Figure 6.21 has an inverse (not shown) in which each of the strings would be on the opposite side of the preparation object. Inverting a weave can significantly alter both the resultant sound and the playability of the instrument.

Spectral Components

String coupling results in a spectrally dense and complex sound that is not nearly as predictable or controllable as that of a single-string attachment. Each individual string involved produces a complex timbre similar to that of a suspended string attachment, including bi-tones and a sub-tone. Because the strings are coupled, however, the components of all strings at play combine to form the composite result.

While sub-tones are present for each string, those for the outer strings tend to dominate. In cases of a woven coupling preparation, the pitch of the sub-tone can be controlled with remarkable precision by altering the degree to which the preparation object extends beyond the strings. As a starting point, we might imagine a metal dowel woven tightly through the strings and positioned so that the end barely extends beyond the sixth string. In this case, the resulting sub-tone will be roughly in unison with the pitch that would be expected—an open-string E2 assuming standard tuning. From this position, increasing the overhang causes the sub-tone to drop in pitch. A demonstration can be found on the companion website [▶ Media 6.17]. Naturally, adjustments to the amount of overhang on one side of the strings will have a reciprocal effect on the other side.

Rigid and Pliable Weave Objects

The rigidity of the preparation object has an effect on both the quantity and quality of coupling resonance. Rigid objects are highly effective at transferring energy to the other strings and tend to cleanly stop the strings at the preparation in much the same way that a bottleneck slide would, resulting in clear and stable spectral components that are largely isolated. For instance, attacking the strings in front of the preparation while altering the fingering behind it results in little variance in the tone. On the contrary, a pliable preparation object will bend when set in motion, absorbing and distorting the forced vibrations as they travel to other coupled strings. Pliable preparation objects tend to produce blurred composite spectra in which the individual components are less clearly defined and the bi-tones less isolated. When very thin objects, such as a snippet of wire or plain steel guitar string, are used, it is possible to hear stopped pitches behind the object when the player attacks the front tone. In addition, pliable objects tend to introduce a buzzing quality to the sounding results.

Implementations

Dowels

Dowels woven through the strings serve as fine coupling objects, particularly when the purity and stability of spectral components is a concern (Fig. 6.20). Typically made of metal or wood, they can be purchased at craft or hardware stores and come in a variety of diameters. The material and pliability both have an impact on the resultant sound. Smooth metal dowels tend to produce bright and focused tones with crisp attacks and maximal sustain, whereas wood has a warmer, more ethnic quality with less sustain. The tones in the composite spectrum will be more stable and resonant if the dowel is rigid. Metal dowels are advantageous in this respect, even when the diameter is small. Wood tends to be more pliable and usually needs to be comparatively larger in diameter to achieve a similarly stable spectrum. A comparison of metal and wood dowels is available on the companion website [▶ Media 6.18].

Flat Weaves

Flat shaped objects such as craft sticks, coffee stir sticks, or flat metal brackets can be woven through the strings with minimal impact on string height. This can render the instrument more playable regardless of whether the strings pass over or under the weave (Fig. 6.22a). However, flat weaves produce heavy and prominent sub-tones when set away from the bridge, which at times can become overbearing, and generally tend to sound less stable and clear than the tones produced with a rigid dowel.

Guitar String Snippets and Metal Wires

A variety of interesting effects can be obtained by weaving a snippet from a guitar string or similarly gauged metal wire through the strings of the instrument. Compared to the more rigid weaves discussed thus far, pliable wire produces a blurred and noisy effect in which the individual tones making up the composite spectrum are less defined. Added to this is a metallic sizzle component that can be quite prominent depending on the weave and its placement along the string. A light gauge plain steel string snippet produces a relatively crisp and thin spectrum, characterized more by a noisy metallic sizzle than the inharmonic bell-like quality of a rigid dowel. Heavy gauge strings yield more coupling resonance, leading to a muddier composite spectrum in which the expected pitches are less clear. Weaving a wound guitar string snippet introduces additional noise as the ridged windings of the two strings rub against each other. Flexible weaves can be set near the bridge so that the instrument can be played in a conventional manner with the fingered pitches sounding as expected, albeit colored by the preparation. Weaving a light gauge string snippet near the bridge produces an effect resembling reverberation, which can be made more prominent by moving the weave away from the bridge.

(a)   (b)

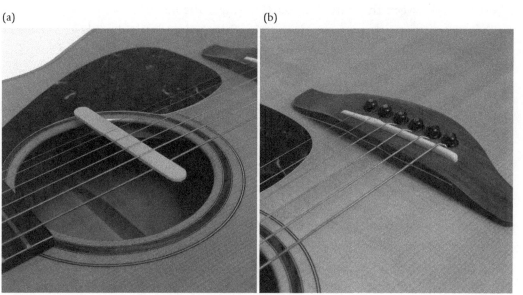

Figure 6.22
(a) a flat wooden craft stick weave that places the inner strings at the same height [▶ Media 6.19]; (b) a woven guitar string set near the bridge [▶ Media 6.20].

129

(a)   (b)

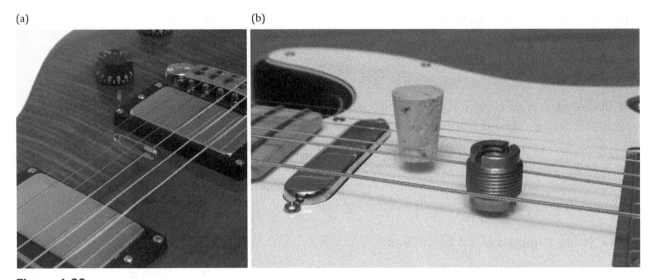

Figure 6.23

Non-woven couplers: (a) a safety pin coupling only two strings [▶ Media 6.21]; (b) a microphone clip adapter and cork wedged between adjacent strings to couple them [▶ Media 6.22].

Non-Woven Couplers

Safety Pins

Appropriately sized safety pins can be installed so that only two strings are coupled, leaving the others unaffected, including those that run through the middle of the pin (Fig. 6.23a). The coupled strings sound bright and metallic with a bell-like timbre similar to that of a suspended string attachment, including bi-tones and sub-tones. As compared to weaves, however, the composite spectrum is considerably more transparent since only two strings are involved.

Wedges

Adjacent strings can be coupled by wedging an object between them, as shown in Figure 6.23b using a microphone clip adapter between the fifth and sixth strings and a bottle cork between the third and fourth strings. The metal clip adapter produces a much brighter tone with considerable sustain. Threaded wedges help to keep the object from slipping. Softer materials, such as the cork, produce a duller, dampened sound.

Notation

The notation of passages involving coupled strings can be approached in much the same way as suspended string attachments. Shape note heads, along with string indications, can be used to denote the fingered pitches when sounding pitches are different. If intonational control is important, then sounding pitches should be denoted using small parenthesized note heads. In most cases these can be limited to just the sounding pitches of the attacked strings. It is generally not necessary to represent coupling resonance in the notation unless the performer is asked to interact with it directly, for example, by damping the strings. In this case, the resonance might be denoted graphically by framing the staff with wavy lines when it is present (Fig. 6.24). The

Preparation Instructions:

Weave a 4–5 inch long, thin diameter metal dowel through all six strings using the following pattern:

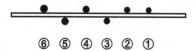

⑥ ⑤ ④ ③ ② ①

The dowel should extend beyond the outer strings by roughly equal amounts.

Position the dowel perpendicular to the strings just above the fretboard so that the following bi-tones are produced on the first string;

Symbol Directory:

▲   Stopped pitch on the fretboard (sounding pitch will be different);

(●)   Prominent sounding pitch;

⊥○⊕   Attack back tones (behind the preparation) while muting the front tones;

⊥○   Attack back tones (behind the preparation) while allowing maximum coupling resonance;

○⊥   Attack front tones (behind the preparation) while allowing maximum coupling resonance;

〜   Indicates that coupling resonance should be evident;

▯   Hit preparation with index finger where it extends beyond the sixth string.

Notation:

Figure 6.24

Possible notation for a passage that implements a metal dowel coupling preparation [▶ Media 6.23].

symbols provided in Figure 6.14 can be used to indicate where the string is attacked in relation to the preparation object. Additional symbols can be defined for other techniques that require the performer to interact with the preparation object itself, such as plucking the end of a weave. Figure 6.24 incorporates a number of possible notational devices.

Buzzes

General Considerations

Buzz effects can be obtained by capitalizing on the repetitive displacement of a string as it vibrates. Broadly speaking, this can be accomplished in two ways: (1) A vibrating string can come into iterative contact with a stationary preparation object that is fixed to the instrument; (2) a suspended string attachment can make iterative contact with a stationary part of the instrument as the string vibrates back and forth. In either case, the trick is to install the preparation object so that it makes contact with the string or instrument whenever the string is near its maximal displacement. Positioned too close to the object, the buzzing collisions significantly dampen the vibrating string. Placed too far, the buzz will only be present at the start of a sound, quickly dying away as the string displacement diminishes. Installed appropriately, the buzz will linger, sounding tight and smooth.

Implementations

Buzzing Instrument Attachments

An object can be fixed to the instrument and set close to a string without touching it so that the string makes iterative contact with it when set in motion. Figure 6.25 offers an example using a short segment of wire with one end fixed to the soundboard with painter's tape and shaped so that the opposite end hovers near the string. Once fastened to the body, it is quite easy to alter the proximity of the wire to the string, and thus, the character of the buzz. Applying these preparations to the outer strings makes reconfiguring the wire more manageable, but similar effects are equally obtainable on inner strings. Unlike string attachments, a buzzing instrument attachment adds a buzz component without altering the timbre or perceived pitch of the vibrating string.

Buzzing String Attachments

A buzz effect can be obtained by attaching an object to a string so it makes iterative contact with some part of the instrument as it swings back and forth with the string's vibrations. Figure 6.26 offers possibilities set over the fretboard using an alligator clip set directly over the fret wire (Fig. 6.26a) and aluminum foil positioned near the fret wire

Figure 6.25

A wire buzz preparation mounted to the soundboard and applied to the sixth string [▶ Media 6.24].

(a)   (b)

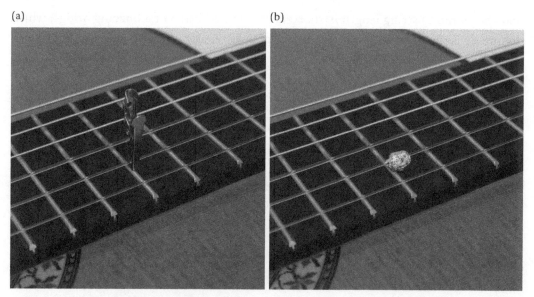

Figure 6.26
Buzzing string
attachments: (a)
an alligator clip
positioned directly
over a fret wire
[▶ Media 6.25];
(b) an aluminum
foil ball set near
the fret wire
[▶ Media 6.26].

Figure 6.27
A metal bottle
cap used as a
buzzing bridge
[▶ Media 6.27].

(Fig. 6.26b). Attaching an object to a suspended string significantly alters the timbre and, in many instances, prevents the expected pitch from sounding. Accordingly, the added buzz component might be considered an adornment to the base preparations, the qualities of which remain salient.

Buzzing Bottle Caps

A metal screw-on bottle cap can be inserted under the strings near the bridge to produce a particularly nasal buzzing effect that is quite distinct from the others presented (Fig. 6.27).[6] The cap should be slightly taller than the string height so that the stings are stretched taut over it and hold it firmly in place, not unlike a third bridge. Set near the bridge of the instrument, the back tones can be treated as the primary string segment that is attacked and the expected pitches will sound with an added buzz component.[7] The effect is most pronounced when the strings are attacked with force. It should be noted that the vibrating string length is shortened by the addition of a buzzing bridge, which slightly disturbs the intonation of fretted pitches on the affected strings. The issue is not significant when the object is set close to the bridge but is magnified as the object is moved away from it.

Buzzing Weaves

Strips cut from sheets of plain writing paper, aluminum foil, or wax paper add a tight, snare-like buzz when woven through the strings. Generally speaking, the width of the weave controls the amount of buzz generated while the location of the preparation along the strings determines the prominence of expected pitches. The flimsy nature of sheet materials minimizes coupling resonance and usually allows the expected pitches to be heard, as opposed to the inharmonic, bell-like timbre typically associated with string coupling.

Plain writing paper weaves produce a prominent buzz effect with snapping, percussive attacks. Set near the bridge, the expected pitches can be heard clearly (Fig. 6.28a). Moving the preparation toward the center of the string gradually diminishes the expected pitches as well as damping the strings, which can ultimately lead to a purely percussive snap-buzz sound with little tonal implication at all. In addition, increasing the overhang beyond the outer strings adds lower frequencies to the spectrum. Johnny Cash used a paper weave set near the bridge to produce a snare-like "boom-chicka" rhythm on a number of early recordings, such as "I Walk the Line" (1956) [▶ Media 6.30].

Aluminum foil weaves produce a bright, yet delicate and smooth buzzing effect with a fair amount of sustain in the buzz itself. Fundamental tones are clear regardless of the preparation location, while sympathetic resonance, bi-tones, and sub-tones are barely audible. A more pronounced buzz can be obtained using wider strips or by folding the overhang back toward the strings (Fig. 6.28b). Wax paper weaves produce results similar to foil, but warmer and lighter. The wax paper can be taped to the soundboard to prevent it from moving when the instrument is played.

Figure 6.28 (a)   (b)

Buzzing weaves: (a) a paper weave set near the bridge [▶ Media 6.28]; (b) an aluminum foil weave set over the sound hole [▶ Media 6.29].

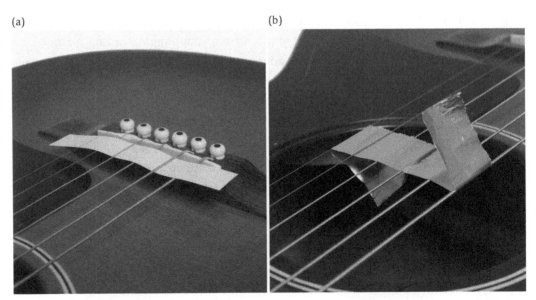

Buzzing Styrofoam™

Styrofoam™ can be used to produce buzzing effects by slotting a small piece to fit on a single string or wedging it between adjacent strings (Fig. 6.29a), or by slotting larger pieces so they can be top-mounted across multiple strings (Fig. 6.29b). Placed near the bridge, the expected fingered pitches sound. The effect becomes more bell-like when moved away from the bridge, as the bi-tone and sub-tone components emerge. Generally speaking, the results have a snare-like quality, similar to the sound of paper woven through the strings.

Notation

The notation for buzzing preparations should indicate that the buzz is present as well as whether the fingered pitch is expected to sound. In cases where the fingered pitch is salient, a normal note head can be used to represent the pitch, with an "x" placed through the stem to denote the added buzz component (Fig. 6.30a). If the preparation prevents the expected pitch from sounding then a crossed ("x") note head might be used, placed on the staff at the fingered pitch (Fig. 6.30b). Of course, strategies such as these must be clearly explained in the score.

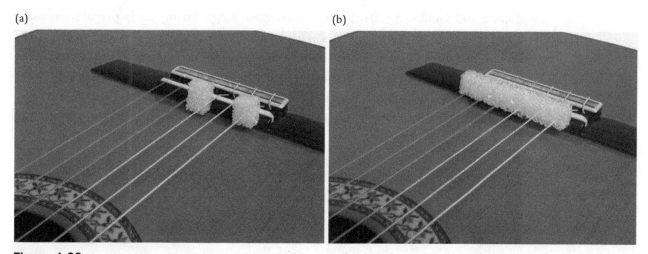

Figure 6.29
Styrofoam™ buzzing preparations: (a) partial buzzing options using small blocks; (b) a top-mounted buzzing preparation applied to all six strings [▶ Media 6.31].

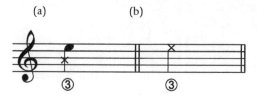

Figure 6.30
Suggested notation for buzzing preparations: (a) when the expected pitch sounds; (b) when the pitch is unpredictable.

Rattles

General Considerations

A rattle effect occurs when a loosely fitted preparation object is allowed to rebound haphazardly off the strings. Unlike the tight and uniform results of a buzzing preparation, the collisions in a rattle are sparser, sounding scattered, inconsistent, and unpredictable. Keeping the preparation object in place is a practical concern that generally needs to be addressed when working with rattling preparations. To achieve a good rattle effect the object must fit loosely on the string so that it can rebound freely. However, the object must also be restrained so as not to fall away from the instrument when deflected. Some solutions for fastening the object to the instrument are provided in the specific implementations introduced below.

When the rattles are light they seem to adorn the performed line. Heavier objects produce a more pronounced rattle in which the attacks can become indistinguishable from those that are performed, thereby obscuring the line being played. The added attacks, however, can be leveraged to produce dense and complex indeterminate textural effects.

Implementations

Wire Rattles

Hopkin and Landman (2012) offer an effective single string rattle preparation using a short segment of light gauge household wire with one end looped around the string behind the saddle. The wire is then bent in an arch and the other end is looped around the same string an inch or two from the bridge (Fig. 6.31a). The loops securing the wire to the string must be loose at both ends so that the wire can rattle freely as the string vibrates. Alternatively, a loose fitting metal ring could be added to an outer string and held in position by a small piece of wire taped to the body of the instrument and fastened loosely to the ring (Fig. 6.31b).

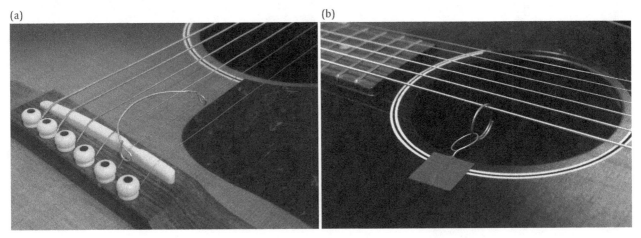

Figure 6.31

Rattlers: (a) a wire rattle with one end fastened behind the saddle and the other in front of the bridge [▶ Media 6.32]; (b) a ring fastened to the soundboard [▶ Media 6.33].

Threaded Objects

Small ring-shaped objects such as jewelry beads, metal jewelry rings, or washers can be threaded by an individual string, producing a rattle that is often more consistent than those mentioned previously (Fig. 6.32). The following generalizations can be made about the sounding results: (1) the smaller the hole, the more rhythmically consistent the rattle will be; (2) setting the object close to the bridge allows fingered pitches to sound clearly and with relative sustain, while moving the preparation closer toward the fretboard can have a more severe damping effect; (3) heavier objects produce more pronounced attacks and dampen the strings more quickly [▶ Media 6.34]; (4) the collisions of the threaded object against the string can produce harmonics if the object is positioned near a node along the string [▶ Media 6.35].

Although a threaded object runs little risk of becoming dislodged, it will travel aimlessly along the string's length as the string vibrates unless confined in some way. When set over the fretboard, threaded objects will often remain within the confines of a single fret, unable to move beyond the fret wires at either end [▶ Media 6.36]. Alternatively, knots made with fishing line can act like bookends around the object, confining it to a region of the string with minimal effect to the tone (Fig. 6.32b).

Notation

The notation for rattle effects can be approached in much the same way as that of buzzes. A normal note head can be used to represent the pitch, with an "x" placed through the stem to denote the added rattle. If the preparation prevents the expected pitch from sounding then a crossed ("x") note head might be used, placed on the staff at the fingered pitch. The unpredictable nature of rattles makes it impossible to notate the rhythmic behavior with any degree of accuracy. However, if the preparations are placed in strategic locations intended to produce particular pitches or harmonics then those should be indicated using small parenthesized note heads.

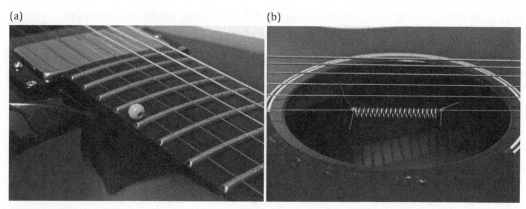

(a)

(b)

Figure 6.32
Threaded rattle preparations: (a) a wooden bead set over the fretboard and confined by the fret wires [▶ Media 6.35]; (b) a spring confined by knots of fishing line [▶ Media 6.37].

Figure 6.33
A bouncing alligator
clip preparation
[ Media 6.38].

Bouncers

A bouncing preparation can be devised by attaching a rigid object to one string in such a way that it falls against and rebounds off other adjacent strings. For the sake of this discussion, we might refer to the string that the object is attached to as the anchor string and those that it bounces off as trampoline strings. Figure 6.33 offers an example of a bouncing preparation using an alligator clip attached to the anchor string, with a dowel added to the other end of the clip for weight. Bouncing effects are characterized by a series of iterative attacks with an orderly trajectory in which the bounce rate gradually accelerates as the volume decays, similar to the sound of a bouncing ball coming to rest. To an extent, the bounce rate can be controlled, making accelerations, decelerations, and a range of simple free-form gestures possible.

General Considerations

Pitch Content

Bounce effects potentially toggle between two distinct pitches: one determined by the fingering on the trampoline string and the other determined by the location where the preparation object collides with the trampoline string. When the trampoline strings are allowed to resonate, the expected note given the fingering can be heard clearly, with the bounce adding a tremolo-like alternation between the two tones. However, the trampoline strings can be muted during the bounce effect to isolate the bounce tone [▶ Media 6.39].

The effect that a bouncing preparation has on the anchor string is similar to that of a single string attachment, inclusive of added spectral components. Note, however, that attacking an anchor string or moving the instrument quickly may prompt the preparation object to begin bouncing off the trampoline strings.

Bounce Rate

Principal factors that influence the bounce rate are the length and weight of the preparation object and the location along the string's length where it is attached. The following generalizations apply: (1) Longer objects bounce at a slower rate than shorter objects; (2) heavier objects bounce slower and persist for longer than lighter objects; (3) bounce rates are fastest when the object is attached to the ends of the vibrating string and slowest when the anchor location is in the middle of the string. The baseline bounce rate can therefore be altered to some degree by modifying any of the above listed attributes. For instance, using an alligator clip, weight and length can be added by inserting a dowel into the end of the clip and crimping the tabs to prevent it from slipping out (Fig. 6.33).

The bounce rate can also be controlled dynamically during performance by altering the vertical angle, or roll, of the instrument. In a standard playing position the soundboard of the guitar is at a near 90-degree angle to the floor with most of the weight of the preparation directed toward the ground rather than the strings. If the player leans forward so that the object dangles slightly away from the strings, this slows the bounce rate further, until eventually the object no longer makes contact with the strings and the effect is lost entirely. Conversely, leaning back so that gravity pulls the object toward the strings accelerates the bounces. Laying the instrument flat on its back produces the most rapid bounces, as the full weight of the object falls directly back onto the strings. Subtle variations in the roll of the guitar can cause significant variations in the bounce rate, and a performer can learn to control the roll with enough accuracy to articulate prescribed contours such as accelerations, decelerations, or simple successions of the two. Importantly, however, the player has no direct control over each iterative attack as the object bounces, and has only limited control over the total number of bounces. As such, any prescribed variation in the bounce rate should be limited to a general contour and duration.

String Buoyancy

One need not play with a bouncing preparation for long to realize that the bounces change unpredictably with each attack. To understand the source of the inconsistency we must take a deeper look at the mechanics behind these preparations. In most cases the trampoline strings provide the force that rebounds the object, referred to here as buoyancy.[8] Generally speaking, more buoyancy leads to a greater rebound of the object, the sounding effects of which are a slower bounce rate and a longer decay time for the bounces. However, the conditions are quite different when the trampoline strings are motionless from when they are in motion. Let us look at each case in turn.

When a bouncing preparation object falls onto a trampoline string that is not in motion, the string will bend, creating an increase in tension that the string will resolve by returning to its normal position, thereby providing the buoyancy that rebounds the object. Importantly, the initial rebound at the start of any bounce effect will set the trampoline strings in motion unless they are muted, and all subsequent rebounds will be off vibrating trampoline strings. The most consistent and articulate bounce effects tend to be achieved when the trampoline strings are muted for the duration of the bounce.

The situation is more complex and unpredictable when a bouncing object collides with a vibrating string because the potential buoyancy varies according to both the preparation location and the string's vibrational pattern. A vibrating string has nodes located at points that mark whole number divisions of the string and anti-nodes between them

(Fig. 6.34). Note that there is little string displacement at the nodes and maximal displacement at the anti-nodes. Clearly, the object will have more rebound potential if it makes contact with the string at an anti-node. However, stopping the string results in a shift of the nodes and anti-nodes, causing the bounce effect to vary considerably from one pitch to the other on the same string.

The phase of the vibrating trampoline string at the moment of impact is the principal source of the inconsistency in bounces. The greatest rebound is obtained when the string is moving toward the preparation object and near its maximum point of displacement when it collides with it. However, it is possible that the trampoline string, in its vibratory state, will be moving in the same direction as the preparation object at the moment of impact, resulting in little or no rebound. Of course, there is no way for a player to coordinate attacks with the phase of the vibrating string, and as a result, any sequence of notes is likely to have varying degrees of buoyancy, with some possibly not bouncing at all.

Activating the Bounce

Bouncing preparations can be set in motion in a variety of ways. The cleanest and most consistent results are obtained by engaging the object directly—either by lifting it away from the strings and releasing it or by plucking the end in a downward motion against the trampoline strings (Fig. 6.35). Alternatively, attacking any of the trampoline strings,

Figure 6.34
Nodes and antinodes of a vibrating string.

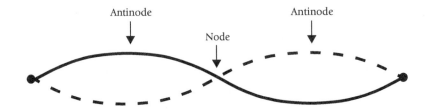

Figure 6.35
Plucking a bouncing preparation directly with the thumb to set it in motion [▶ Media 6.40].

depressing and quickly releasing trampoline strings, or depressing the anchor string near the preparation will all set a bouncing preparation in motion, although these latter methods produce less consistent outcomes [▶ Media 6.40].

Notation

Any attempt to notate the resultant sound of a bouncing preparation can only be a rough approximation since the behavior is somewhat unpredictable. However, some indication of when the bounce is occurring and when it is not is essential. Shape notes, wavy lines, small parenthesized note heads, or plain text can all suffice. If the player is expected to alter the bounce rate during performance, then that must be indicated as well. Figure 6.36 addresses many of these considerations. Pitches affected by the preparation are represented with triangular-shaped note heads to distinguish them from those that sound normal. A string indication is also used in the second measure to stress that the upper line should be played on the first string. Finally, the graphic notation below the last measure represents the angle of the guitar, and consequently, the bounce rate. It is present only when relevant.

Preparation Instructions:

Attach a 2-inch alligator clip with teeth to the second string approx. 3.5 inches from the bridge. The clip should grip the second string at its tip (in the first tooth) so that it hangs down and bounces freely against the first string. The bounce tone should be a high B.

Figure 6.36

Possible notation for a bouncing preparation using graphics below the staff to specify the angle of the guitar [▶ Media 6.41].

Symbol Directory

• • • • • • Indicates that the alligator clip should be actively bouncing.

  Depress string with a right hand finger on the front side of the preparation and then release quickly so that it causes the clip to bounce. The left hand fingers the string as written.

  Graphic notation below the staff represents the angle of the guitar, which is used to control the rate that the alligator clip bounces at. The lower line indicates that the guitar should be held in the standard playing position. The upper line indicates that the guitar should be angled forward, resulting in slower bounces. Assume standard playing position in the absence of graphic indications.

Notation

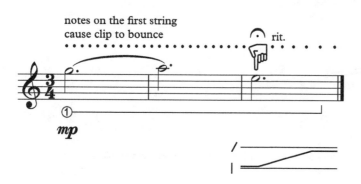

Mechanical Oscillators

Long and rigid objects can be woven through the strings so that, when set into motion, they teeter about a fixed point like a seesaw, creating a pulsating effect (Fig. 6.37). What is striking about these effects is how long they last—slower oscillators could continue for minutes. Moreover, the pulsations often crescendo and decrescendo over relatively long time spans, imbuing the effect with a self-propagating quality. As intriguing as mechanical oscillators sound, they tend to occupy most, if not all, of the instrument and offer little opportunity for the performer to engage with it. In fact, any contact with the strings will quickly dampen the oscillation. Instead, one is tempted to just set them in motion and leave them alone, perhaps playing along on another instrument.

General Considerations

A mechanical oscillator uses a weave pattern to set up opposing forces from the strings that create a rocking motion similar to that of a pendulum. As the object teeters to one side, the strings that pass under the weave on that side are bent toward the body of the instrument, while those passing over the weave on the other side are bent upward. The added tension of the bent strings is released as they return to their normal position, thus propelling the object in the other direction (Fig. 6.38). This process alternates from side to side as the object rocks back and forth, which is what causes the oscillation to sustain for so long.

Figure 6.37
A cooking skewer set over the fretboard and weighted toward the higher strings, producing relatively slow oscillations [▶ Media 6.42].

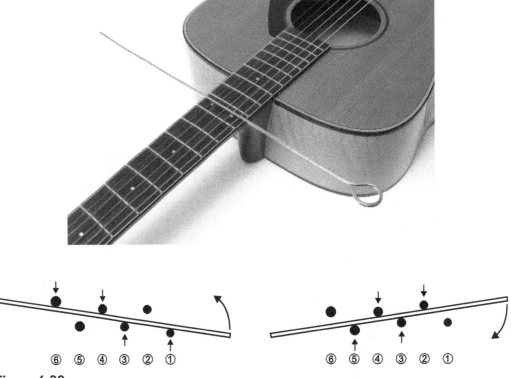

Figure 6.38
Opposing forces exerted on a woven object from the strings as it oscillates from side to side act to propel it back in the other direction.

Controlling the Rate of Oscillation

The rate of oscillation is determined by a number of interacting factors. The first is the length of the object; all other attributes being equal, longer objects will oscillate slower than shorter ones. Second, objects woven so that the weight is equally distributed on both sides of the strings will oscillate fastest, while shifting the weight more to one side or the other slows down the oscillation rate. Finally, the tension of the strings affects the amount of potential buoyancy that they have. String tension is obviously affected by the tuning employed, but also by the thickness of the woven object and by the number of strings added to the weave. Tight weave patterns like the basic under-over pattern produce comparatively rapid oscillations, while weaving only a single string over the object produces much slower results. Furthermore, the tension can be modified dynamically by exerting pressure on any of the strings with the hand or by stopping and/or bending any notes on the fretboard.

Controlling Timbre

Mechanical oscillators produce timbrally complex sounds, comprising coupling resonance, bi-tones for each string affected, and bounce tones for the trampoline strings. The collective results tend to be somewhat cluttered. Front tones tend to dominate, and specific harmonic relationships can be obtained using alternate tunings. Shifting the distribution of weight to the bass or treble strings will give emphasis to those components in the composite sound. Front and back bi-tones can also be muted to achieve a range of different timbral effects. In addition to the tonal content, mechanical oscillators often add percussive elements as the object knocks against the body of the instrument or the edge of the fretboard. These are most prominent when longer objects are used, especially when set over the body of the instrument.

Shared Nut Slots, Crossed Strings, and Snarled Strings

Shared Nut Slots

It is possible for strings to share a nut slot (Fig. 6.39), which has little impact on the sound of the strings but causes the space between them to gradually diminish until they ultimately converge at the nut. Such close string spacing allows both strings to be stopped under a single fingertip in the lower frets, similar to the manner in which the double courses of a 12-string instrument are stopped. Unison and octave tunings create

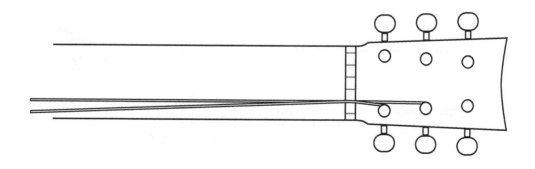

Figure 6.39
First and second strings sharing the same nut slot
[▶ Media 6.43].

143

a natural chorus effect, while other intervals result in parallel harmonic motion reminiscent of a harmonizer effect pedal. The tighter spacing may also be leveraged to hold a wedged preparation in place, particularly when it is set over the fretboard.

Crossed Strings

The strings of the guitar can be installed so that they cross each other to produce a buzzing, percussive effect. While this preparation is extremely stable, it requires that strings be removed from their designated tuning posts and wound around others. In Figure 6.40, string one is wound around tuner two while string two is fixed to tuner one, causing the two strings to cross at their midway point, typically between the 10th and 12th frets. The space between crossed strings is tighter than normal over the entirety of the fretboard, so it can be difficult to target individual strings. Crossed strings produce a noisy, buzzing quality with inharmonic timbre and coupling resonance when the crossing point is contained within the vibrating portion of the strings. Stopping the strings above the crossing point essentially gives the same effect as a shared nut slot, producing two normal sounding pitches that are timbrally unaffected by the crossing.

Snarled Strings

To snarl strings, one of them must be removed from the machine tuner, twisted around another, and then re-installed back onto its appropriate tuner (Fig. 6.41). When fingered near the crossing point the sounding result is noisy and inharmonic, similar to that of crossed strings but more pronounced since the strings are entangled to a greater extent. Stopping the string at a distance from the crossing point often results in a clear double stop with minimal interference. Interesting effects can be

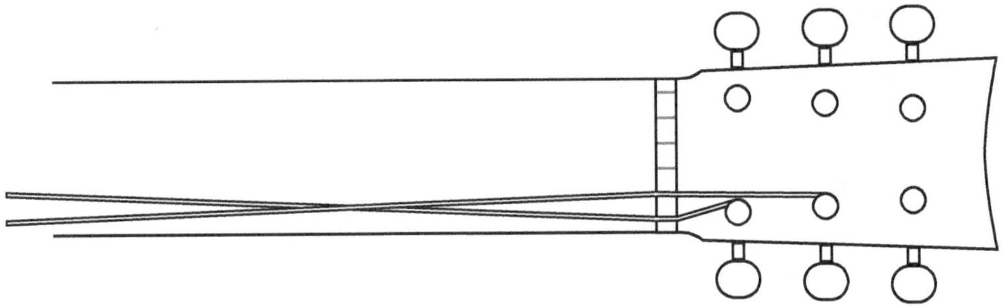

Figure 6.40
String crossing, with string one wound around tuner two and string two fixed to tuner one
[▶ Media 6.44].

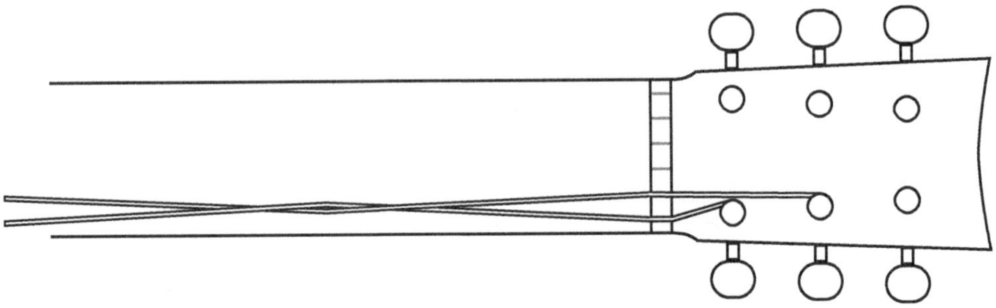

Figure 6.41
Snarled strings
[▶ Media 6.45].

obtained by experimenting with string tensions. For instance, slack strings produce a flapping quality reminiscent of a rubber band. However, intonation is particularly problematic with snarled strings since any adjustment to the tension of one of them affects the force pulling on the other. Moreover, both strings typically settle on the same pitch.

Body Preparations

Objects can be attached to the resonant body of an acoustic guitar to achieve a variety of non-pitched effects. Because body preparations do not engage the strings or impact the player's ability to play the instrument in a conventional manner, they offer sound materials that can supplement the natural output of the instrument. When objects are placed on the body, the precise location has a significant effect on the resulting

145

Figure 6.42
Body preparations: Velcro and sandpaper scratch surfaces and tines made from snippets of guitar string [▶ Media 6.46].

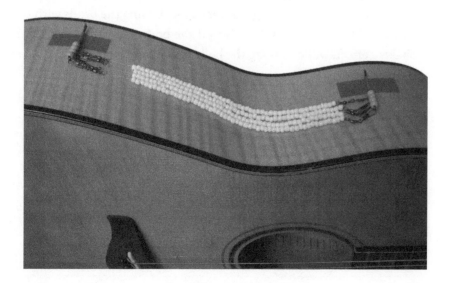

Figure 6.43
Plastic beads threaded on fishing line and fixed to the top of the instrument, producing shekere and shaker effects [▶ Media 6.47].

sound, which must be balanced with a concern for the object being easily accessible to the performer.

Implementations

Scratch Surfaces

Scratching or scraping the body of an acoustic guitar with the fingers or pick is not uncommon in contemporary compositions. Textured materials such as Velcro or burlap can be attached to the body to provide additional scratch surfaces with distinct sounds (Fig. 6.42). If you don't want to attach sticky glue materials directly to the soundboard, then painter's tape or non-stick scratch guards (golpeadores) can be used.

Body Bouncers

Tine-like objects can be taped to the edge of the soundboard and set in motion to create a bouncing effect similar to that of plucking a ruler over the edge of a desk (Fig. 6.42). Heavy wire and heavy-gauge string snippets are good candidates. For best results, the object must be securely taped to the body of the instrument roughly an inch or more from the edge so that it is free to flap against it. The amount of overhang determines the bounce rate. Figure 6.42 offers a few implementations using guitar string snippets. The lower preparation uses a single string and produces articulate bounce effects in which the pitch can be changed dynamically by anchoring the tine at various points closer to the edge of the instrument with a finger. The upper preparation involves a group of strings cut to varying lengths so that each bounces at a different rate. When plucked together, the result is a more complex, irregular cluster of attacks.

Shekere and Shaker Effects

Shekere and shaker effects can be obtained by attaching loosely hanging strands of threaded beads to the body of the instrument. In Figure 6.43, plastic beads threaded on fishing line are fixed to bobby pins to create four strands. The bobby pins are then taped to the top-side of the guitar using painter's tape. Pulling the beads with the fingers toward one of the bobby pins so that they lift off the body and then releasing them creates a good shekere effect, while shaking the body of the instrument imitates maracas.

7

Amps, Effects, and Signal Chains

A remarkable characteristic of the electric guitar is the flexibility of its sound, as this can be altered electronically in extreme ways. Indeed, the timbral diversity of the instrument is so vast that one might question what a "normal" guitar sound refers to. In the context of well-established musical genres conventions breed stereotypes that may guide a player toward a particular tone, but in less established musical contexts there are no rules. Even more, the contrast between two guitar sounds can easily be as stark as that between any two orchestral instruments. Likewise, an ensemble of guitars can be every bit as colorful and timbrally rich as any other collection of instruments if proper attention is given to diversifying tones.[1]

The tone quality of an electric guitar is the product of a chain of distinct but interconnected components that begins with the instrument, usually includes a number of effects devices, and ends with an amplifier. Guitarists refer to this instrument-effects-amplifier tripartite system as their "rig," and they pay considerable attention to the contribution of each component. Instruments and their hardware are the subjects of Chapter 1. Here, we are concerned with the effects and amplification components of a rig, with particular attention placed on the preservation of tone throughout the signal chain.

Amplifiers

A guitar amplifier takes a signal from a pickup and projects it from a speaker so that it can be heard. The amp contributes more than mere volume, however. It can play a central role in defining the tone of the guitar and also reflects the strategy underlying the rig's design. One approach strives for amp transparency, leaving the modification of tone primarily to pedals and other external processors. More often, however, an amp is chosen for its particular sound. Amp circuitry is designed to color the tone in deliberate and unique ways, with the starkest distinctions to be found in the overdrive or distortion characteristics of different models. Other reasons for selecting a particular amp may include its technical features, number of channels, power, or speaker configuration.

While other amplifiers could be used to project the electric guitar, none can compare to the sound of a high-quality, purpose-built guitar amp, and for good reason. Guitar amps are designed to accept a high-impedance, instrument-level signal, precisely like that originating from electromagnetic pickups. Most other amplification systems—a keyboard amp or PA system, for instance—expect a line-level, low-impedance signal. As we will see, mismatched signals generally lead to a degradation of tone quality.

Amp Types

Guitar amps have historically been based on either vacuum tube or solid-state technology. Tube amplifiers are coveted for their warmth and for the way they color and ultimately distort the signal when overdriven. However, they are more expensive, heavy, fragile, require regular maintenance, and generate a fair amount of constant hiss from the speaker. Solid-state amps, on the other hand, are considerably cheaper to manufacture, require little maintenance, run quieter, and are generally more robust. Newer hybrid amp designs employ both tube and solid-state components in the different amp stages. For instance, tubes may be employed in the preamp to provide the sought-after tube overdrive while the power amp stage uses solid-state circuitry to move the speaker and project the sound. Although tone connoisseurs may cherish the authenticity of vacuum tubes, many of the newer solid-state and hybrid amps are designed to sound tube-like and do indeed come close.

The most significant innovation transforming the amplifier market in recent years has been the introduction of modeling technology. Modeling amps contain digital circuits designed to emulate a range of classic amplifiers, speakers, or conventionalized guitar tones, all at the turn of a dial. The emulations are not entirely convincing, but they do come close, and having access to so many different tones in a single unit has clear advantages for the working musician.

Acoustic Guitar Amps

If an acoustic instrument needs to be amplified, a high-quality acoustic amp offers the most natural solution. Acoustic guitar amps differ from those made for the electric instrument. They usually have a closed back and a wider frequency response; they are designed to be neutral, in contrast to the intentional coloration that most electric amps add. An acoustic guitar played though an electric guitar amp tends to sound unnaturally amplified, whereas an acoustic amp does a much better job of capturing the acoustic character of the instrument. Needless to say, the inverse is also true: it is generally not a good idea to pair an electric guitar with an acoustic amp.

Combo Amps, Heads, and Cabinets

Within an amplifier a distinction can be made between the preamp, power amp, and speaker stages. A combo amp has the amplification circuitry and speakers built into a single unit for convenience. These amps are relatively small and contain one or two speakers, although many provide an output jack for an external speaker cabinet. Alternatively, amps can be assembled from separate head and cabinet components. The head contains the amplification stages while the cabinet encases the speakers. The principal advantage of a head and cabinet system is that the amp can be paired with different speakers.

Inputs, Channels, and Channel Switching

The simplest of guitar amps offer a single channel and are limited to only one tone setting. Others provide an input for just one instrument but have two or more selectable channels that can be configured for distinct tones. For example, one channel might provide a clean sound while the other is used for amp-based distortion. Still other amp designs offer two discrete channels with separate inputs to allow multiple instruments to be connected to the amp simultaneously. For instance, a guitarist who uses two different guitars in different works can have both connected to the amp with separate volume and tone settings for each. While technically feasible, it is generally not a good idea to allow two musicians to share an amplifier on stage because the instruments will be localized to a single point source, which obfuscates segregation of the parts and muddies the mix.

Hi-Z and Lo-Z Inputs

Many guitar amps provide high-impedance (Hi-Z) and low-impedance (Lo-Z) inputs in a single channel. In such cases, input one is typically high impedance and input two is low impedance.[2] Since guitar pickups output a high-impedance signal it usually makes sense to connect a guitar to input one. Connecting a Hi-Z signal to the Lo-Z input results in a volume reduction and a squashed tone, with significant loss of detail. The low-impedance input may be more appropriate for some active pickups or when connecting other sources to the amp such as an audio interface or electronic keyboard. Although both inputs can often be used simultaneously, the two inputs should not be confused with a two-channel design. When both are used the signal level and impedance typically get normalized to the characteristics of the Lo-Z input, which is not ideal for the guitar's tone. Furthermore, both instruments must share the same volume and tone controls.

Non-Master Volume and Master Volume Amps

All amplifiers boost the signal of the guitar in two stages: the preamp and the power amp. The preamp increases the instrument-level signal to something more appropriate for subsequent electronics in the amp. The power amp stage is where the signal is boosted to a level that can drive a speaker and be heard. Some amplifiers have a single volume control linked to the power amp stage. Conventional wisdom is that these so-called non-master volume amps sound cleaner than those with multiple gain stages, attributed to the minimal circuitry that the signal passes through. The Fender Twin Reverb and Fender Deluxe Reverb amps are industry standards in this category. However, such a clean sound comes at the expense of distortion features. In order to overdrive a non-master volume amp the volume must be turned up near maximum, which is too loud for practical purposes in most instances. By contrast, master-volume amps provide a gain control for the preamp stage and a separate volume for the power amp stage. Given this scenario, the gain can be used to overdrive the preamp while the volume is set low to keep the loudness under control. If amp-based distortion is preferred to that of a pedal, then a master-volume amp with a preamp gain is essential.

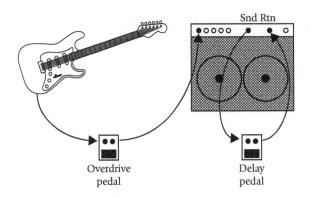

Figure 7.1

Placing wet effects in an amplifier's effects loop.

Effects Loops

Many amplifiers are equipped with an effects loop that allows external devices to be inserted into the signal chain between the amplifier's preamp/tone circuitry and the power amp stage. It is common to put wet effects such as reverbs or delays in the effects loop so that they do not hamper the interaction between an overdrive or distortion pedal and the amplifier's preamp (Fig. 7.1). Plus, having fewer pedals between the instrument and amplifier leads to a stronger and more preserved signal when it reaches the amp.

Signal Chains

Effects devices can be inserted into a guitar's signal chain to alter the sound of the instrument. Commercial devices are available that range from single function foot pedals, or so-called stomp boxes, to multi-effects and rack mountable units. Some devices are used to enhance the natural sound of the instrument while others invoke more radical transformations. Still others serve utilitarian functions, such as splitting, rerouting, or boosting the signal. It is not uncommon for a working guitarist to have a chain of effects devices in the rig, used in varying combinations to achieve a range of different sounds.

The following discussion is concerned with the application of guitar effects in a live rig. It does not cover topics of post-production, that is to say, effects added to a pre-recorded guitar track during the mixing stage of a production. While processing units designed for studio production offer many of the same effects as those found in pedals, they usually do not sound as good when added between the guitar and amplifier because they are not designed to handle the type of signal that a guitar pickup generates. To understand why, we will need to examine analog audio signals in greater depth.

Analog Audio Signals

Line Level and Instrument-Level Signals

Electronic audio devices are designed to operate at different nominal signal levels. When sending an analog audio signal from one device to another it is important to be mindful of the device's operating level, as mismatched levels can lead to excessive noise, distortion, and a generally poor quality guitar tone. Understanding the level at which the input and output of each device operates is essential for preserving the tone through the signal chain.

The vast majority of electronic devices—those ranging from smartphones and home DVD players to electronic keyboards and pro audio equipment—operate at line level, of which there are two standards. Consumer line level measures –10 dBV at unity gain, that is, when the device's VU meter registers 0 dB. Professional line level measures +4 dBu at unity gain, giving it a better signal-to-noise ratio. The convention is to express consumer line level in decibel volts (dBV) and professional line level in decibels unloaded (dBu), which obscures the actual difference in loudness. Using a common reference, we find that professional line level is nearly 12 dB louder than consumer line level.[3] Audio interfaces and mixing consoles will often provide a +4/–10 dB button near the connection jack to switch the mode of operation between professional and consumer levels.

Unlike most electronic devices, a guitar pickup outputs an instrument-level signal that is considerably lower than consumer line level, measuring around –20 dBu.[4] Accordingly, most guitar amplifiers and effects pedals are designed to operate on an instrument-level signal. Connecting an instrument-level signal to a device that expects a line level creates a mismatch that results in a poor quality tone. Fortunately, there are direct injection (DI) and reamping boxes that can be used to convert to and from an instrument level. The signal level, however, is not the only difference between a guitar pickup's output and that of line-level devices. We now turn to impedance.

Impedance

Impedance, denoted with a "Z" in engineering equations and expressed in Ohms (Ω), is a measure of the total opposition to current flow in an analog circuit. Device connections are classified as "Lo-Z" when they have an impedance of up to 600 Ω and "Hi-Z" when impedance measures several thousand Ohms or more. Electric guitars with passive magnetic pickups output a high-impedance signal ranging from roughly 4k to 15k Ω. Active pickups will often have a low impedance of around 100 Ω. When connecting analog devices it is best to send a low-impedance signal into a much higher-impedance input, a practice known as impedance bridging; otherwise the signal-to-noise ratio and frequency response suffer. As a general rule, the impedance on the input of the next device should be at least 10 times greater than the impedance of the source being fed into it. Guitar equipment is typically designed with impedance bridging in mind. For instance, effects pedals usually have a 1 Megohm (MΩ) input impedance and 1,000 Ω output impedance, while amplifiers typically have a high-impedance input of around 1 MΩ (Fig. 7.2).

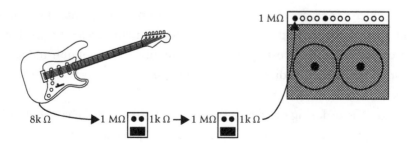

Figure 7.2

Impedance bridging in a typical electric guitar signal chain.

Analog Buffers and the True-Bypass Revolution

The sad truth is that most pedals degrade the quality of the guitar's signal, even when the pedal is in bypass mode. Guitarists refer to this as "tone sucking" and it can easily be tested by comparing the sound of the instrument connected directly to the amp with that when it runs through a pedal in bypass mode.[5] A few pedals in series may be tolerable, but the degradation is cumulative and increasingly squashes the sound as more pedals are added. The main reason for the loss of quality is an improper or overuse of buffering devices.

From an engineering standpoint, high-impedance signals such as those coming from passive guitar pickups are problematic. For one thing, a high-impedance signal loses high frequencies if the total cable length from guitar to amplifier is greater than around 15 feet. On the contrary, a low-impedance signal can travel farther while preserving the full bandwidth of the signal. Second, it is difficult to design an analog audio device that operates directly on a high-impedance signal, and for this reason nearly all pedals convert the signal to low impedance before running it through their internal circuitry, a process referred to as buffering. Buffering the signal at the start of the chain or before a long cable can help to preserve the tone as it makes its way to the amp. For years it was common practice in pedal design to buffer the signal regardless of whether the effect is bypassed. As a result, a pedal board with many pedals is always buffering the signal multiple times, even when the effects are not being used. Overbuffering or sending a low-impedance signal into an effect designed for a high-impedance signal are common culprits of poor tone.

Many pedals are now being made with true bypass circuitry, which simply means that when the pedal is bypassed the signal flows directly from the input to the output unbuffered. When the pedal is engaged it will convert the signal to low impedance, but when it is not being used it has no effect on the tone. Many tone connoisseurs swear by true bypass, but it is not without issues of its own. A high-impedance signal cannot travel too far down a cable before it deteriorates; 15-feet is a good rule of thumb for a maximum cable length. When a number of true bypass effects are chained together and all bypassed, it is as if the signal is being sent down one long cable with a total length equal to the sum of its individual segments. The point of true bypass, however, is not necessarily that the guitar makes its way through the effect chain and to the amp as a high-impedance signal. Rather, it is that a chain can include many pedals while only buffering the signal once or twice at any given time.

Pedalboard Design

Order of Effects

The order in which pedals are chained together can significantly impact the output, both in terms of signal strength and in the way the effects themselves interact. For instance, a compressor placed after a booster pedal will limit any added volume and simply sound more compressed. Likewise, a distortion pedal placed after a reverb will distort the reverberation itself.

To assist in the ordering of effects the signal chain might be conceptually divided into three categories: pre-distortion, distortion, and post-distortion (Fig. 7.3). Pedals

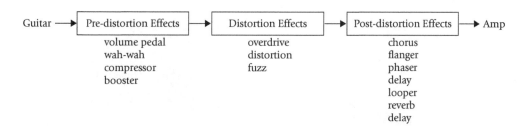

Figure 7.3
Common ordering of effects pedals.

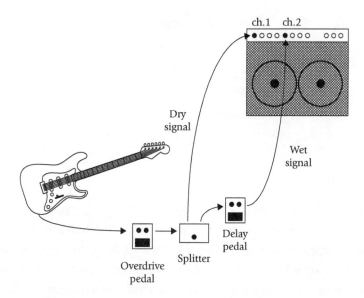

Figure 7.4
Using a splitter to separate wet and dry signals.

153

that are typically placed before distortion include compressors, equalizers, wah pedals, envelope followers, filters, and boosters when used to overdrive the next device in the chain. The distortion category includes overdrive, distortion, and fuzz effects. It is important that the signal hits these pedals hard, and to that end, they are typically placed near the start of the signal chain without much in front of them. If multiple overdrive or distortion pedals are used it is sensible to place the milder ones before those that are more severe. Wet effects such as chorus, delay, and reverb are usually placed after the distortion stage, along with booster and volume pedals when functioning purely for volume. Although informed by common practice, these are merely guidelines, as there is no correct way to order pedals. Players must configure the signal chain to meet their own needs and are encouraged to experiment with unconventional arrangements.

Isolating Wet and Dry Channels

Using a splitter box after the distortion stage, it is possible to divide the signal into dry (unaffected) and wet (affected) paths, each feeding into a separate channel on a two-channel amp, or a separate amp for that matter (Fig. 7.4).[6] Unlike using the amplifier's effects loop, splitting the signal has the advantage of truly reducing the number of effects in each chain. The two channels also offer independent tone controls that can be applied to each signal. When working with separate wet and dry signals, the mix control on all wet effects should be set to 100% wet since the volume controls on the amplifier now determine the balance between dry and wet signals.

Figure 7.5

Using a loop insert pedal to enable or disable a particular section of the signal chain.

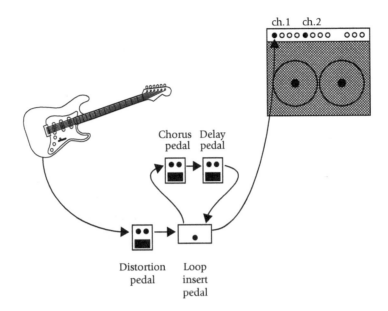

Loop Insert Pedals

An alternative means of minimizing the number of buffering pedals active at any given moment is to use a true bypass loop insert pedal, which provides an effects loop within the signal chain. Engaging the loop routes the signal through any pedals connected to it. However, when the loop is bypassed, the signal is sent from the input to the output unbuffered, effectively removing those pedals from the chain. Apart from alleviating buffering concerns, a loop insert pedal can be used to activate a number of effects with a single click, as shown with a chorus and delay in Figure 7.5. Note that pedals in the loop should always be enabled, as the switch on the loop insert pedal now functions as the bypass. The companion website offers an example of a true-bypass pedalboard [▶ Media 7.1].

Catalog of Effects

Volume Pedals

A volume pedal provides a treadle-style foot controller used to expressively alter the signal level over time. Passive pedals do not require power but are incapable of boosting the signal. Rather, the signal passes through at unity gain when the treadle is fully open and is attenuated as the treadle is closed. Some allow a minimum volume to be set; otherwise the signal is attenuated to silence. Using a passive pedal, the guitar's tone is best when the treadle is fully open, as that essentially passes the signal through with the level unchanged.[7] Attempts to ride the pedal at a lower position so that it can also be used to boost the signal will produce the intended volume effect, but the tone of the guitar will be compromised at those lower levels. Active volume pedals require power and are capable of boosting the signal as well as attenuating it. These pedals often provide control over the upper and lower volume limits and tend to do a better job of preserving tone.

The unique offering of a volume pedal is its ability to control dynamics over time. Applied to an extended passage, crescendo and decrescendo effects can be created that have a distinctively smooth quality. The fact that these are electronically induced dynamic modifications becomes evident when applied over numerous attacks. At the event level, the envelopes of individual sounds can be modified to evade the expected attack-decay morphology of a plucked string. One such technique is to attack the string with the treadle all the way down and then fade it in quickly, replacing the natural attack with one that is elongated [ⓟ Media 7.2]. The hand and foot coordination required to execute such detailed envelope transformation places limits on the speed at which it can be performed; quarter notes at 120 BPM is a safe upper limit for a player not accustomed to the technique. Of course, the amount of envelope shaping that can be applied is limited by the relatively quick decay of the note. Paired with an EBow, however, sustain is infinite and the dynamic changes can become the primary dimension of interest [ⓟ Media 7.3].[8]

Marc Ribot makes interesting use of a volume pedal using a hollow body electric guitar in his rendition of Leonard Bernstein and Stephen Sondheim's "Somewhere" (2001). Leveraging the acoustic projection of the instrument, he is able to blend and crossfade between the amplified and acoustic sounds. Apart from a swelling effect, there is a striking timbral difference due to the electric signal being from a pickup and the acoustic from a microphone. A volume pedal can be paired with any acoustic guitar equipped with a pickup to create a similar effect, leading to some interesting possibilities for imaging and sound projection on the concert stage.

Volume pedals behave differently depending on where they are placed in the signal chain. At the end, the pedal functions as a master volume for the whole pedalboard. By contrast, placing a volume pedal earlier in the chain alters the signal level going into the next effect, which will make a difference if that device is an overdrive, delay, or reverb, for instance.

Booster Pedals

A booster pedal functions to amplify the signal by a user-specified amount, which can exceed 20 dB on some boxes. The two most common uses for a booster pedal are to increase the level during solos or to create a hotter signal that overdrives the next device in the chain, whether it is an amp or another pedal. The placement of the booster in the pedal chain depends on its intended function. If the booster is used to increase overall volume, then it makes sense to place it at the end of the chain. On the other hand, if it is used to overdrive another device then it must be placed immediately before that device.

Boosters are labeled "clean" when all frequencies are affected by the same amount, producing a louder but otherwise unaltered guitar tone. Consider, however, that the signal then enters the next device in the chain at a higher level and that is likely to alter the way it responds. Other booster pedals have a contoured frequency response in which the low-, mid-range, or high frequencies are accentuated more than the others. Of these, the treble booster is most commonly applied to the guitar, as the added presence helps it cut through an ensemble during solos.

Overdrive, Distortion, and Fuzz

A dirty tone is as much a character of the electric guitar as the clean sound that originates from the instrument, and players can generally be expected to have some form of it at the ready. The term "distortion" is broadly used in reference to any dirty guitar tone. In actuality, there are distinct circuit designs used to transform the signal, namely, overdrive, distortion, and fuzz. They all offer similar parameters: the gain controls the amount of clipping or dirt added to the signal; the level determines the output volume; the tone offers basic control over brightness.[9] While overdrive, distortion, and fuzz produce similar transformations to the guitar's sound, there are idiosyncrasies of each worth considering.

Overdrive

A device is overdriven when the signal exceeds its maximum operating level. As a result, the peaks of the waveform are clipped, adding spectral richness to the sound that is particularly noticeable in the higher frequencies (Fig. 7.6). The original overdrive effect was obtained from the earliest tube amps by turning the volume up to a point at which the power amp tubes clipped, a level too loud to be practical for most contexts. Master-volume amps address this issue with a channel gain that can be turned up to overdrive the preamp while keeping the master volume low and the overall loudness at a reasonable level. In any case, tubes are generally preferable when obtaining overdrive from an amplifier, as the result is soft clipping characterized by a rounding of the edges around the clipped segments, producing a warmer, and often more transparent effect in which the natural tone of the instrument can still be heard (Fig. 7.6a).

The overdrive pedal was developed to act as an external gain before the signal reaches a tube amp or other dirt-producing pedal, boosting the level so that it hits the next device hard and overdrives its circuitry. To be clear, the actual dirt is added to the signal by the device immediately following the overdrive pedal. If that device is a tube amp then the overdrive should be placed at the end of the effects chain, just before the amp input. If it is another pedal then the overdrive must be placed immediately before that pedal. Used in this way, the overdrive pedal's level is of utmost importance, as it determines the strength of the signal feeding into the next device. The drive can be kept to a minimum, used mainly to add subtle coloration to the tone.

Alternatively, a dirty tone can be produced solely within the overdrive pedal, relying on its internal drive circuitry for the effect. Some overdrive pedals work well on their own, while others are designed to be paired with an amplifier and do not offer much in the way of internal clipping. None reach the degree of clipping obtainable with most distortion or fuzz boxes. If the pedal is used as a stand-alone overdrive it should be placed near the start of the chain so that the instrument's signal feeds directly into it.

Figure 7.6
(a) Soft clipping;
(b) hard clipping.

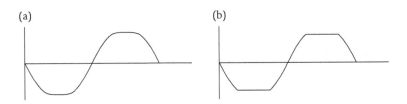

(a)   (b)

A unique attribute of overdrive is that the process is inherently sensitive to the level of the input signal. Clipping is mild when the instrument is played at softer dynamics and more severe when attacked harder. This correlation between energy input and timbral richness is ubiquitous in the realm of acoustic sounds and is probably the reason that many guitarists describe the overdrive effect as feeling more natural than distortion or fuzz.

Distortion and Fuzz

Distortion circuits typically use solid-state diodes and op-amps to produce their effect, resulting in hard clipping that is characterized by sharp angles at the clipped edges and a brighter, more buzz-like tone quality (Fig. 7.6b). Distortion treatments range from a light, transparent coloration to a thick and heavy saturation that shrouds the natural tone of the instrument. Unlike overdrive, distortion is not sensitive to dynamics and remains consistent regardless of the input level. While arguably less natural, this allows the guitar to be played at soft dynamics without compromising the effect.

The fuzz pedal was developed in the 1960s using transistors to clip the signal. Vintage pedals used germanium transistors, which are favored by many players for their warmer tone and sensitivity to dynamics. Newer designs use silicon transistors, producing a brighter, sharper tone that clips more evenly at varying dynamics. The fuzz effect is more severe than overdrive or distortion, leading to a thick and raspy tone. The guitar sound used by Jimi Hendrix in "Purple Haze" (1967) serves as a classic example.

Generalizations

Concern for distortion is often at the center of a rig's design. Signal clipping can be obtained at the amp, in pedals, or some combination of the two, and the method chosen for obtaining a dirty tone will influence the devices employed and their ordering in the signal chain. Tube amps are the de facto standard if overdrive is preferred, with the possibility of some sort of overdrive or booster pedal placed immediately before the amp. On the other hand, the amplifier is less crucial when a distortion or fuzz box is used, and the pedal is typically placed near the start of the signal chain.

The sonic differences between overdrive, distortion, and fuzz are difficult to pin down and verbalize. Broadly speaking, overdrive produces the mildest effect, while fuzz is the most severe. Thick and heavy tones are achievable with distortion, but some pedals and amps are equally capable of a mild and transparent treatment. To complicate matters, a wide array of dirt-producing pedals and amplifiers is available and each possesses a truly distinctive character. Players may have several different pedals in their chain, used individually or in varying combinations to achieve a variety of tones. When describing a dirty tone, the distinction between overdrive and distortion/fuzz is perhaps most relevant, as it has dynamic implications that may be relevant to a performer. Beyond this, descriptors such as thin, thick, heavy, or transparent might be used to convey the general direction of the sound, allowing the player to devise a suitable response.

Implementations

Harmonic Richness

Any amount of clipping adds spectral richness to the instrument's tone. Using a pedal with the drive set near the minimum yields a guitar tone that is practically clean, but with lightly accentuated spectral components that give it significantly more bite and presence. Such a subtle treatment might be used to facilitate hard-to-obtain harmonics, to brighten up the sound of instrumental preparations, or simply to help the guitar cut through an ensemble [▶ Media 7.4].

Compression/Sustain

Clipping inherently compresses the dynamic range of a signal, as the peaks of the waveform are suppressed proportional to the gain setting. A side effect of the reduced dynamic range is increased sustain, as softer portions of the signal tend to be amplified. Limiting the dynamic range of the signal is useful when delicate sounding preparations are employed or to maintain presence of soft background activity. However, the compression effect also increases the level of any noise in the signal, most noticeable when the instrument is resting. Needless to say, a distortion pedal should not be used as a compressor, but the compression effect of clipping is significant enough that it is rare to use a compressor along with dirty effects, unless the dirt is kept to a minimum.

Feedback

Feedback from an electric guitar occurs because the sound pressure waves coming from the amp's speaker hit the instrument and cause it to vibrate sympathetically. These vibrations ultimately make their way to the strings and are amplified through the pickups. In most live sound contexts, feedback is something to avoid. However, electric guitarists have been treating it as a viable element of the instrument's sound for decades and have even developed some techniques for controlling it. Volume and distortion are key ingredients to generating feedback, the latter due to its compression qualities. Although it is difficult to control the pitch, a change can be invoked by altering the angle and/or proximity of the instrument to the amplifier and will typically settle on a lower-ordered harmonic of the string length. Rock guitarist Ted Nugent allegedly used to place tape on the stage to mark the locations that would produce particular tones.

Choruses, Flangers, and Phase Shifters

Choruses, flangers, and phase shifters are modulation-based effects that utilize a low frequency oscillator (LFO) to impose a swirling motion onto the instrument's sound, adding a sense of inner liveliness. It is also possible to get some far-out sounds from these pedals when parameters are taken to extremes. Let us now look at each effect in turn.

Chorus

Discrepancies in timing and intonation are inevitable whenever two or more musicians play together in unison. A chorus mimics these irregularities by adding a copy of the input back into the signal path, but slightly delayed and pitch modulated, the latter introducing intonational discrepancies. It is the pitch modulation that gives the effect its characteristic swirling motion. In addition, chorus adds thickness to the sound and seems to distance it from the listener. The effect is more often used on clean or only slightly distorted guitar tones, as can be heard in the opening to Nirvana's "Come as You Are" (1991).

The important parameters of a chorus effect are the delay time, rate, depth, feedback, and mix. The delay time determines the time discrepancy between the dry and wet signals. The rate determines the frequency of the LFO, which adds a bi-polar, vibrato-like pitch change to the copied signal. The depth determines the amount of deviation in pitch, both sharp and flat, around the original signal. If a feedback loop is implemented, the feedback control determines the amount of signal returned to the input, which leads to a more pronounced effect. Finally, the mix control sets the balance between the dry input and the processed signal. Importantly, the classic chorus effect is created by interference between the dry and processed signals, and as such, the most pronounced effect tends to be when the mix is at 50%, with both signals roughly balanced.

Flange

A flange effect is created when the input signal is copied, sent through a time-varying delay, and then added to the original signal, inducing phase cancelation at evenly spaced peaks and notches in the spectrum. The delay time is modulated by an LFO, which causes the peaks and notches in the spectrum to shift back and forth, producing the characteristic swishing effect. In a flanger, the rate determines how quickly the delay time changes, while the depth determine the range of that change. A flange effect can be heard on an isolated distorted guitar in the introduction to Rush's "Spirit of the Radio" (1980).

Phase Shifting

A phase shifter is similar in principle to a flanger, although it utilizes a series of all-pass filters to produce peaks and notches in the spectrum that oscillate according to the rate and depth controls. Unlike a flanger, the peaks and notches in a phase shifter are not necessarily evenly spaced, leading to a subtly different sound. The number of filter stages employed determines the number of notches in the spectrum, where n stages results in n/2 notches. For instance, a two-stage phase shifter will produce a single notch in the output spectrum, while an eight-stage phase shifter results in four notches. Jonny Greenwood uses a classic phaser effect in Radiohead's "The Tourist" (1997).

Implementations

Classic Swirling Modulation

Modulation effects are most often used to add subtle inner activity to a guitar tone, brought about through the swirling behavior of the LFO. In this classic implementation, all parameters are kept at modest levels. In particular, intonation discrepancies created by the depth control should not be so pronounced as to cause the instrument to sound out of tune. The mix is roughly balanced between dry and wet signals, favoring the dry signal if anything [▶ Media 7.5].

159

Poor Intonation

Intonation discrepancies between the wet and dry signals of a modulation effect can be exaggerated by turning the depth control up high while keeping the remaining parameters at modest levels. The result is akin to that of two guitars playing out of tune with one another, although clearly a mechanical emulation [▶ Media 7.6].

Flanger Sweeps

A prominent filter-sweeping effect can be obtained using a flanger with the rate set fairly low, the depth fairly high, and the mix set to nearly 100% wet. The effect should be so pronounced that the moving filter grabs the attention of the listener, imposing a sweeping gesture onto the sound. Flanger sweeps are often used over short passages, such as the last few measures of a section, using the gesture to propel the music into the subsequent downbeat, at which point the effect may be removed [▶ Media 7.7].[10] Note that it can be difficult to coordinate the sweeping gesture with the timing of the music, since the flanger's LFO is constantly oscillating. Software flangers often have the ability to sync the phase of the LFO, which solves the problem.

Propeller Sounds

When the rate and depth are turned way up, the oscillating behavior of the LFO becomes the salient characteristic of the sound, producing a propeller-like effect with ill-defined pitch. Setting the mix to 100% wet isolates the LFO, but at that point the performer's contribution to the music is marginalized [▶ Media 7.8].

Electronic Tremolo

Tremolo describes a regular fluctuation in loudness. As an electronic effect, it is obtained by modulating the amplitude of a signal with an LFO. A rate control sets the frequency of the LFO, while the depth determines the amount of amplitude reduction in each oscillation. A depth set to maximum causes the amplitude to fall to zero, the most pronounced effect. While such a heavy treatment works well to transform the envelope of a single sound, it can suppress events when applied over an extended passage and the tremolo rate is slower than the rate of performed materials. Tremolo units often provide a number of basic wave shapes that can be chosen for the LFO. Those closer to a sine wave produce a smooth tremolo, whereas shapes such as a square wave produce hard-cutting pulsations. Although an electronic tremolo bears some semblance to a performed repeat tremolo, it is not intended as a substitute for the manual technique. Rather, it is far more mechanical and usually applied over extended passages of music to produce a blanketing effect that is distinctly mechanical.

Implementations

Classic Electronic Tremolo

The classic tremolo effect adds a pulsating quality to the sound, which usually remains stable in terms of the rate [▶ Media 7.9]. In pulse-based music it is sensible to set the rate to a subdivision of the working tempo. If it can be defined specifically it will most likely be presented as a frequency in Hertz, which can be computed by dividing the beats-per-minute by 60. For instance, at a tempo of 110 BPM a rate of 1.83 Hz will pulse at the quarter note, while a rate of 3.66 Hz would pulse at the eighth note. Unfortunately, many pedals simply provide an unmarked rate knob with no means of specifying a precise setting. Others offer a Tap button that can be used to set the rate by tapping with the foot at the appropriate tempo.

Accelerations/Decelerations

Clear acceleration and deceleration trajectories can be obtained with tremolo by gradually changing the rate over time. Some analog tremolo pedals support an external expression pedal controller that can be used in this way. Otherwise, the effect can be implemented in a software environment such as Cycling '74's Max with a MIDI expression pedal mapped to the tremolo rate [▶ Media 7.10]. It is not uncommon to link the rate and depth so that faster tremolo speeds invoke a greater amplitude fluctuation.

Electronic Vibrato

Vibrato refers to a repeated fluctuation in pitch. As an electronic effect, it is obtained by modulating the pitch of the input signal with an LFO. The modulation is bi-polar, creating fluctuations both sharp and flat of the original signal. The rate controls the speed of pitch oscillation while the depth determines the amount of deviation. Electronic vibrato adds a shimmering quality to the sound, which can help to bring out a line when the guitar is playing with an ensemble. It also masks intonation discrepancies between instruments.

Implementations

Classic Electronic Vibrato

Musicians add vibrato, especially to longer notes, for expressive purposes. Keeping the pitch variance within a semitone and the speed of oscillation under 4–5 Hz, both parameters are altered in complex ways according to the musical phrasing. Electronic vibrato devices have little of this expressive quality, as the oscillation is mechanical and static. As with tremolo, it would be more appropriate to think of electronic vibrato as an effect distinct from the performance technique. In fact, it is often applied to extended passages of music comprised of materials that would not be amenable to the performance technique [▶ Media 7.11].

Accelerations/Decelerations

Using an expression pedal, vibrato effects can be made to accelerate or decelerate in a manner similar to that of electronic tremolo. While changes in the rate define the trajectory, it is natural to link the depth to the rate such that the pitch variance is greater at faster rates and diminishes as the vibrato slows. Controlling both with a single pedal usually requires that the effect be implemented in a computer, where parameters can be linked accordingly.

Ring Modulation

Ring modulation is achieved by multiplying two audio signals. In the case of the guitar, the instrument's signal is usually modulated with a basic waveform generated within the effect unit.[11] The multiplication of two signals results in spectral energy at frequencies that are the sum and difference of the spectral components present in the two inputs. As a simple example, ring modulating a sine wave at 300 Hz with another sine wave at 100 Hz results in a spectrum with two components: 400 Hz (300+100) and 200 Hz (300-100).[12] Given a more complex signal at one of the inputs, sum and difference tones will appear around each of its spectral components. Figure 7.7 shows a hypothetical spectrum of an open A2 on a guitar being ring modulated with a sine wave at 50 Hz. The guitar tone should have harmonics at 110 Hz, 220 Hz, 330 Hz, 440 Hz, and so on, yet the resultant spectrum shows energy at tones that are 50 Hz above and below each of those harmonics. Importantly, the original signal is not present in a ring-modulated output, which creates a highly electronic sound, almost reminiscent of synthesis. The results of ring modulation are predictable, assuming that the input spectra are known, and this lends the technique to formal methods of compositional control.

Like other modulation techniques, the principal parameters of ring modulation are those that define the modulator tone, namely, frequency and amplitude. However, the frequency is not confined to low frequencies as it is in the other techniques. The amplitude affects the loudness of the resultant sidebands. There may also be options for different wave shapes, although any waveform other than a sine wave leads to a very dense spectrum when applied to a guitar.

Implementations

Harmonic and Inharmonic Spectra

When tones in simple whole number frequency ratios are ring modulated, the resultant sum and difference tones will also be harmonic, producing a relatively consonant spectrum [▶ Media 7.13]. By contrast, when the tones being modulated are in a complex frequency ratio, the resulting components will be inharmonic and dissonant, sounding somewhat metallic and bell-like [▶ Media 7.14]. It is important to note that modulation of a varying input signal with a static tone generated within the ring modulator leads to

Figure 7.7

The spectral result of an open A2 (110 Hz) ring modulated with a sine wave at 50 Hz, showing sum and difference tones straddling the expected harmonics [▶ Media 7.12].

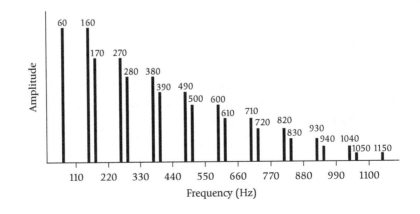

constantly changing frequency ratios, and consequently, timbral diversity. Greater control over the ratios can be obtained by changing the modulator's frequency whenever the pitch of the guitar changes. This is not something that a guitarist could do easily while performing. However, a second musician could play tones on an electronic keyboard that serve as the modulating signal. Alternatively, automated changes to the modulating frequency could be implemented in a computer. If calculated appropriately, a constant frequency ratio can be maintained over a pitch-varying guitar signal, resulting in a more homogenous timbre.

Cause/Effect Relations

The multiplicative property of ring modulation leads to one of its more interesting idiosyncrasies. If one of the inputs is silent, then the output of the ring modulator is also silent. German composer Karlheinz Stockhausen exploits this peculiarity in many of his works, including *Mikrophonie II* (1965) for choir, Hammond organ, four ring modulators, and tape. Four microphones are placed in front of a choir and connected to four ring modulators. The output of the Hammond organ is also connected to the four ring modulators. It is only when both the choir and the organ sound at the same time that the ring modulation is heard, as if to electronically highlight moments of overlap in the work.

Delay

A delay splits the input signal into wet and dry paths, postpones the wet signal for a specified amount of time, and then mixes it back with the dry to produce a single repetition of the input. More repetitions can be obtained using a feedback loop, in which the output of the delay is routed back to the input. The feedback knob is used to attenuate the signal before returning it to the input, thereby affecting the number of repetitions that will be heard before the signal fades away. This simple delay algorithm is at the heart of many commonly used guitar effects, including echo, slapback, doubling, reverb, and most filters. Many delay units also incorporate an LFO, allowing for modulation effects such as chorus, vibrato, and a wide range of bizarre, pitch-bending echoes.

Implementations

Echoes

Setting the delay time long enough that the repetitions are heard as distinct events creates an echo effect. The feedback control determines how long it takes for the echoes to fade away. The mix controls the balance between the dry signal and the echoes. Under natural acoustic conditions echoes are considerably softer than the source, and would typically never be louder than it. A mix setting of around 10% to 15% wet provides a good starting point [▶ Media 7.15].

When a player is using a delay in music with a regular pulse, it may be desirable to synchronize the echoes to a subdivision of the tempo. Delay times are typically expressed in milliseconds, but can be calculated from the tempo using the following equation: MS=60,000/BPM. For instance, at a tempo of 120 BPM a quarter note would occur every 500ms, while an eighth note would occur every 250ms. Some newer pedals provide a tap button that allows the user to set the delay time by tapping along with a foot.

Slapback

A slapback effect should sound like a single reflection from a nearby wall. It is created using a short delay time, roughly 80–140ms, with no feedback so that only a single repetition of the input is produced. The mix is usually set so that the echo is almost as loud as the dry signal. Slapback effects are characteristic of traditional country and rockabilly guitar sounds [⊙ Media 7.16].

Doubling

Delay times on the order of 50–70ms produce a doubling effect, as if two instruments are playing together, but not perfectly synchronized. Like a slapback effect, the feedback should be set to zero so that only a single repetition of the input is produced, and the mix control should be adjusted so that the wet and dry signals are nearly balanced. If the delay unit offers modulation controls, subtle pitch variation might be added to mimic discrepancies in intonation. The doubling effect is similar to a chorus, but oriented more toward timing discrepancies than intonational discrepancies [⊙ Media 7.17].

Cheap Reverb

A reverb-like effect can be produced using a delay with a short delay time and a fair amount of feedback, the latter determining the decay time. Delay times of around 30ms produce a relatively smooth reverb, while longer times cause the effect to sound increasingly rough until it eventually becomes a clear echo. It should be noted that this is not a realistic reverb effect, but there is a certain charm to the cheap imitation quality of it [⊙ Media 7.18].

Comb Filter

A comb filter is obtained by adding a signal to itself with a very short delay time, on the order of 1–25ms. A signal delayed by such a short time will not be heard as a separate event, but instead behaves like a filter by inducing constructive and destructive interference in the spectrum. The filtering can be heard best when the feedback is set near the maximum, producing a resonant, electronic sound with long decay [⊙ Media 7.19]. Resonant comb filters generate a sense of pitch that is correlated with the delay time. For example, if a sound repeats 100 times per second, the repetition itself generates a tone at 100 Hz. Accordingly, longer delay times produce lower resonant nodes, while shorter times produce higher nodes. While a comb filter can impose a resonant tone onto non-pitched materials, any performed pitches may be obfuscated by the periodicity of the filter. The degree to which a comb filter imposes pitch is ultimately determined by the dry/wet mix.

Vari-Speed Echoes

Original delay devices such as the Echoplex employed tape loops that would record the sound and play it back repeatedly. Since the tape was of a fixed length, different delay times were achieved by changing the speed at which the tape cycled around the loop. In such a system, if the tape speed is altered after sound has been recorded, the pitch and speed of the sound are both affected. Many digital delays maintain this link between pitch and duration, and players have learned to exploit it to create bizarre pitch-bending effects. For instance, increasing the delay time while sound is caught in the delay causes it to play back at a slower speed and lower pitch, while decreasing the delay time will play the sound at a faster speed and higher pitch. Tabletop guitarists will often set the feedback high so that sounds get caught in the delay and then "play" the delay time knob to alter the pitch and rhythm as the sound echoes on. A similar technique can be achieved in software while playing the guitar by mapping a MIDI expression pedal to the delay time [⏵ Media 7.20]. Linking an LFO to the delay time creates a mechanical variant of the effect. Some newer delay algorithms attempt to evade this pitch-bending behavior, but often introduce glitches or unusual zippering artifacts when the delay time is changed. More sophisticated devices offer different modes of operation that implement these varying approaches all within a single pedal.

Ping Pong (Stereo Delays)

A stereo delay unit has two discrete outputs, usually considered the left and right channels of a stereo signal.[13] Pedals intended for use with the guitar can take a mono input and split it into two channels. These devices typically implement two distinct delays. When the two channels are configured the same, the effect is essentially that of a mono delay, but when delay times are different the echoes bounce back and forth between the two outputs, an effect referred to as a ping-pong delay. Simple whole number ratios between the left and right delay times create polyrhythms, while more complex ratios tend to produce a more irregular quality. Of course, for the ping-pong effect to be heard the outputs need to be sent to distinct destinations, such as amplifiers positioned on the left and right sides of the stage.

Texture

As delay time is increased, the echoes eventually become dissociated from the input signal, functioning more as a distinct voice in the musical texture.[14] As a simple example, a two-voice canon can be rendered by setting the delay time equal to the canon offset. Dense and rhythmically irregular textures can also be generated with the help of a delay. Using a stereo pedal with independent controls for the left and right signals, pulse can be obscured by setting the long delay times in a complex numeric ratio. Combining these techniques with irregular playing can significantly marginalize the periodicity of the delay effect [⏵ Media 7.21]. It should be noted that a delay device always has a maximum delay time that is limited by its memory capabilities. A relatively long delay time is required in order for the echoes to seem dissociated with the input.

Reverb

Reverb is a common effect applied to the electric guitar intended to mimic the acoustic response of an imagined space. Indeed, most guitar amps have a built-in reverb unit, typically of the spring variety. Spring reverbs function by sending an audio signal down a spring and picking it up on the other end. As the sound travels through the spring it disperses and creates the effect. Spring reverb is not a natural sounding reverb treatment, and in terms of parameters, it only offers control over the wet volume. Nonetheless, it is such a common component of an electric guitar sound that many guitarists prefer it to all others. Some newer amplifiers implement digital reverb, which has the advantage of being able to employ a variety of different algorithms, emulating spring, plate, and more natural room and hall effects. Reverb can also be obtained from a pedal or rack unit, both of which offer more control over the effect.

Reverb is an effect unlike most others in the sense that it is not perceived so much as transforming the sound but rather as establishing the space where the sound occurs.[15] The principal parameters—reverb time, pre-delay, tone, and mix—define that virtual space. The reverb time determines how long it takes for the reverb to decay, which, in a natural space, correlates with the size of the room. The pre-delay defines the time between when the dry signal enters the input and when the wet signal arrives at the output. In an acoustic space, the pre-delay is a factor of the time it takes for the sound to bounce off the nearest wall and arrive at the listener's ear. While larger spaces have the potential for greater pre-delay times, a source positioned close to a wall in a large space would have a short pre-delay and long decay time. Accordingly, the relationship between the reverb time and the pre-delay loosely defines the position of the source within the virtual space. The mix parameter offers the usual control over the dry/wet balance, although in a reverb this translates to the listener's position in relation to the source of the sound within the space. As a listener approaches a source, the balance tips in favor of the dry signal. In a physical space, reverb will never be louder than the dry signal, and in fact, it is usually much lower. A good rule for balancing reverb is to turn it up just to the point where the ear can hear it overtly in the mix, and then from that point turn it down so that it falls below that threshold. It is also important to consider that the space created by reverb will ultimately be projected into a physical space and acquire the natural reverberant characteristics of that room as well.[16] Accordingly, electronic reverb added to a signal can make a small room appear larger, but it cannot make a large reverberant space seem smaller.

Low-Pass, High-Pass, and Band-Pass Filters

A filter is a frequency-dependent amplifier capable of altering a sound's spectrum by boosting or attenuating frequencies within a specified band. Some filters, such as equalizers, allow frequencies outside of the defined band to pass through unaffected, while others block everything outside of the pass band, inducing a more severe spectral transformation. The study of filters is a broad and complex subject, and in the digital domain many varieties are available. This discussion is confined to the basic filters found in hardware effects units, namely, low-pass, high-pass, and band-pass types.

A low-pass filter passes the low frequencies through while blocking the higher ones. Conversely, a high-pass filter passes the higher frequencies through while suppressing the lower ones. In both cases, a cutoff frequency determines where in the spectrum the stop band begins. Technically, a filter's cutoff frequency is defined as that at which the amplitude has been attenuated by 3 dB. As such, frequencies will pass beyond the cutoff frequency, albeit attenuated (Fig. 7.8a). Low- and high-pass filters also have a Q (quality factor) control that determines the steepness of the amplitude roll-off. In addition to a steeper slope, a higher Q produces a resonant node around the cutoff, amplifying those frequencies. Filters are commonly employed for this resonant effect. Filtering removes,

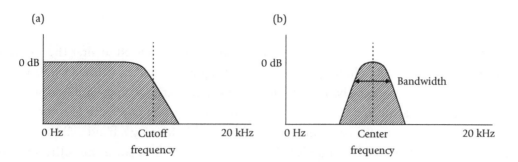

Figure 7.8
(a) A low-pass filter;
(b) a band-pass
filter.

or in the case of a resonant node, boosts energy in the spectrum, and consequently, can significantly alter the overall signal level. A gain control is therefore provided to recalibrate the amplitude.

A band-pass filter can be thought of as overlapping low- and high-pass filters, rolling off frequencies on both sides of a defined center frequency (Fig. 7.8b). The bandwidth control determines the width of the pass band at points attenuated by 3 dB, essentially controlling the Q for both sides. Again, a gain control is provided to readjust the output level.

Implementations

Wah Pedals and Envelope Followers

A common application of filtering involves changing the pass band over time to produce a sweeping effect over the spectrum. Two filter-based guitar effects—the wah pedal and the envelope follower—address the issue of a moving pass band in distinct ways. Wah pedals have a treadle that the player manipulates with the foot to move the cutoff frequency upward or downward in the spectrum, usually between 400 Hz and 2.2 kHz (Hunter, 2004) [▶ Media 7.22]. An envelope follower sounds similar to a wah pedal, but rather than providing manual control over the cutoff frequency, it is linked it to the amplitude of the signal, typically configured so that louder levels shift the pass band higher in the spectrum [▶ Media 7.23]. From a performer's perspective, the dynamic response of an envelope follower feels natural, with the tone sounding muffled and bass-heavy at softer levels and brighter when the instrument is played harder. Some pedals allow the correlation between signal level and pass band to be inverted such that louder signals shift the pass band lower in the spectrum, although this behavior contradicts a listener's expectations of the link between dynamics and timbre.

Talk Box

The talk box is one of the more unusual effects in the commercial guitar gear arsenal. It consists of a pedal with a small built-in speaker that has a rubber tube connected to it. The other end of the tube is attached to a microphone. When the guitar is played, the sound from the pedal's speaker is projected through the tube and into the performer's mouth, where it is "filtered" by the shape of the vocal cavity and then captured through the microphone and projected through a sound reinforcement system. A talk box is technically not an electronic filter, but the effect that the mouth has on the spectrum of the sound is analogous. Similar devices were used as early as the 1940s, but the effect was popularized by Peter Frampton in his hit song "Show Me the Way" (1975).

Equalizers

An equalizer, or EQ, is essentially a series of peak-notch filters used to alter the spectral contour of a signal by amplifying or attenuating frequencies within defined bands while leaving those outside of the bands unaffected. There are various types of EQs, the most common being graphic and parametric. A graphic EQ consists of a bank of filters, with each band fixed at a particular frequency and bandwidth. Moving a band's slider control alters the gain at that band. A graphic EQ requires many bands to cover the entire audible frequency range (20 Hz—20 kHz) with any reasonable degree of resolution. Because of their compact size, stomp box devices are limited in this respect. Nonetheless, graphic EQ pedals up to at least 10-band are available and provide far more tone-shaping control than the amp alone. A parametric EQ offers fewer bands, but each is definable in terms of frequency, bandwidth, and gain, which ultimately offers greater flexibility in a compact unit.

In a live rig, equalizers are most often used to enhance the natural sound of the guitar, and they do provide far more timbral control than the tone knobs on an amp. These are not transformational effects, however. Even when pushed to extremes, the tone-shaping capability afforded by most EQ pedals only causes a modest alteration of the sound, as the gain for each band is limited in terms of how much it can boost or attenuate the signal.

An EQ can also be used to thin the spectrum of the guitar so that it blends more clearly with other instruments in an ensemble, a technique known to sound engineers as mirror equalization. The idea is to identify areas of spectral overlap between two sources and use an EQ to attenuate those frequencies in one of the sounds, clearing spectral space for the other to cut through. While mirror equalization is more often associated with post-production sound mixing, the technique can be highly effective on the concert stage, particularly when working with a large ensemble.

Compressors and Limiters

A compressor reduces the dynamic range of an input signal by attenuating the amplitude whenever it goes above a defined threshold. Signals below the threshold pass through unaffected. Compressors are typically used to stabilize the signal level over time so that individual attacks do not pop out in the mix. However, they can also be used to obtain more perceived loudness and increased sustain. Due to the inherent level reduction, a gain control is provided to return the signal to its original level. When the gain is increased, softer dynamics end up being louder than they were without the effect.[17]

Threshold, ratio, and gain are the principal compressor parameters. The threshold defines the signal level at which the compressor kicks in. This is typically set relatively high so that only the loud peaks in the signal are affected. The ratio determines the amount that the signal is attenuated when it goes above the threshold. For example, a ratio of 3:1 indicates that every 3 dB of input above the threshold will output at 1 dB above the threshold; 6 dB above the threshold would amount to 2 dB at the output. Turning the ratio up all the way causes the compressor to function more like a limiter, in which nothing passes more than 1 dB above the threshold. Compressors may also provide attack and release controls that determine how quickly the device responds to a signal when it goes above the threshold, and how quickly it then releases the signal when it drops below the threshold. Applied to the guitar, a short attack time will compress the percussive start of each note, while a longer attack time allows the natural transient of the plucked string through before the effect kicks in.

Compressors are not transformational effects. Rather, they are used to enhance the natural sound of the instrument, and applied correctly, they should be transparent. Employed in a live guitar rig, a compressor can be easily misused, or it can be configured so that it does more harm than good. Over-compression causes a significant loss of dynamic range and can add a pumping quality to the signal as it crosses the threshold. Furthermore, the effect is typically applied to clean or only slightly dirty guitar tones since heavier distortion results in significant compression of its own. Finally, a compressor should be placed near the start of the chain and always before wet effects such as reverb or delay.

Implementations

Stabilizing Dynamics

To use a compressor for the purpose of stabilizing dynamics, the threshold control should be set high so that only the loudest peaks are affected. The ratio is usually set to a modest level, such as 4:1. Setting the ratio too high will negate performed dynamics. The attack time should be kept short to ensure that it catches the sharp transients at the start of plucked or picked notes. When the gain is used to return the peaks to their maximum loudness the softer dynamics appear more present in the mix while the level of loud transients is more consistent.

Country Twang

Country players use compression to accentuate the attack of each note, contributing to the characteristic "twang" guitar tone. There are two approaches. In the first, the attack time is set to the minimum so that the compression acts on the initial attack of the string. This produces a popping effect that resembles the snap of a string against the fretboard and pairs well with hybrid picking, as every note sounds with considerable presence. An alternative and somewhat more natural approach sets the attack time just long enough to allow most of the natural attack through unaffected. The compressor then kicks in after the attack and further suppresses the decay of the note, causing the attack to seem even more pronounced. Both techniques work best when applied to a clean signal from a single-coil pickup [▶ Media 7.24].

Noise Gates

An electric guitar signal is highly susceptible to noise and interference. While largely attributed to the electromagnetic pickups, the high-impedance, instrument-level signal and the use of unbalanced cables throughout the chain all contribute to the notorious amp buzz problem. In a live guitar rig, a noise gate is most often used to quiet the signal when the instrument is not being played. Gates have no means of differentiating the guitar signal from unwanted interference. Rather, they work by attenuating the signal to silence whenever it passes below a specified amplitude threshold. When used with a guitar, the threshold should be set very low so that the gate has minimal impact on the natural decay of the instrument. Of course, any guitar tones or chords allowed to ring long enough will eventually fall below the threshold and get truncated by the gate. In ensemble contexts or busy musical passages this may not be an issue, but it does tend to be more noticeable in solo works or musically sparse moments.

In addition to the threshold, the other key parameter of a noise gate is the release, which determines how fast the signal ramps to silence once the gate kicks in. Longer release times can help to mask the amplitude suppression by mimicking a more natural decay. On the other hand, a hard-cutting effect can be achieved by setting the threshold relatively high and the release extremely short so that the sound is abruptly truncated [▶ Media 7.25]. Regardless of how a noise gate is used, it is typically placed near the end of the signal chain so that it suppresses the output from all pedals before it. It is important, however, to put reverb and delay pedals after the noise gate to prevent it from operating on their decays.

Pitch Shifters/Harmonizers

Pitch shifter and harmonizer pedals transpose the input signal by a specified interval. Some transpose only in octaves, while others allow specific intervals to be selected. Advanced pedals allow the key of the music to be selected and ensure that transpositions are diatonic. Alternatively, quite a few pitch shifters allow an external expression pedal to be used to change the pitch freely. The DigiTech Whammy Pitch-Shifting Pedal has a built-in treadle and produces a range of bends and dive-bomb effects reminiscent of those obtained from a whammy-bar.

The basic difference between a pitch shifter and harmonizer is that the former removes the original signal from the output, rendering a single, transposed voice. By contrast, a harmonizer retains the dry signal in the output, mixing it with the transposed signal to create the impression of two or more parts playing together in parallel harmony. Both effects can usually be obtained from the same pedal simply by setting the mix control appropriately: 100% wet for a pitch shifter and 50% or less for a harmonizer. That said, pedals designed around concerns for harmonization sometimes offer more features, the most notable being options for additional voices.

Loop Pedals

A loop pedal records an input signal and then repeats it continuously. Once the performance is captured in the pedal, the loop can be stopped, restarted, or sometimes reversed, all using the feet. Some pedals have an overdub feature that allows additional layers to be recorded. The amount of material that can ultimately be added is limited by the pedal's memory, which is likely to be on the order of minutes in a modern device. Parameters tend to be limited to just a volume knob, which determines the loudness of the looped output.

Loop pedals are often used in solo works to develop complex textures using accumulative processes in much the same way that tape loops were used in the 1960s [▶ Media 7.26].[18] Fausto Romitelli employs a loop pedal in *Trash TV Trance* (2002) to create an underlying pulse that is frequently interrupted by other material. The player is also required to change the material in the loop throughout the piece. Aside from use in performance, the ability to instantly lay down a rhythm track and then play along to it has truly revolutionized how electric guitarists practice. In a similar way, a loop pedal can serve as a compositional tool, allowing materials to quickly be heard in combination.

Modeling Pedals

Digital modeling pedals emulate the stereotypical sound of particular guitars, amplifiers, speaker cabinets, and pedals, all within a single device. While most players would agree that the emulation is not entirely convincing, these pedals, using minimal equipment, offer an extremely wide range of common guitar tones that come close to the real thing. Modeling pedals that provide amp emulation usually have a line-level output for connection directly to a sound reinforcement system or mixing board. Indeed, some guitarists are playing without a stage amplifier today, instead monitoring their performance through floor monitors. If a stage amplifier is used in combination with amp modeling, it is sensible to set the amp to the cleanest setting possible, with all tone controls flattened.

Multi-Effects Pedals

Multi-effects pedals offer a wide selection of effects, essentially replacing a number of individual stomp boxes with a single device. Many such devices are literally laid out like a pedal board, each effect with its own set of controls and bypass button. More advanced units allow the pedal chain to be reconfigured and saved as a preset. The storage and recall feature alone is tremendously valuable for changing parameter settings or reconfiguring the rig for different pieces. Using a multi-effects device, one gives up the ability to cherry pick pedals for their unique character. However, having the effects chain within a single hardware unit reduces the number of buffers that the signal passes through, and of course, makes travel and set up much easier. Furthermore, some units provide an effects loop to allow external devices to be added between the overdrive and wet stages of the chain.

Multi-effects devices can pose a dilemma in terms of ordering the signal chain. Many players prefer to place dirty and dry effects before the amp and wet effects in the amp's effects loop so that they are inserted after the preamp stage. If the multi-effects unit is used for overdrive or distortion it should be placed between the guitar and amp, which also places any wet effects before the amp. On the other hand, inserting a multi-effects pedal in an amp's effects loop suggests that it be limited to wet effects, as you typically would not want other effects after the preamp. Assuming that both the multi-effects pedal and the amp have effects loops, the dry and wet stages of the multi-effects unit can be divided as follows: (1) connect the guitar to the multi-effects' input; (2) connect the multi-effects' loop send to the amp input; (3) connect the amp's loop send to the multi-effects' loop return; (4) connect the multi-effects' output to the amp's loop return. Voila! The overdrive stage of the multi-effects unit is now in front of the amp input while the modulation and wet effects are patched into the amp's effects loop.

Scoring Effects

Describing Tone

Guitar rigs are assembled around concerns for particular guitar tones and, short of modeling technology, no rig is good at achieving all of them. It is important that composers provide some indication as to the sort of tone required for a given work so that the performer can assemble a suitable rig. Descriptors such as clean, dirty, heavy distortion, transparent distortion, raw, thin, round, mellow, twangy, over-produced, expensive, or cheap might be written in the score, leaving it to the performer to conjure up an appropriate response. In *Vampyr!* (2004), Tristan Murail compares the desired guitar tone to that of other well-known players, in particular, Carlos Santana and Eric Clapton. Of course, the actual equipment and settings required could be provided in detail. While it is impractical to expect a performer to assemble a complex rig verbatim, listing suitable brand names and models in the score can give the player a better sense of the intended sound and help him or her choose a viable substitute.

Effects Notation

A verbal description of the effects required and intended tone is adequate if the effects are simply applied and remain static through the work. However, processing is often applied in a more dynamic manner, with individual pedals turned on and off at different points in the work or parameters altered over time. Any manipulation of an effect that requires action on the part of the performer must be clearly called out in the score. Boxed text might be used to indicate that an effect is to be enabled, while similar boxed text with a horizontal strikethrough could denote that the pedal is to be bypassed (Fig. 7.9). The manipulation of a parameter over time, such as the treadle on a volume or wah pedal, requires special symbols. In *Trash TV Trance* (2002), Fausto Romitelli uses an "x" beneath the staff to indicated that a wah pedal should be closed and an "o" to denote that it should be open, with arrows suggesting a gradual transformation from one state to the next. If greater notational precision is required, a graphical line may be added below the staff with the vertical dimension representing the position of the treadle, as shown in Figure 7.9. A similar graphical approach could be adopted for any time-varying parameters. As there are no conventions for

Figure 7.9
Suggested notation for electronic effects.

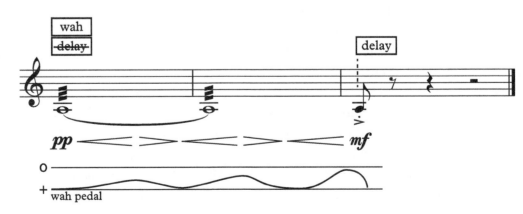

the notation of effects, any strategy adopted will need to be explained in instructions accompanying the score. This should include a full description of the signal chain as it runs from the instrument, through the effects, and to the amp, along with settings for important effects parameters and some account of the expected sonic results. A description of what the amp should sound like with all effects bypassed is also helpful.

8

Computer-Based Processing and Instrumental Augmentation

Adding a computer to a guitar rig inspires a wealth of possibilities otherwise unavailable to the instrument. Used as an effects device, a computer is capable of providing processing far beyond that which is available in a traditional hardware pedalboard. But it is ultimately the ability to design customized algorithms with parameters that can be manipulated over time that sets computer-based processing apart from its hardware-based heritage. Control signals taken from a player's deliberate actions or incidental movements can be mapped to effects parameters, providing the performer with an unprecedented level of control over the dynamism of the processing. This chapter focuses primarily on applications of the computer that extend the timbre or instrumentality of the guitar. In most cases, the resultant electronics are strongly linked to the live instrument's part, if not musically inseparable from it. Applications of a computer that lead to more autonomous electronics are addressed in Chapter 9.

Computer-Based Processing

The personal computer has the potential to be the mother-of-all pedalboards, offering processing capabilities far beyond what is available in conventional pedals and hardware effects. First, the entire gamut of digital signal processing techniques is available, either through off-the-shelf software applications and plugins or by developing custom-built algorithms using an audio programming environment such as Cycling '74's Max.[1] Convolution, comb filtering, wave shaping, bit depth decimation, spectral domain processing, ring modulation, stutters, and granulation are just some of the sound transformation techniques not typically offered by conventional guitar gear. Moreover, control signals from expression pedals, foot switches, various sensors, or the live audio signal itself can be linked to parameters in the sound-processing algorithm, offering the guitarist an unprecedented ability to engage and "play" the effects as a part of the performance. Finally, because the processing is software-based, the effects can be reconfigured at the click of a button: parameters can be saved and recalled ad infinitum and processing units can be added, removed, or rearranged in the signal chain on the fly, all without having to run the signal through numerous pedal buffers.[2] The signal does, however, have to pass through the computer, and special care must be taken to preserve the quality of it at both the input and output stages.

Adding an Audio Interface to a Rig

In order to process the guitar with a computer, an audio interface is needed to convert the input signal from analog to digital, and once processing has been performed, to convert it back to an analog signal that can be sent to a guitar amp, mixing console, or other destination. It is important to keep in mind that conventional guitar equipment operates at instrument level. Not all audio interfaces accept instrument-level signals at their inputs, and few, if any, are designed to output a signal appropriate for a guitar pedal or amplifier later in the chain. Whenever an interface is inserted directly into a guitar's signal chain—that is, between the instrument and amplifier—it is important to ensure that signals match the inputs that they are connected to in terms of level, impedance, and cable type; otherwise the tone can suffer considerably. This may require the use of direct injection (DI) or reamp boxes to provide the necessary signal conversions; those are discussed below. Let us first examine issues pertaining to the input and output stages of the audio interface, with special concern for the preservation of tone. We then explore some possibilities afforded by the addition of a computer to the rig.

The Input Stage—Direct Signals and Microphones

The first step in any computer-based processing involves obtaining a digital representation of the guitar signal. Digitization can either be performed on a direct signal taken straight from the signal chain or a signal captured through a microphone placed in front of the instrument or amplifier. There are merits to each approach worthy of consideration.

A direct signal originates from electromagnetic pickups and first appears at the output jack of the instrument. However, a direct signal can be taken from any point in the signal chain prior to the power amplifier stage, including the output of a pedal or the effect send on an amplifier (Fig. 8.1), or in the case of an acoustic guitar, from piezo-electric transducers or contact microphones attached to the instrument. Direct signals have the benefit of being clean and free from extraneous sounds. However, they do not

Figure 8.1

A direct signal can be obtained from any point in the signal chain prior to the power amplifier stage.

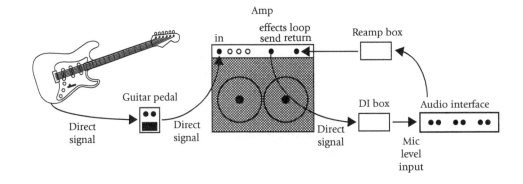

accurately account for the sound of the instrument as typically heard by a listener. The amplifier, a siginificant component of any rig, is removed from the equation, and in the case of the acoustic guitar, the signal originates from specific points on the body and does not reflect the whole sound of the instrument.

Whenever devices are added to a guitar's signal chain care should be taken to preserve the integrity of the signal. A direct signal from a guitar should only be connected to an audio interface equipped with an instrument-level input. If the interface only provides options for microphone and line-level inputs a direct injection (DI) box should be used to convert the guitar's unbalanced, high-impedance, instrument-level signal to a balanced, low-impedance, microphone-level signal that the interface can handle (Fig. 8.1). DI boxes provide benefits beyond mere level changes. The conversion to a balanced signal allows for extended cable runs with less risk of interference. They also offer a ground lift to prevent hum caused by multiple ground paths.

An alternative way to obtain a direct signal for processing without having to add the interface to the signal chain is to use a splitter, thereby dividing the signal along two paths. In Figure 8.2, one path goes straight to the amplifier without compromising the tone while the other runs to an audio interface, which can either be output to a mixing console or returned to an independent channel on the amplifier.

Rather than processing a direct signal, the sound of the instrument or amplifier can be captured with a diaphragm microphone and sent to an audio interface for digitization. Microphones tend to render a more realistic representation of the guitar since they capture the entirety of the sound: the sliding of hands over strings, the rattling of preparations against the fretboard, and in the case of the electric guitar, the product of the whole rig, including the amplifier and speaker. Furthermore, distal perspective can be altered by changing the microphone's placement in relation to the source, as opposed to the unnaturally close and fixed perspective of a direct signal. The use of a microphone also negates concern for signal degradation since the audio interface is left out of the guitar's signal chain. Of course, microphones are not without issues of their own: they are prone to feedback, can intrude on a performer's space, and are susceptible to extraneous sounds. To this latter point, it may be difficult to get an isolated signal from a microphone in an ensemble context with other instruments played in close proximity.

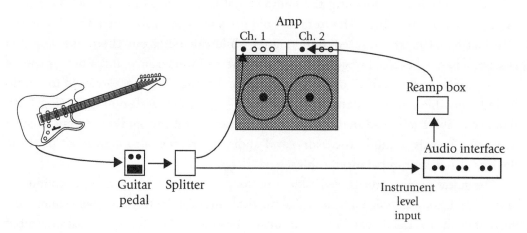

Figure 8.2

Using a splitter to side-chain an audio interface.

177

The Output Stage

The output of an audio interface will typically operate at line level or higher. Many devices provide a +4/–10 dB switch near the output jack to toggle between professional and consumer levels. Line-level outputs can be connected directly to a mixing console, but connecting a line-level signal to conventional guitar hardware or any other device that expects an instrument-level signal at its input generally leads to a less-than-optimal tone. A reamp box converts a low-impedance, balanced, line-level signal to a high-impedance, unbalanced, instrument-level signal appropriate for guitar gear (Figs. 8.1 and 8.2) and should be used whenever the signal from an audio interface is sent back into the guitar's signal chain. Most reamp devices have a potentiometer that allows the level to be scaled manually, as well as a ground lift switch. Note that some audio interfaces provide controls for scaling the output levels within the interface and can produce similar results in terms of level, although without the impedance and cable conversion. The companion website offers a presentation of a guitar rig with a computer added to the signal chain [▶ Media 8.1].

All the power that the computer wields can easily be overshadowed by an uninspiring guitar tone, and in this regard the importance of level matching cannot be overstated. When a signal from an audio interface or reamp box is sent to an amplifier or any other conventional guitar equipment the level should be calibrated to match that of a guitar. To do this, the input level to the interface should first be set so that the signal enters strong, but without clipping. The output on the interface or reamp box can then be adjusted until the loudness of the signal running through the interface and to the amp is equal to that of the guitar connected directly to the amp. The cable switching required to perform this comparison can be clumsy, but the procedure is tremendously helpful when the player is trying to calibrate levels, and the benefits it has to tone are well worth the effort [▶ Media 8.2].[3]

Balanced and Unbalanced Cables

There are two types of analog audio cables: balanced and unbalanced. A balanced cable contains three wires: hot (+), cold (–), and ground. The hot and cold lines carry the same audio signal, but with the polarity inverted. As the signal travels along the cable it picks up interference on both lines. At the destination, the polarity of the cold line is inverted, returning the audio signal to its actual polarity while inverting the noise on that line. The hot and cold lines are then combined, which has the effect of boosting the wanted audio signal while canceling out the noise. For this reason, balanced cables are generally less prone to interference and a better choice for any cable longer than 15 or 20 feet. Common balanced connectors used for audio include the XLR and the balanced quarter-inch TRS (tip-ring-sleeve) types (Fig. 8.3). Balanced cables are used mainly with microphones and pro audio equipment such as mixing boards, studio processors, and audio interfaces, although most of these devices also accept unbalanced cables.

The guitar uses an unbalanced cable consisting of only two wires: a center conductor and a shield. The audio signal is carried along the center conductor. The shield completely surrounds the central line and carries a constant ground that intercepts most unwanted

(a)

(b)

(c)

Figure 8.3
Common balanced and unbalanced audio cables: (a) balanced XLR; (b) balanced ¼-inch; (c) unbalanced ¼-inch.

interference as long as the cable is relatively short, not more than 15 or 20 feet. While a conventional guitar rig uses all unbalanced cables, the option to inject balanced cables may emerge when adding an audio interface to the signal chain or when sending a direct signal to a mixing console. Given the option, balanced cables are preferable, particularly when dealing with long cable runs. Needless to say, a balanced cable can only be used if both ends are connected to devices that support balanced signals.

Latency

Most real-time digital audio systems have some degree of latency, experienced as a short delay between the time a signal enters an audio interface and when it reaches the output. Several components within the digital system may contribute to latency, including the audio conversion procedure and software drivers. However, the main culprit is digital buffering, which should not be confused with the analog buffering that occurs in effects pedals. A digital buffer is simply an amount of memory allocated to handle the signal and provide time for the system to perform any necessary processing. The first sample received does not reach the output until the buffer is completely full, and all audio from that point forward is delayed by the time required initially to fill the buffer, plus any additional latency caused by the other components of the system. Buffers ensure smooth play-through in the event that the operating system interrupts the audio application to perform system-level tasks. As an analog signal is digitized the sample values begin to fill the buffer. Without a buffer, or with an insufficiently small buffer, interruptions to the continuous data throughput result in anomalies such as pops, clicks, stutters, or audio dropouts.

While latency cannot be completely eliminated, the user does have control over the buffer size within the software application used for processing. Larger buffers offer more time for the computer to process the signal but result in greater latency. When performing live with an audio interface in the signal chain, the performer must keep latency to a minimum. A delay greater than 10–20 ms can make it difficult to perform the music.

Striving to keep latency as low as possible while maintaining uninterrupted audio at the output is an important step in the calibration of a rig when a computer is inserted into the signal chain. Note that latency is less of an issue if the audio interface is side-chained via a splitter box or when a microphone is used to obtain the signal, another reason to consider these options.

Applying Effects

Once a guitar signal has been digitized, effects can be applied within a computer in a number of ways. Stand-alone software applications such as Native Instrument's Guitar Rig are designed specifically for this purpose, appearing like a virtual pedalboard on the screen and offering a wealth of classic effects, along with amp, speaker, guitar, and microphone simulations. To complete the setup, a multi-pedal MIDI foot controller can be integrated to toggle the effects on and off analogous to a conventional pedalboard (Fig. 8.4). Alternatively, commercial plugins can be applied to a live signal within digital audio workstation software such as Ableton Live by simply inserting the plugin on a track and arming the track for recording.

Tone connoisseurs may argue that software-based pedals generally yield unconvincing emulations of their hardware models. While the tones may not be authentic, they do get close. Issues of poor tone are more likely to result from mismatched signal levels or impedance when the audio interface is added to the chain. Given a properly calibrated rig, software-based pedalboards can sound surprisingly similar to their hardware counterparts, and what may be given up in terms of quality is exchanged for the myriad of benefits offered by these systems—the ability to store and recall presets, to reconfigure the signal chain in a instant, and to access hundreds of different virtual pedals within a single device—all features particularly appealing to the gigging guitarist who requires a different tone for each song in a set, for instance.

While off-the-shelf software processors such as those mentioned above do offer functionality beyond what is available in conventional hardware pedals, possibilities really open up when the processing is done within an audio programming

Figure 8.4
A Behringer FCB1010 MIDI Foot Controller, offering 10 footswitches and two expression pedals.

environment such as Cycling '74's Max. Audio programming environments offer a wealth of pre-programmed functional units that perform specific tasks, including signal processing, MIDI data manipulation, and logical operations. These units can be connected together to create a seemingly endless variety of complex processing procedures. Classic effects can certainly be emulated, but more innovative are the non-traditional algorithms that can be established. Moreover, logic can be scripted into the algorithm causing the effect to react in particular ways to qualities inherent in the input signal. For instance, the mix and depth parameters of a chorus might be linked to the amplitude of the signal so that louder events introduce a greater wavering disturbance to the sound. Finally, and perhaps most important in terms of instrumentality, controllers such as foot switches and expression pedals can be mapped to any parameters in the sound engine, offering performable control over the processing. While there is a learning curve associated with audio programming languages, the payoff is well worthwhile for those seriously interested in adding a computer to their rig.

Customized Pedalboard Controllers

Much of the potential afforded by computer-based processing lies in the flexibility to customize a control interface so that a player can manipulate effect parameters over time as an integral part of the performance. Following the classic pedalboard model, a MIDI foot controller like the one shown in Figure 8.4 might be used. Each foot switch and expression pedal transmits data over a unique MIDI controller number that can be mapped to any parameter in the sound engine. For instance, an expression pedal might be linked to the cut-off frequency of a high-pass filter, the feedback of a delay, or the rate of a modulating LFO. Of course, mappings can be one-to-one or one-to-many and ranges can be uniquely scaled for each destination parameter.

Foot switches are more limited in terms of instrumentality since they output only two values associated with down and up states. Switches are primarily used to bypass particular units or step through a series of saved parameters. They can also be used to trigger events such as a sound file or a stored automation line that modifies some parameter of an effect over time. The foot maneuvering that is needed to engage effects can quickly become complex, requiring rehearsal, and perhaps even representation in a score. However, guitarists, and particularly electric guitar players, are more accustomed than most musicians to these sorts of requirements.

Extracting Control Data from a Guitar Signal

Rather than incorporating controllers that the performer engages directly, effect parameters can be driven by data extracted through analysis of the live audio signal. Three basic music information retrieval (MIR) techniques are examined here: envelope tracking, onset detection, and pitch estimation. These techniques can be combined with a bit of logic to detect higher-level musical features such as tempo, meter, harmonic structures, or motive and theme recognition. It should be noted that MIR is an active and growing area of research and the present discussion only touches on these matters. For a more robust description of MIR techniques the reader should consult the literature. For those less interested in the implementation, one can look to user groups for ready-made tools capable of accomplishing the task at hand.

Envelope Tracking

Envelope tracking provides a data stream representative of how the amplitude of a signal changes over time. It forms the basis of the classic envelope follower effect, in which the center frequency of a bandpass filter is linked to the amplitude of the input signal. Of course, once the changing envelope is captured it can be mapped to any parameter. For instance, the rate of a tremolo effect could be tied to the envelope so it oscillates more energetically at louder dynamics or a cheap overdrive can be devised by linking bit depth reduction to the amplitude of the signal.

Envelope tracking can be accomplished by polling an input signal at a regular interval and then interpolating between those sampled values. The rate of polling determines the resolution of the resultant envelope; intervals of 10–50 ms tend to yield suitable results on the guitar, but this parameter may need to be adjusted for the specific signal and musical content being analyzed. Because an audio signal contains both positive and negative amplitude values, either the signal needs to be rectified before polling or the absolute values of the polled data points can be used. A variation of this strategy involves squaring all polled values, which at once rectifies the signal and exaggerates the envelope contour.

An alternative approach to envelope tracking involves sending a rectified input signal through a lowpass filter, which has the effect of smoothing the contour. Greater smoothing is achieved using a lower cut-off frequency, but at the expense of an increased response time.

Onset Detection

The ability to identify and distinguish events in an incoming audio signal is a fundamental first step to any significant analysis of a performance. Solutions to the problem of segregating an audio signal into its constituent events generally focus on the detection of onsets, which are characterized by a sudden increase in amplitude and/or flux in the spectrum. Precompiled tools for onset detection, such as Miller Puckett's bonk~ object for Max, can be leveraged for the task. For those wanting to implement the algorithm, a few common approaches are discussed below. The musical content that is being analyzed will often determine the strategy most suitable for event detection, and in many cases reliability can be improved by combining techniques in order to corroborate the evidence.

Onset detection algorithms generally consist of three stages: pre-processing, data reduction, and peak selection. In the pre-processing stage the signal is modified to accentuate particular characteristics important to subsequent stages in the analysis, which might include filtering, expanding the dynamic range, or dividing the spectrum into multiple frequency bands. In the second stage, the data from the pre-processing stage is reduced in order to obtain a lower-resolution function in which onsets appear as clearly identifiable peaks. Peak selection then becomes a matter of determining which of the transients are actual event onsets.

One strategy for onset detection looks for a sudden rise in the amplitude of the signal, which can be measured in the time domain by polling the signal at an interval within the temporal range of an attack—on the order of 10–20 ms for a plucked string—and comparing the current reading to the previous to see whether the amplitude has risen sufficiently to be considered an onset. The two important parameters—the rise time and the delta between neighboring amplitudes—are crucial to the effectiveness of the algorithm and will need to be adjusted for the particular signal and musical content.

Amplitude flux can also be identified in the spectral domain as a sudden change in energy. A common strategy is to divide the spectrum into five or six frequency bands, sum their energy individually, and then combine the results to yield a single value representative of the energy at that moment in time. Bello et al. (2005) point out that transients are typically characterized by high frequency energy and suggest weighting those bands proportional to the bin number before summing in order to accentuate them in the analysis.

Onset detection based on amplitude flux is fairly reliable when applied to events that have pronounced attacks, such as a plucked string. However, some guitar techniques, such as string bends, slides, or legato, clearly lead to the perception of a new event, yet with no significant spike in amplitude. These transient-less events can be detected by looking for flux in the spectrum, which would be expected whenever a note changes. Spectral flux can be measured by taking a series of short-term spectral analyses and comparing successive frames. Rather than running through a complex comparison of frequencies in each data set, it is more convenient to reduce the spectral data to a single value such as the spectral centroid, an average of the frequency spectrum. Onsets are then identified as significant changes in neighboring centroid measurements.

The methods discussed so far have been oriented toward generic event detection. More sophisticated systems can be devised that are capable of recognizing event types. As a case in point, Reboursière et al. (2011) have developed algorithms for detecting a number of particular guitar techniques from the audio signal, including string bends, legato, slides, palm muting, harmonics, and attack location.[4] The detection algorithm also discriminates between left and right hand activities, which it uses to help identify the technique. The authors present a number of possibilities for mapping the extracted data to sound, shown in Figure 8.5.

Palm Mute > Octaver: a detected palm mute invokes a pitch shift down one octave, allowing the player to switch between a normal guitar tone and a 'bass' sound by applying and removing the palm.

String Bend > Filter Q: the amount of string bend is mapped to the Q-factor of a bandpass filter such that the band narrows the more the string is displaced, giving those notes a 'wailing' character.

Harmonics > Reverse Delay: a detected harmonic triggers a reverse delay.

Legato > Cross-synthesis: legato techniques are cross-synthesized with a pre-recorded percussive sound (a slap-tongue effect from a clarinet) to re-introduce some attack to the notes, while also imbuing the instrument with a unique timbre.

Attack Location > Wet/Dry Mix: the attack location is mapped to the mix of a granular synthesizer such that normal attack locations produce no effect, while those near the bridge add granular artifacts that are pitch shifted upwards and locations over the fretboard add granulations that are lowered.

Figure 8.5

Possibilities presented by Reboursière et al. (2011) for mapping data extracted from a guitar signal to sound processing algorithms.

Pitch Estimation

The ability to detect the pitch content of a live audio signal has tremendous value in terms of computer interaction and score following, yet it remains a challenging task, particularly in polyphonic contexts. There are several precompiled tools in circulation that accomplish real-time monophonic pitch estimation with a fair degree of accuracy. Of these, IRCAM's gbr.yin~ object and Miller Puckett's fiddle~ and sigmund~ objects for the Max environment stand out. Polyphonic pitch detection is generally less reliable, and the more effective approaches currently in use are not conducive to a real-time environment. Autocorrelation and harmonic product spectrum (HPS) are two common approaches to real-time monophonic pitch estimation that have proven to be effective on a guitar signal. They are briefly introduced here, but a full account of their implementation is beyond the scope of this book. The reader is encouraged to consult the literature for an in-depth account of these techniques.

Autocorrelation

Time domain algorithms often implement autocorrelation functions that look for a repeating pattern in the waveform. The strategy involves incrementally delaying a copy of the incoming signal one sample at a time and comparing its shape to the original signal. The correlation will be at a maximum when the delay time is zero, decreasing until the two signals are 180 degrees out of phase, and then increasing until the waveforms are back in phase alignment. The point of maximum correlation reveals the period, from which the frequency can be computed. While quite effective on monophonic signals, autocorrelation is not successful in polyphonic contexts.

Harmonic Product Spectrum

The harmonic product spectrum (HPS) approach to pitch detection is quite effective on monophonic sounds and computationally inexpensive. The signal is first converted to the spectral domain using an FFT. The HPS technique is then applied in two steps. In the first, copies of each frame of spectral data are downsampled by successive integer values, which has the affect of compressing the spectral content toward DC (0 Hz). This can be achieved by creating a new array using every other value in the original spectral array, then every third value, and so on. HPS algorithms typically employ around five downsampled versions of the spectrum. Assuming a periodic sound, downsampling the spectrum by half will align the second harmonic with the fundamental in the original signal, while downsampling by one third aligns the third harmonic with the fundamental in the original signal. Harmonic alignment occurs regardless of the fundamental frequency since spectra are always distributed in whole number multiples of the fundamental. In the second step, the original and downsampled spectra are multiplied and the highest peak in the output is assumed to be the fundamental frequency. HPS tends to be poor at estimating low frequencies and can often produce octave errors, where the estimated pitch is reported as being an octave higher than it actually is.

Instrumental Augmentation

Instrumental augmentation refers to the practice of attaching sensors to an instrument or to a player's body in order to capture data streams that in some way affect the timbre or behavior of the instrument. Accelerometers, potentiometers, pressure sensors, push buttons, sliders, and tilt sensors are available using electronics prototyping hardware kits and can be paired with an audio programming environment such as Max to make the endeavor relatively straightforward.[5] Sensors might be employed to track ancillary movements associated with playing the guitar, such as the strumming motion of the right hand or the angle at which the instrument is held. Linking ancillary data streams to processing parameters adds life to the electronics that is drawn from the performance itself, as opposed to, say, the use of an LFO to arbitrarily animate an effect. Tracking natural movements also places no additional burden on the guitarist; the instrument can simply be played in a conventional manner.

In contrast to capturing ancillary gestures, sensors can provide additional control mechanisms to be engaged directly by the performer. Direct controllers demand that the instrument be approached in novel ways, and taken to extremes, can lead to performance actions that bear little resemblance to conventional guitar techniques. Implementations of this sort shift the paradigm from guitar augmentation to alternative controller development, lending import to considerations of instrument design, ergonomics, and a spectator's interpretation of the links between physical and sounding gesture.

Hardware and Software Solutions

A number of electronic prototyping platforms are commercially available for building computerized interactive objects. Adafruit's Arduino board and Infusion Systems' iCube are current favorites among composers and musicians, but similar products are available from other vendors, including Libelium's Waspmote, Eowave's Eobody, Electrotap's TeaBox, and Phidgets. Kits consist of a microcontroller board with multiple connectors for sensors and actuators (Fig. 8.6). Figure 8.7 provides a generic list of sensors commonly used for musical applications, but a variety of others also exist. The prototyping hardware unit connects to a personal computer via a USB port or wireless network and the Open Sound Control communications protocol (OSC) is typically used to stream

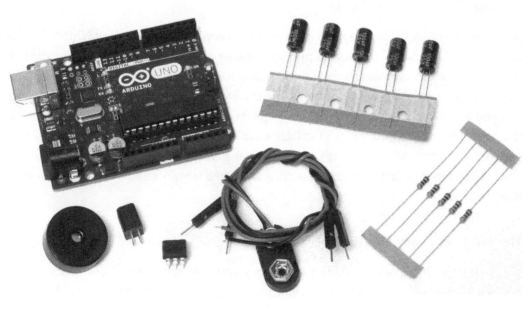

Figure 8.6
Arduino Uno
Starter Kit.

185

Figure 8.7

Common sensors available in electronic prototyping platforms.

Accelerometers	An accelerometer measures acceleration forces, but can be used to obtain information about which direction an object is facing, how it is tilted, or how fast it is moved. Accelerometers come in two- and three-axis varieties.
Pressure sensors	A pressure sensor, or force-sensitive resistor (FSR), responds dynamically to force applied to its surface. FSRs come in various shapes and sizes and can be used to detect events such as tapping on the instrument or to generate a continuous data stream that can be routed to a processing parameter.
Flex/bend sensors	Flex sensors output a range of values as they are bent. They might be attached to the body joints of a player to track movements during performance.
Rangers	Infared and ultrasonic rangers measure distance. Close proximity rangers can be mounted to the instrument to measure hand and finger movements. In a more theatrical performance, long-range sensors could measure choreography on stage.
Optical sensors	Optical sensors output voltage depending on the amount of light that enters.
Buttons and switches	Push buttons and switches provide two-state control signals, which might be used to trigger electronic events or advance through a series of saved presets.
Sliders and knobs	Sliders and knob-style potentiometers offer tactile interfaces that can be engaged directly to produce a continuous stream of control data.

the data into the audio programming environment. The microcontroller board could be encased in a protective box and mounted with Velcro to the body or strap of the guitar to avoid numerous cables running from the instrument. All of these platforms are designed to be easy to use and one need not have an extensive knowledge of electronics to employ them.

Commercial Game Controllers

Accelerometers are built into most modern game controllers, including Nintendo Wii Remote and Nunchuk devices, and provide a cheap and easy means of getting started with instrumental augmentation. Game controllers typically communicate with a computer via Bluetooth wireless technology and the Open Sound Control protocol can then be used to stream the data into an audio programming environment. In addition to the accelerometer data, these controllers usually have a few buttons that can act as two-state switches. The main impediment of game controllers is their size—the device needs to be securely fastened to the instrument or performer's body without hindering the performance.

Tracking Ancillary Gestures

Verfaille et al. (2006) coined the term "ancillary gestures" to refer to movements by the performer that are not directly involved in sound production. To the extent that such

Spectral panning	Shifts in body weight were mapped to a spectral stereo panning effect so that more bodily movement would increase motion in the stereo field, while less bodily movement would render the panning still in the center of the field.
Stereo delay	Shifts in body weight were used to control the stereo spread of two delay channels, similarly to the spectral panning application. Head movements were mapped to a tremolo applied to the delay lines.
Adaptive filter	Weight shifts were mapped to a filter's cutoff frequency and head movements to the filter's Q-factor.
Drive and granulation	Weight balance was connected to the saturation level, and head movements to the Q of a low pass filter. A variation of the effect was implemented that introduced granulation instead of saturation.

Figure 8.8

Possibilities presented by Lähdeoja (2008) for mapping ancillary gesture data to sound processing algorithms.

187

bodily movement is guided by the music, ancillary gestures carry performance-related information that could be used to enhance the liveliness of digitally processed sound. Mapping such gestures to sound establishes a hierarchy in the physical-sounding gesture relationships of the instrument: the core elements of the performance—the raw musical materials—are controlled by deliberate gestures and direct mappings, while secondary transformations are induced by ancillary, perhaps even unconscious, movements that provide a complementary level of control (Otso, 2008).

Otso Lähdeoja (2008) has developed an approach to guitar augmentation that focuses primarily on ancillary gestures. His system employs three sensors: a two-axis accelerometer on the headstock of the guitar and four pressure sensors on the floor, two per foot. Three distinct variables are calculated from the raw sensor data: the general amount of head movement, left/right weight distribution, and back/front weight distribution. The system is also able to detect a limited number of body postures, such as standing on one foot or on the toes or heels, by looking for weight distribution signatures in the analysis data. Lähdeoja establishes "loosely causal" links between ancillary gestures and sound transformations (Fig. 8.8). Body movements alter the sound in subtle and slightly unpredictable ways, achieved through the use of complex, multi-layered mappings and indeterminacy in the physical-sounding gesture pairings so that the same action does not always yield the same transformation. The stated objective was to find an equilibrium in the mapping of gesture to sound that would not be so obvious that the performer is tempted to take control, yet not so distant from the physical gesture that it appears intrusive and disturbing. Lähdeoja's augmented guitar can be heard on his solo album *Yonder* (2011).

Direct Controller Augmentations and Instrumentality

The guitar can be augmented with control mechanisms that the player engages with directly. Buttons, pressure strips, sliders, or a tilt sensor that requires that the player deliberately angle the guitar in unusual ways all fall into this category and require the performer to take actions not typically associated with guitar performance. It is worth noting that these actions will often hinder the player's ability to engage the instrument in conventional ways. A performance, then, becomes a matter of switching between engagement with the guitar and with the added controllers. Taken to the extreme, the actions required to perform a work with direct controller augmentations could be so removed from established guitar performance practice that it would be more appropriate to view the system as a new instrument entirely. For those interested in developing such alternative controllers, it is worthwhile to consider performance attributes associated with traditional instrument designs as well as current thinking on the design of digital musical instruments.

The sound produced by an acoustic instrument is coupled directly with the performer's physical gestures. There is, by necessity, energy transference from the gesture to the sound such that, for example, more forceful gestures produce louder, brighter, and generally more aggressive results. The link between physical and sounding gesture is important for a musician learning to play the instrument, but it is also essential for a spectator to be able to comprehend and evaluate a performance, recognize virtuosity, and identify error.

Richard Moore (1988) elaborates further on the issue of virtuosity, recognizing that performers learn to subtly modify sound for expressive purposes. The more an instrument allows such subtlety to be reflected in the sound, the more musically expressive that instrument will be. However, such control intimacy is "simultaneously what makes such devices good musical instruments, what makes them extremely difficult to play well, and what makes overcoming that difficulty well worthwhile to both the performer and the listener" (Moore 1988, p. 22). Acoustic instruments offer a tremendous amount of subtle control over the sound, and it does indeed take many years of practice to master control of it.

In the case of electronically mediated instruments there is an inherent division of labor between the performance interface—the controller—and the sound engine. It is possible to establish links between physical and sounding gesture, but those connections must be made explicitly and can easily be overlooked as a developer's attention shifts toward technical matters. The relationship between physical and sounding gesture can be further obfuscated by the fact that the sonic parameters under a performer's control in an electronically mediated instrument may bear little resemblance to those typically associated with the guitar, and the mappings may be complex one-to-many or many-to-one configurations. To get the degree of control intimacy that Moore refers to with a new performance interface, many parameters need to be under the performer's control; and the more that are added, the more difficult it becomes to play the instrument.

Inspired by traditional notions of instrumentality, David Wessel and Matthew Wright (2002) provide a number of features deemed desirable in a computer-based instrument. First, there should be a correlation between the performance gesture and the sounding result. The expectation of both performer and audience is that subtle actions taken by the performer will result in subtle changes to the sound, while larger, more forceful actions produce more stark contrasts. Second, the mapping of gesture to sound should be one-to-one; otherwise the relationship is at risk of being too complex to be deciphered by a spectator. Third, the results of the instrument should be predictable, which is not only necessary for a performer to develop skill on the instrument but also clarifies the links between physical and sounding gesture for the audience. Given the technical possibilities now available, considerable restraint is required in order to abide by such design principles.

Any new performance interface inevitably leads to a classic chicken-and-egg dilemma. Who will devote the time to learn to master an instrument that has so little repertoire? And who will choose to compose for an instrument with so few performers available? In fact, when works for new electronic instruments appear on concert programs, the composer/developer usually performs them. The strength of the augmented instrument paradigm lies in the fact that the performance interface remains familiar, allowing a player to bring skills acquired over years of experience to the realization of the work. However, this strength is only harnessed to the extent that the instrument is played in a conventional manner. If the performance requirements of a work do not leverage established guitar techniques then one might question whether the piece is a guitar work at all, or whether a non-guitarist musician might be able to perform it equally well.

Augmented Guitar Systems: Case Studies

Dan Newton and Mark Marshall have developed a system referred to as the Augmentalist, which offers a nearly plug-and-play method for adding sensors to any instrument (2011). The system employs Phidgets sensors that connect to a computer via USB and stream data into Max, where it is converted to MIDI continuous controller data. They map the MIDI data to plugin parameters in Apple's Logic digital audio workstation software, although any software that accepts MIDI controller data would suffice. Examples of guitar augmentations used by Newton and Marshall include (1) an accelerometer attached to the neck and used as a tilt sensor to track the angle between the neck and the ground; (2) a slider attached to the body of the guitar below the pickups so that it can be comfortably accessed with the fingers of the right hand; (3) a distance sensor attached to the body of the instrument so that the strumming hand passes over it. The sensor was configured as an on/off switch to detect strums.

Jon Robert Ferguson has worked extensively with game controllers to augment the electric guitar. In collaboration with Robert van Heumen under the label "Whistle Pig Saloon," Ferguson attaches a Nintendo Wii Remote to the headstock of the guitar, another to the lower cutaway, and a Nintendo Nunchuk to the strap button. Tilt information and button controls are used to provide direct control data that is then processed in Max. Ferguson's performances are quite physical, as he crouches and maneuvers the instrument in various angles and directions to engage the sound.

Guaus et al. (2010) propose an Arduino-based system that tracks left hand movements in guitar performance using capacitive sensors placed on the fretboard at each position. The sensors measure distance between the fingers and the fretboard and are therefore capable of detecting the presence of a finger on a string even when it does not actually touch the fretboard. The system is able to detect barré, legato, and vibrato, as well as string and fret locations for individual notes, the number of fingers in a given fret, the position of the fingers, and the pressure of the fingers to the strings.

Reboursière et al. (2010) developed the Multimodal Guitar Toolbox, in essence, a set of tools for guitar augmentation that includes polyphonic pitch estimation, fretboard visualization and grouping, pressure sensing, modal synthesis, infinite sustain, looping, and "smart" harmonization. The pressure and MIDI sensors were design by Interface-Z. They use a Roland GK3 hexaphonic pickup with a Keith McMillen StringPort interface to get distinct signals for each string. The use of a hex pickup greatly simplifies the task of polyphonic pitch detection, since it can be achieved using a set of accurate monophonic pitch detectors. To this end, they settled on Miller Puckett's sigmund~object, which is freely available for both Max and PureData software platforms. They attach three pressure sensors to the back of the guitar's body, intended to provide expressive control from information related to natural movements of the performer. In the process of their research they discovered that the behavior of the rear sensors was affected by the body and playing position of the player. Cleverly, they attached a block of foam along the array of sensors between the guitar body and the player's body. While this solution was excellent from a technical standpoint, they suggest that something more durable would need to be used for a long-term solution. From the three sensors they obtained a measure of the total pressure, the position of the center of the pressure (weighted average), and the velocity of the movement. They mapped the total pressure and center of pressure to the Q and center frequency of a bandpass filter, respectively. The velocity of the movement controlled the amount of feedback added to a delay. Of course, the sensor data streams could be mapped to anything; that's the beauty of the hardware augmentations. Unlike the other systems discussed earlier, the Multimodal Guitar Toolbox uses physical modeling synthesis techniques to produce the sound.

Composing for the Future

Technology becomes obsolete rather quickly. Tethering a work to any particular hardware or software platform will inevitably impact whether the work can be performed in the future, as those tools become antiquated and increasingly difficult to obtain. Rather than composing for particular tools, one might take an open-ended approach to technology that makes a conceptual distinction between the technical processes at play and the tools used to realize them. A work for guitar and Max that exploits idiosyncrasies of particular Max objects will only be performable in Max, whereas a work for guitar, tilt sensor, ring modulator, and high-pass filter can be performed using any tools capable of those functions. An open-ended approach toward technology demands that the processes be limited to those that are well understood, can be accurately described in a score, and can be reproduced in other environments. Pseudo-code can be documented that describes the signal flow and logic of the algorithm while avoiding reference to specific functions of any particular application. Ultimately, it will be the ability to describe the system and how it interacts with the instrument or performer that will enable the work to be reproduced at a later date and with different tools.

9

Performing and Recording with a Computer

Mixed works that combine traditional live instruments with non-live, electronically mediated sounds have become commonplace in modern music practice.[1] In Chapter 8 we saw how a computer can be used to extend the timbre or instrumentality of the guitar. In this chapter we take a broader view of the computer's contribution to a mixed work, examining a range of potential relationships between a live performer and non-live materials, including those in which the electronics assume a more autonomous role in the musical texture. In addition to musical concerns, issues regarding the implementation of electronics, sound projection on the concert stage, and mixed work recording strategies are also addressed.

The discourse remains focused primarily on works for solo instrument and electronics, as that is where the relationship between live and non-live sources is most salient. In an ensemble context, the contribution of non-live components tends to get diluted by the web of interrelations that occur between the multiple instruments on stage. Moreover, relationships between live and non-live components can be highly dynamic, formed on a moment-by-moment basis and constantly shifting. Concurrent sounds can assume varied roles in the musical fabric, and the function of even a single sound may change as it unfolds over time. This complexity is multiplied when several players are on stage since electronics can fuse with any of the individual instruments, function as an autonomous voice in the texture, or serve to extend the ensemble as a whole. And of course, the relationship that an electronic component has with one instrument in the ensemble may not reflect the relationship it has with others. A focus on solo works allows relationships between live and non-live components to be examined in a more direct and one-dimensional context, bringing clarity to concepts that can then be applied to larger groups.

The Mixed Work Format

Musical Relationships between Live and Non-Live Materials

A heightened concern for the relationship between live and non-live components arises in mixed works and is motivated by the loudspeaker-based presentation of the electronics. In a concert setting, a spectator is able to see a performer on stage, yet hear sounds that are clearly not sourced from the instrument. This leads to a perceptual dissonance that draws attention to the relationship between live and non-live components. Beyond merely heightening awareness of these relations, the mixed work format presents opportunity for relationships that would be less effective in the context of multiple live instruments, precisely because the source of the electronics cannot be seen. Indeed, exploiting the peculiarities of loudspeaker-based listening is idiomatic of the mixed work format and electroacoustic music in general.

Three relationships between live and non-live components that are particularly poignant in mixed works have been identified as extension, causal, and independent (Frengel, 2010). Importantly, these categories reflect musical relationships as perceived by the spectator and may differ from what is technically happening. In fact, one might argue that the mixed work composer is ultimately concerned with creating the illusion of particular relationships, with matters of implementation a secondary consideration.

Electronic Extensions

Extension is concerned with a fusion of live and non-live components into a single, musically inseparable sound complex. The apparent elongation of a decaying guitar note with a non-live tone at the same pitch provides a simple hypothetical example.[2] Live and non-live components need not be perceptually indistinguishable to qualify as extension. The listener may be conscious of an electronic presence, in which case the notion of extension is only figurative. In other instances, live and non-live sources may be much more ambiguous. While there would seem to be a predilection toward ambiguity when working with modes of extension, it is important to note the reciprocal correlation between the degree of extension and the potential for ambiguity between sources. In general, ambiguity is greatest in conservative extensions that maintain much of the timbral and behavioral characteristics of the live instrument. After all, if a listener is to believe that a sound came from an instrument then she or he must believe that the instrument is capable of producing such a sound. As the sound complex is further removed from the expected character of the instrument, the presence of non-live components becomes increasingly apparent. In this regard, the use of instrumental preparations and extended performance techniques in the live part can raise the potential for ambiguity by diminishing a listener's familiarity with the instrument and disrupting expectations of its sonic capabilities.

The mixed work format is ideally suited to electronic extensions of a live instrument because the source of the non-live sounds cannot be seen, which in turn, encourages a musically inseparable interpretation. However, attempts at extending a more dominant non-live component with a live instrument tend to fall short on the concert stage due to the perceptual bias toward the performer. Regardless of how musically insignificant a live instrument's contribution may be, the performer's presence on stage captivates attention and places everything he or she does at the center of the musical activity. If proof is needed, one might simply imagine the difference between two guitarists performing a canon as compared to a solo guitarist performing the same canon along with an electronic second voice. In the former, both parts would appear more-or-less equal, while in the latter, attention would clearly be weighted toward the performer on stage, regardless of whether the live instrument serves as leader or follower in the canon. Of course, perceptual bias toward the performer is only a factor when experiencing a mixed work live. Listening to a recording of the same work may lead to a different interpretation.

Causal Relations

In a causal relationship one component appears to directly affect the behavior of another. The intervention can be instigative, with one part triggering activity or inducing change in another. Inversely, it can be terminative, with one part appearing to halt activity in another. Such points of intersection between live and non-live materials elevate the perceived collaboration between components and draw attention toward the relationship itself. While there often appears to be a mechanical basis for causality, this need not be the case. The effect can be equally convincing when the electronics are manually triggered or halted at the appropriate times.

Independent Relations

Complete independence of voices is somewhat rare in music. Simply framing a group of sounds as belonging to a composition gives rise to the expectation that they will be coordinated in some way, leading a listener to form connections between events.[3] We most often experience sound sources behaving independently of one another in ambient settings. This, again, is a matter of expectation. Listeners do not assume coordination between disparate elements in a soundscape and are therefore not inclined to seek out connections. In fact, in our daily lives we tend to tune out ambience altogether when focusing attention on foregrounded events. A similarly selective listening also occurs in the concert hall, where listeners draw a distinction between the sounds of the music and those that are external to it, such as the occasional cough of an audience member or the ebb and flow of outside traffic. Concertgoers generally recognize that these sounds are extraneous to the music and omit them from any interpretation of the work.[4]

One of the significant contributions that recording technology has made to concert music is the ability to bring sounds from the outside world into the performance space. Mixed works often employ ambient recordings to set the stage, so to speak, transforming the concert hall into another space. When such transplanted soundscapes are realistic there is a similar sense that the ambience exists outside the primary boundaries of the music, and like a naturally occurring ambience, a listener may exclude it from the moment-to-moment interpretation of the music. It is largely this tendency to neglect ambience, reinforced by our natural expectations and facilitated by the acousmatic presentation of the electronics, that allows it to remain independent of foregrounded components. As soon as there is a sense that the ambience is being controlled or manipulated deliberately, a listener will likely begin to search for connections between it and the other sounding materials in the work.

Implementation Models

Implementation models are concerned with technical issues regarding the production and management of non-live components. Two common computer-based strategies employed in mixed works are sound file triggering and real-time processing. Although distinct, these approaches are complementary in many ways and can be operative simultaneously within a given work.

It is important not to equate the musical objectives of a work with its technical underpinnings. From a design perspective, implementation details are clearly important—the performance environment must accomplish the required tasks. But an audience may find it difficult to distinguish between real-time processing and sound file triggering, and the distinction is arguably not all that important. It is ultimately the perceived relationships that spectators deal with, and one's interpretation of what is going on may not always correspond with what is actually happening, a point that can be leveraged for powerful effect.

Sound File Triggering

The earliest mixed works were written for an instrument that would play along with a pre-composed tape. Under such conditions, performers often report feeling straitjacketed by the fixed chronometer of the electronics, forced to relinquish much of their interpretive freedom. Nowadays, a single sound file played from a computer or compact disc replaces the tape medium, but the temporal constraints associated with fixed electronics delivered on a single continuous track remain.

Temporal freedom can be granted to the performer by dividing fixed electronics into multiple sound files, or indices, that are instigated at particular moments in the work. Given enough indices, the temporal constraints associated with fixed electronics are hardly noticeable to the performer. Indices can be instigated by an off-stage technician or by the performer on stage using a foot pedal or other easily accessible controller. Management of the electronics from the stage puts the player in complete control of the music's temporal flow but burdens the performance. By contrast, the use of an additional person to trigger the indices absolves the performer of technical tasks but usually requires some amount of rehearsal time to coordinate the live and non-live components. More concerning than the rehearsal demands, performers are often unable to practice the piece on their own with the electronics, having to wait until the few pre-concert rehearsals to hear the music as it will ultimately be presented.

Musically speaking, a principal advantage of working with pre-composed sound files is that they are not timbrally or behaviorally tied to the live instrument. Rather, they can be derived from any source material and can function entirely apart from the instrument. Of course, pre-composed sound files are equally capable of fusing with an instrument on stage, and with some careful crafting can sound as if sourced directly from it. In terms of production quality, files prepared in advance tend to sound superior to real-time generated electronics. In a studio it is possible to engage in a level of critical listening and attention to production fidelity that is simply not attainable in a live setting. And even when the same processing techniques are used, a composer working out of real time is able to be selective about the sounds that end up in the work. For instance, large amounts of material can be generated and the composer can sift through it, retaining only the best moments. By contrast, on the concert stage there is little choice but to accept whatever non-live materials are generated on the fly.

Real-Time Processing

Real-time processing derives non-live components from the live instrument's output on stage. Chapters 7 and 8 identified a range of hardware and computer-based processing techniques that can be placed in a guitar's signal chain. Under such conditions, the processed sound may be projected from a stage amp, in which case it would likely be interpreted as a transformation of the instrumental tone rather than serving as a separate non-live component in the musical texture. If autonomy of electronics is the objective, real-time processing could be performed on a signal captured through a microphone or split from the signal chain. Separating live and non-live signals leaves the unprocessed sound of the instrument intact and allows the electronics to be projected from alternative locations, such as sound reinforcement speakers.

Many of the issues regarding coordination between live and non-live components are alleviated under the real-time processing model because the electronics are generated in direct response to a live instrument's signal. Having said that, real-time processing does not necessarily eliminate the need for the performer or a technician to manage the electronics. It is common for processing algorithms or parameters to change over the course of a work, and those changes are typically invoked in a manner analogous to that used when sound files are triggered, either by the performer using a foot pedal or by a technician off stage.

Real-time processing offers great potential for coherence between live and non-live sounds, as nuances specific to a particular performance can make their way into the electronic part. This is particularly valuable in indeterminate contexts where it is not possible to predict what the performer will be playing at any given moment. In works that involve improvisation, for example, real-time processing may be the only way to obtain similarity between the instrument on stage and the electronics. On the other hand, the timbral and behavioral potential of the non-live components is significantly limited when compared to the seemingly infinite possibilities afforded by the use of pre-composed sound files, precisely because the electronics must be derived solely from the instrumental material in real time. Real-time processing also poses challenges to rehearsals similar to those encountered when working with fixed sound files. Performers must have the required technical equipment and the capability to operate it or they will not be able to practice the work in its totality. However, the complexity of real-time implementations can make it more difficult for performers to get the system up and running on their own.

Performance Software, Score Sequencing, and Score Following

While off-the-shelf software and hardware products can be leveraged for both sound file triggering and real-time processing, most mixed works today implement electronics within an audio programming environment such as Cycling '74's Max. In addition to the ability to fully customize processing algorithms and controller mappings, tailor-made software allows for a sequence of actions to be scripted, essentially functioning as a score for the non-live components. A simple counter can be employed that increments each time a footswitch is pressed. Distinct actions can then be assigned to each count. A single advance of the counter may initiate a variety of technical maneuvers such as parameter changes, automation lines, reconfigurations to the live processing signal chain, or the playback and/or halting of pre-composed sound files. The performer can then step through the non-live action sequence manually using a single footswitch, minimizing the amount of footwork required to manage the electronics.

Score following is very similar to sequencing, except that the software advances through the non-live action sequence automatically. To do this, a score follower must be able to interpret a live performance, compare it to an internal representation of the live part, and then advance at the appropriate times. Assuming that an audio signal is fed to the computer, the interpretation stage will likely involve onset detection and pitch estimation, as well as the ability to identify specific techniques that may serve as milestones within a given work. As discussed in Chapter 8, the ability to analyze a continuous audio signal and extract such information is no trivial task. In particular, real-time polyphonic pitch estimation is problematic, and it is generally necessary in the case of the guitar, given that it is a polyphonic instrument. To be sure, polyphonic pitch tracking can be performed with relative success on the guitar using a hexaphonic pickup to isolate the monophonic signal from each string, or by using a MIDI pickup to perform the pitch estimation, but both techniques require specialized hardware that most instruments do not possess.

Score following is a complex task that is difficult to implement unless one is willing to devote significant time to the software development. Fortunately, there are pre-compiled tools for the task, most notably, IRCAM's Antescofo for the Max audio programming environment. It is capable of detecting individual pitches, trills, glissandi, and simple chords from an audio signal, as well as accepting MIDI data. Note, however, that even Antescofo is not entirely reliable, and functions best when the musical materials are conventional and fairly simple.

Mixed works are inherently burdened by technological demands, as live and non-live components must be coordinated in some manner. One might argue that the ideal strategy absolves the performer of all technical responsibilities, allowing his or her full attention to be placed on the realization of the live part. Score following offers precisely that. However, the need to liberate a performer from purely technical tasks should not be overstated, and certainly should not be pursued to the extent that it compromises the quality of the sounds or the reliability of the performance. Musicians are accustomed to taking actions while playing that are not directly tied to the realization of their part. In instrumental music, performers may cue the entrance of another performer, turn pages in their music, or pick up and put down objects while playing. Asking a performer to depress a footswitch at specific moments in a work can be no more distracting than any of these activities, so long as the requirements are kept within reason. This is especially true for electric guitarists who are accustomed to engaging foot pedals during performance. Even more, there are situations in which it is desirable to place the temporal flow of non-live components under the performer's manual control, such as when the electronics enter after a long rest.

Concert Sound Design

The manner in which live and non-live components are projected to an audience takes on particular significance when a mixed work is presented on the concert stage. A source projected from wide-field sound reinforcement speakers has imaging characteristics quite distinct from that of an unamplified acoustic guitar or from sources projected through an instrument amplifier on stage. This difference in imaging can be harnessed to emphasize the intended musical relationships at play. For instance, non-live components that function to extend the live instrument are most effective in that role if projected from a location near the performer, so as to appear to emerge from the instrument and encourage a musically inseparable interpretation. Conversely, more autonomous relationships between live and non-live components benefit from the segregation obtained by distinct imaging. With an understanding of the practical and sonic implications of various projection options a strategy can be devised for both live and non-live components that best compliments the musical demands of a particular work as well as the acoustics of the concert venue.

Imaging and Perspective

A sound projected in space presents a sonic image of the source object, an important part of which is a sense of listening perspective. One way to think about a sound's image and perspective might be for a listener to close his or her eyes and envisage where the source seems to be positioned relative to the point of listening. Is it close or distant? Centered or off to one side? Focused to a specific location on stage or diffused? And finally, is the projected image proportional to an instrument on stage or artificially magnified? All of these image qualities are attainable given the proper approach to projection, and they all have a place in the presentation of mixed works on the concert stage. The key is to pair an appropriate projection strategy with the musical relationships at play.

An unamplified acoustic guitar or instrument amp acts as a point source, projecting sound from a precise and clearly defined location on stage (Fig. 9.1). Point sources tend to produce a realistic image of the object, proportional to an instrument on stage and somewhat distanced from the audience. Moreover, when a number of point sources are

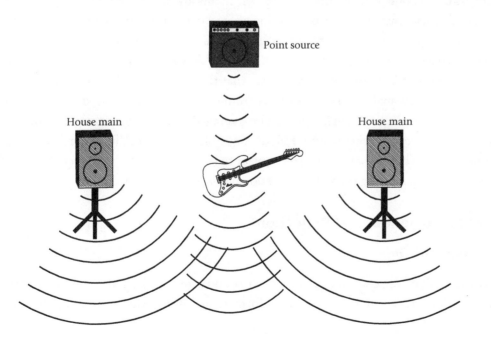

Point source

House main

House main

Figure 9.1

Point source and wide-field projection images.

distributed across a stage their physical separation aids in perceptual segregation, adding clarity to the overall blend of sounds.

A principal drawback of a point source approach to concert sound design is that the balance between instruments changes depending on the listener's position in relation to the stage. Listeners situated at the far right will mainly hear the instruments on the right side of the stage, while those at the left will hear primarily the instruments on the left side. This is less of a concern in the case of a solo work since there are not competing sources on opposite sides of the stage, and it is not even much of an issue in the context of a purely acoustic ensemble since those instruments radiate sound in all directions. It is, however, particularly problematic when working with stage amps. Instrument amps are highly directional, sounding different to listeners in front than to those off to the sides, leading to substantial variation in volume and tone at different positions relative to the amp.

A sound reinforcement system, often referred to as a "house system" when supplied by the venue, consists of a mixing console, power amplifier, main speakers, and stage monitors, along with all the necessary cabling and supportive gear. The two principal functions of a sound reinforcement system are to make the sound from the stage louder and to distribute it evenly to the audience. This latter point is often overlooked. Even in a small venue where volume is not an issue, an ensemble may choose to run instruments through the house system in order to project a more consistent mix to both sides of the audience seating area. Sound reinforcement systems provide additional benefits: they allow a sound technician to control the balance of sources from a mixing console positioned within the audience; they offer players a monitoring system on stage so that they can better hear other instruments or electronics; they reduce the potential for feedback by allowing levels on stage amps to be kept low; and they often provide common effects such as equalization, compression, or reverberation, should they be needed.

House mains are typically positioned at the front-left and front-right edges of the stage (Fig. 9.1). The wide placement of the speakers and their close proximity to the audience results in a larger-than-life image that can seem artificially magnified, enveloping, and diffuse, all of which are intensified as the mains are distanced from the performer or spaced farther apart. This image enlarging effect can be employed to obtain more weight and power from sources, which is fitting to grand or forceful moments in a work. Indeed, electroacoustic composers often embrace such wide-field imaging for its surreal perspective. However, it is important to recognize that the close and wide-field imaging characteristics of house mains are quite distinct from the narrow and focused image of a point source. While the contrast in images can be leveraged to encourage segregation of components, it may also prevent sources from fusing or blending naturally. In particular, sounds projected from house mains will often appear to be in front of those projected from point sources on stage, giving them disproportional presence in the mix.

Live Instrument Sound Projection

The Acoustic Guitar

Acoustic guitars are crafted to project their sound acoustically, and while that may seem like a self-evident statement, many performers are all too willing to plug the acoustic instrument in. Any method of amplification tends to diminish the natural quality of the acoustic guitar by degrading the tone and potentially interfering with its projection characteristics. If enough volume is obtained from the instrument in its acoustic state, then further amplification may be avoided entirely. Of course, there are situations when amplification is desirable, for purposes of volume, sound distribution, or any of the other functions that a sound reinforcement system provides. In such cases, an acoustic guitar can be amplified using either a stage amp, by sending its signal through the mixing console to the house mains, or some combination of the two.

A stage amp acts as a point source and offers a fairly natural image for an acoustic instrument when positioned close to it. Ideally, the amp should be placed several feet behind the performer so that the sound appears to emanate from the instrument itself. When an amp is placed far off axis from the performer, the projected image loses much of its localized quality, as there are now two distinct point sources: the instrument itself and the amp. Moreover, if the amp is considerably louder than the acoustic sound emanating from the guitar, the projected image can seem detached and projected from a distinct location. Placing the amp several feet behind the instrument also allows the player to hear it accurately. An amp positioned in front, to the side, or too close to the instrument puts the performer's ears outside the amp's beam of projection and gives a false impression of the sound, both in terms of dynamics and timbre, which in turn, can affect the player's performance.

Rather than using a stage amp, an acoustic guitar can be amplified through a sound reinforcement system and projected from the house mains. In terms of getting a signal to the house system, diaphragm microphones prevail. First, they capture all the sounds from the instrument, including those not adequately detected by pickups, such as non-pitched sounds originating from the body or those produced over the fretboard or at the headstock. Equally important, the captured signal can be modified by moving the microphone in relation to the source. Distance can be added to obtain a more realistic perspective than that achieved from a pickup, and the location of the source within the stereo field can be altered using stereo placement configurations.[5] As a general rule, condenser microphones are preferable for acoustic instruments because they are highly sensitive to subtle amplitude fluctuation, which translates to a better ability to capture high frequencies and detail.

Microphones do pose complications when used in a concert setting, the most pressing of which is the potential for feedback. Despite the power capabilities of a sound reinforcement system, the level to which a miked instrument can be raised is usually limited by feedback and will only be a fraction of what the system is capable of delivering. Finding that breaking point and keeping the level in the mains well below it is an important step in feedback prevention. Additional measures to minimize feedback include using microphones with unidirectional polar patterns, positioning the mics well behind the line of the house mains, and keeping monitor levels on stage as low as possible. Signal isolation can also be an issue when using microphones, especially in an ensemble context when other instruments are in close proximity. A microphone with a unidirectional polar pattern attenuates sound entering the mic from the sides and rear and will minimize, but may not completely eliminate, peripheral sounds.

199

As an alternative to using a microphone, the signal from an acoustic guitar pickup could be sent directly to the house system. Direct signals are free of extraneous sounds and are less susceptible to feedback. In terms of tone quality and imaging, however, they provide a less-than-optimal representation of the instrument, appearing disproportionately close and magnified when projected from house mains. If a direct signal is sent to the mixing console, a direct injection (DI) box should always be used to convert the unbalanced, high-impedance, instrument-level signal to a balanced, low-impedance, mic-level signal.[6] This conversion should be done on stage so that the long cable run from the stage to the mixing console carries a balanced signal less prone to radio frequency (RF) interference.

Point source and wide-field projection strategies may be combined to obtain greater volume and more even sound distribution, or to alter the image characteristics of the instrument. As long as the level of the point source on stage remains dominant, adding a small amount of guitar signal to the house mains has the effect of enlarging the image while maintaining its point source character. Of course, an unamplified acoustic guitar is not very loud, and significant restraint is needed to keep the level of the mains below its sound. If more volume is required, a stage amp can be employed to help keep the image anchored to the instrument. For instance, an acoustic guitar fitted with a pickup can be connected to a stage amp positioned behind the performer for the purpose of establishing a louder point source on stage. The guitar might then be miked and projected from the house mains at higher levels while remaining attached to the instrument on stage. Careful use of stereo miking techniques can also help to bond the projected image to the instrument on stage, as the source can appear to be localized between the speakers. However, when the level in the house mains overpowers that from the instrument or amp on stage, the mains become the dominant source that the audience hears, at which point the projected image shifts from a defined position on stage to the enlarged and more diffused quality of the wide-field speakers. It is important to recognize that a performer's presence creates a focal point that anchors perception to his or her position on stage and provides a reference against which the projected image is evaluated. When the house mains function as the primary source of the guitar, a sense of disembodiment can emerge due to the discrepancy between the visual percept and sonic imaging, with the projected sound appearing in front and detached from the instrument.

The Electric Guitar

Projection strategies for the electric guitar are guided by the same principles outlined above in relation to the acoustic instrument. Of course, the electric guitar projects such a minimal amount of acoustic sound that amplification of some sort is always necessary. Projecting a direct electric guitar signal through house mains is not recommended, as it generally results in an unsatisfactory tone as well as an unnaturally magnified image that will likely be detached from the instrument on stage. An amp and speaker cabinet plays a crucial role in defining an electric guitar tone and should always serve as the source of the projected signal. This can only be accomplished using a diaphragm microphone placed in front of the amp. Projection options are therefore limited to point sourcing the guitar to an amp on stage or miking the amp and also sending the guitar signal through the house mains.

Electric guitar amps can project substantial volume, and unless the venue is very large, they are usually capable of filling the space with sound. Amps are, however, highly directional in their projection. Specifically, high frequencies tend to be overly pronounced to a listener situated in front of the amp and to roll off quickly at positions off axis, a phenomenon referred to as beaming. Beaming is a result of destructive interference between the same sound waves emanating from different points on the surface of the speaker. When the listener is on axis, these waves hit the ear at roughly the same time. When he or she is listening off axis, however, the waves arrive at the ear at different times, leading to phase cancellation at certain frequencies in the spectrum. Cancellation starts at the frequency that has a wavelength twice the width of the speaker—roughly 1,130 Hz for a 12-inch cone when listening 45 degrees off axis—and continues upward since there is an infinite number of closer points on the speaker's surface.[7]

Guitar amplifiers sometimes employ multiple speakers to mitigate beaming. Two speakers positioned side by side widen the beam vertically, placing the performer's ears within the beam when he or she is standing at locations closer to the amp. By contrast, vertical speaker configurations enlarge the beam horizontally, which is appropriate if the concern is to distribute the sound more evenly to an audience. As might be imagined, four-speaker cabinets enlarge the beam in both dimensions. Regardless of the speaker configuration, all amps beam their sound, and while multi-speaker cabinets widen the beam's projection area, they do not eliminate the phenomenon of beaming.

There are various ways to mitigate the effect of beaming from an amplifier. A simple method is to raise the amp up and/or shim the front of it so that it projects the beam over the audience rather than directly at them, thereby placing all listeners off axis. Alternatively, speaker designer Jay Mitchell has suggested placing a donut-shaped object cut from foam in front of the speaker (Mitchell, 2015). [8] Referred to as a Mitchell Donut, the foam has the effect of absorbing high frequencies from within the beam, essentially causing the amp to sound off axis even when the listener is directly in front of it. Taking more radical measures, the amp might be turned around so that it reflects off a wall behind the stage. This diffuses the sound considerably and removes much of the bite from the tone, which can help the electric guitar blend more naturally with unamplified instruments. All of these techniques dull the timbre considerably and may need to be compensated for through use of the tone controls on the amplifier. Of course, a final means of eliminating beaming is to mic the amp and project some of the guitar signal through the house mains.

As with an acoustic instrument, further amplification of the electric guitar through house mains has the effect of diminishing point source localization and shifting the projected image to the closer, wide-field speakers. The image will remain anchored to the instrument as long as the stage level exceeds that in the mains; and because an electric guitar amp is capable of producing considerable volume, it is possible to retain a point source image at substantially higher levels than is the case with acoustic instruments. However, once the signal in the mains overpowers that from the amp on stage the quality of the projected image shifts to that of the wide-field speakers.

When miking an electric guitar, it is worth noting that the microphone is positioned in front of the amp and not in front of the instrument. Only sounds that make their way through the pickups and to the amp will be captured. Pickups often exclude elements emanating from over the fretboard or at the headstock. Additional microphones in front of the fretboard or contact microphones attached to those particular areas on the instrument offer possible solutions for capturing such sounds.

Ground Hum and Radio Frequency Interference

Guitar rigs are inherently noisy, largely because of the magnetic pickups and the use of unbalanced cables throughout the rig, both of which are susceptible to RF interference. The noise is less troublesome when the instrument is played continuously at loud dynamics. However, in moments of rest or at softer dynamics the buzz and hum emanating from the amplifier is exposed and can disrupt the listening experience. Noise problems are difficult to eliminate completely when you are using a traditional electric guitar.[9] There are, however, measures that can be taken to reduce them. For starters, some equipment is more prone to noise and interference than others: single-coil pickups are more susceptible to RF interference than double-coil humbuckers; longer cables pick up more noise than shorter cables; tube amplifiers tend to hiss more than solid-state amps; spring reverbs tend to pick up interference, which gets louder as the reverb is increased. Selecting gear that is less prone to noise issues can go a long way to quieting the rig. In addition, effects like distortion and compression increase the presence of any noise in a signal. Bypassing these effects during moments of rest in the live part saves the audience from having to hear the exposed noise.[10]

Power conditions in the venue pose another obstacle to a quiet rig. Ideally, all electrical devices engaged in sound production, including the mixing console, mains, stage monitors, guitar rig, and any computer-related equipment, should be powered by a single electrical circuit that is isolated from lighting, fans, or other non-musical devices. A good music venue will have considered this when installing the electrical system. If, however, one ends up in the all-too-familiar situation of experiencing more amp buzz than normal or having changes in lighting affect the noise from the amplifier, then a solution is to find a wall outlet that is on a clean circuit. The house sound technician may have an idea of how the outlets are divided in the venue, or you may have to determine it through a tedious trial-and-error process. It is a good idea always to carry a long extension cord in the event that power needs to be sought from a location off stage.

A ground loop occurs when multiple electrical devices are connected to a common ground through different circuits. This often occurs when a direct signal taken from a guitar rig powered by an on-stage outlet is sent to a sound reinforcement system that is positioned far from the stage and powered by a separate circuit. The telltale sign of a ground loop is a 50 Hz or 60 Hz hum from the guitar amp. Flipping the ground switch on a direct injection box will likely quiet the amp but move the hum to the house mains. A "ground-lift" adapter that removes the ground prong from the power plug will usually solve the problem, but all devices in the signal chain need to be lifted. Connecting the entire rig to a single power strip allows the ground to be lifted from all devices with a single adapter. Note that lifting the ground from the power supply should be a last resort, as it can lead to electric shock when someone simultaneously touches the guitar and other electrical devices on stage. The proper way to resolve a ground loop is to power the guitar rig from the same circuit that supplies the reinforcement system, which may require a long extension cord.

Projecting Non-Live Components

Point source and wide-field projection strategies are also available to non-live components with similar implications for imaging and localization. However, the loudspeaker-based presentation of non-live components, and in particular, the fact that there is no performer on stage to establish a point of reference for the sound image, offers greater freedom in terms of both spatial movement and imaging. For instance, the projection strategy for non-live materials might change from one sound to the next, with some projected from a point source and others projected from the house mains. Without the presence of the performer on stage to anchor perception there is nothing for the image to be dislocated from. Instead, the source of the sound simply seems to move from a point farther back on stage to the closer position of the mains.

The careful management of projected images can play an important role in supporting, or even establishing, musical relationships between live and non-live components. If the intention is for the electronics to fuse with the live instrument, then it is important that they be projected from roughly the same physical location. On the other hand, if the non-live materials are to function as a separate voice in the musical texture, then projecting them from a distinct location can encourage segregation. In practice, a strategy should be devised for the projection of both live and electronic sources that compliments the relationships at play in a particular work. Five hypothetical models are presented below that provide a range of opportunities available to mixed works.

Models for Sound Projection in Mixed Works

Model 1: Point Sourced Instrument with Non-Live Materials Projected through House Mains

Point sourcing the guitar on stage while projecting non-live materials through house mains offers the most natural treatment of the live instrument and provides clear separation between live and electronic components. The same spatial discrepancy between sources that aids in segregation, however, discourages fusion and ambiguity. Even more, the close and magnified image of electronics projected from house mains, along with the volume potential of a sound reinforcement system, can easily overpower and envelop a point source on stage, with the result that the instrument seems like a small component of a much larger, all-encompassing virtual ensemble. Careful balancing at the mixing console along with a fair amount of volume restraint is usually required for the live instrument to remain dominant in the mix, and consequently, the overall dynamic potential of a piece may be limited under this model.

Model 2: Live and Non-Live Components Projected through House Mains

Projection of both the live and non-live components through a sound reinforcement system unifies the two sources spatially by bringing the instrument's sound to the electronics. Although the natural image of the instrument is compromised, conditions are now in place for relationships that rely on fusion of the live and non-live components. In addition, a greater dynamic range can be obtained through a sound reinforcement system and the sources will be projected more evenly to the audience. This strategy is well suited to large venues or works containing grand, forceful moments that demand power and weight. Of course, it offers no contrast in imaging, and therefore no ability to use the projection strategy to support the musical objectives in a work.

Model 3: Point Sourced Instrument and Point Sourced Non-Live Materials

Point sourcing both the live instrument and all non-live components provides the most natural option in terms of imaging. The instrument retains its point source character, and non-live components blend well with it, appearing comparable in scale and perspective to an instrument on stage. Non-live components can be projected from a stage amp, which might be the same amp that the guitar is using or a separate amp positioned in close proximity.[11] A two-channel amp is preferable if it is shared by live and non-live components, as each then has its own volume and tone controls. Otherwise, the live and non-live components must be balanced within the audio software used to perform the piece.

There is a loss of fidelity when projecting non-live components from a guitar amp that should be considered when producing the materials. Aside from the point source image, amps typically only take a mono signal and and are limited in terms of frequency range. Broad-spectrum sounds produced in the studio tend to be considerably duller and bass-heavy when heard from an amp. While not ideal for all electronics, the effect that an amp has on the tone and image might be embraced as a means of pushing non-live components to sound more guitar-like. And of course, non-live components derived from guitar recordings sound perfectly natural when projected from a guitar amp.

Sound reinforcement speakers could also be used for point source projection of non-live components if positioned close to the performer on stage (Fig. 9.2). This enables stereo sounds to be projected with full spectrum, larger imaging, and greater force while remaining focused to a precise location on stage. Although this is an attractive option, chances are that no other works on the concert program will need the main speakers in this location, in which case a second pair of speakers is required.

Model 4: Point Sourced Instrument with Point Sourced and Wide-Field Non-Live Projection Options

A more flexible projection strategy allows non-live materials to be projected from either a point source near the performer or from the house mains on a moment-to-moment

Figure 9.2

Multi-channel frontal imaging, with two speakers near the performer and two wide-field mains.

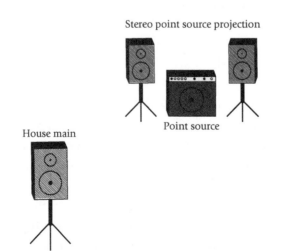

Stereo point source projection

Point source

House main

House main

basis (Fig. 9.2). The projection of each non-live element can then be chosen to support its intended relationship with the instrument. For instance, electronic sounds meant to function as extensions of the live instrument can be sent to the point source, while those intended to provide a more autonomous role can be projected from the house mains. Having different images available for the non-live materials also allows for spatial motion in the electronics. Sounds that originate in the amp can spread out to the house mains, or vice versa. Shifting a live instrument's projection between a point source on stage and the house mains during the work is also possible, but it draws attention to the discrepancy between the visual anchor of the performer and the sounding image. It is generally more sensible to choose a consistent projection strategy for the live instrument and then work out the projection of non-live materials around it.

Model 5: Multi-Speaker Surround Sound Systems

The spatial dimension of music remained relatively underexplored until the second half of the 20th century, when it began to receive considerable attention, especially from electroacoustic composers. Surround sound systems are now customary at electroacoustic concerts, with eight speakers distributed around the audience representing a small configuration. Large systems can utilize dozens of speakers, ranging in size, fidelity, and imaging characteristics.[12]

In a mixed work, it is reasonable to maintain a frontal image for the live instrument so that the projected sound bonds to the performer on stage. If the sound of an instrument is projected from speakers in the rear, for example, listeners will not believe that the source is behind them since they can see the performer on stage. Rather, there is an unsettling sense of dislocation. Non-live materials do not share the same spatial constraints. Without a physical source to anchor perception, the movement of a sound to different speakers creates the impression that the source actually moves in the venue. Still, the presence of the performer orients perception toward the front, which can cause non-live components to feel tethered to the stage. Although sources are free to move in space, the effect is often more one of sounds radiating outward to the speakers from a fixed frontal position.

Stage Monitors

To counter feedback from microphones, performers are typically seated on stage behind the house mains, a position from which it is difficult to hear what is coming from the speakers. This can be particularly problematic when instruments or non-live materials are sent directly to the mains, as there will be no source on stage for the performer to hear. Stage monitors are small speakers that face back at the performers, allowing them to hear sources running through the house system. Monitors can also allow a player to hear instruments on the opposite side of the stage, which is especially helpful when directional amps are being used.

The balance of sources on stage is essential to a good performance, as musicians will play to the blend that they hear. Accordingly, the same care afforded to the house mix should be given to the monitor mix. It is imperative that performers be able to hear their own instruments clearly. As a general rule, if a musician can hear the sound of his or her instrument from a point source on stage there is no need to also add it to the monitor mix. Doing so will likely require the level of other sources in the monitor to be raised even more, leading to excessive volume on stage and potential feedback issues. If the instrument does need to be monitored, it is best to set that level first, keeping it as low as possible. The non-live components can then be brought up to an appropriate level to provide a balanced mix on stage.

Recording Mixed Works

Before embarking on any recording project one must decide whether the objective is to obtain an idealized studio version of the work or a live recording. To a large extent, these divergent approaches to music production are a matter of convention within genres. The commercial music industry tends to view the recording as the fruit of a composer's labor. As a consequence, the recording has come to represent the definitive and idealized version of the work against which live performances, either by the original artist or others, are compared. With so much emphasis placed on the recorded product, a studio-oriented approach strives for perfection, usually by assembling the performance one part at a time so that meticulous attention can be given to each instrument.

By comparison, the classical composer has historically worked toward the publication of a score, essentially a set of instructions detailing how to realize the work. Scores are inherently incomplete, leaving considerable room for interpretation by a performer; and without a definitive sounding version of the music to reference, performers will produce a range of interpretations, all of which would seem equally valid. Interpretation is embraced in the classical music tradition and it is at the core of score-based music-making.

Aesthetic considerations aside, live- and studio-oriented approaches to recording demand diverse production strategies. A studio-oriented approach generally utilizes all the tools and techniques available to render the best possible performances and production quality. What we hear as an uninterrupted performance of the work is almost never that but rather a piecemeal construction assembled from extracts of numerous takes and isolated punch-ins. If there are multiple parts to the music they are typically "tracked" in turn, which not only makes it easier to assemble flawless performances but also tends to render the highest fidelity productions because all of the engineering effort can be focused on one part at a time. Tracking can also benefit solo works. As a hypothetical example, imagine a work for solo electric guitar in which distinct tones are used in different sections of the piece: one clean, one with light distortion, and one with heavy distortion. The guitar part might be spread over three tracks, divided by tone and recorded in turn. The instrument can then be configured to achieve the best tone for each section of the work without having to worry about obtaining the other tones from the same rig setup. In fact, different amplifiers might be used for the clean and dirty tones, or the recording engineer may want to switch microphones, place them in different positions, or apply individualized post-production effects such as equalization to each tone. This degree of attention to production quality is typically attainable only by overdubbing tracks one at a time.

In contrast to the flawless, sparkling complexion of studio recordings, a live-oriented approach to music production strives for authenticity—a sense that the recording represents a genuine performance. This can certainly be achieved by capturing the work as it is performed in its totality. If there are multiple instruments they all perform together, and if there are non-live components they too need to be present during the recording. But authenticity can also be illusory. Live recordings are frequently made in a studio, and while the musicians play synchronously, they may be in different rooms for purposes of signal isolation, unable to see each other and relying on headphones to monitor the other parts—anything but a typical performance situation. Moreover, the best passages from a number of different takes may be edited together so that the final version of the work is an assembled performance that never actually took place. Despite such sleight of hand production tactics, a live-oriented approach to recording tries to capture as much of the music in its totality as possible, and importantly, the aim is for the final product to sound live, with all instruments seemingly in the same space and heard from a similar perspective. Perhaps the greatest obstacle to obtaining a good live recording is getting all players to execute a suitable performance in the same take. If one player fumbles the entire group has to do it again.

Studio- and live-oriented approaches to recording are by no means mutually exclusive. It is not uncommon to record a small group of core instruments live and then track additional parts one by one on top of that foundation. Such a hybrid approach is often adopted in pursuit of a more natural feel. It also makes it easier for the initial parts to be performed, as it allows the musicians to signal and play off one another. After all, when laying down each part one at a time, being the first person to record can be difficult. The performance requirements for a given work will often point to one recording strategy over the other, and in the case of mixed works—and much of the contemporary music literature for that matter—tracking parts is simply not an option. Music that lacks a regular pulse, requires visual interaction between players, or contains indeterminacy in either the live or non-live components can often only be recorded live.

Recording the Guitar

Preliminary Preparations

A guitar should be configured to sound as good as possible before any attempts are made to record it. In the case of an acoustic instrument, preliminary preparations may be limited to changing the strings, but what a difference that one step can make. New strings sound bright and resonant compared to when they are worn. Strings can take a few days to stretch and hold their pitch so they should be changed well in advance of a recording session. Additional preparatory measures are available to the electric guitar, such as reducing the signal chain to only those devices required for the particular take, using short and high-quality cables, and dialing in the tone on the amplifier and any effects. Because of their directional projection characteristics, stage amps should be adjusted while the adjuster is listening from a position similar to where the microphone(s) will be placed. More likely than not, this will be somewhere in front of the speaker.

Microphones

Once the proper instrument tone has been established it can be captured most naturally using a diaphragm microphone. Mics allow the entirety of the sound to be captured and at a perspective that is akin to how we would expect to hear the instrument. The type of microphone and its position in relation to the source both play a crucial role in determining the quality of the captured tone. To these topics we now turn.

Types and Polar Patterns

Microphones used for audio production are typically classified as dynamic or condenser.[13] Technically speaking, the difference between the two is that dynamic mics are passive and require no power, while condenser microphones require phantom power (+48v) to operate. Although condensers are more complex and generally more expensive, it would be erroneous to assume that they are better. Different mics simply sound different. Dynamic microphones tend to capture less high-frequency content, which contributes to a warmer and less detailed sound. In addition, they have a slower transient response time, making them more resilient to loud events with sharp attacks. Finally, dynamic mics lose sensitivity relatively quickly as the mic is distanced from the source, which can exaggerate the distal perspective and/or aid in signal isolation. By comparison, condenser mics tend to be more sensitive to subtle amplitude fluctuation, which translates to a better ability to capture high frequencies and detail. Furthermore, their fast transient response allows rapid changes in amplitude to be captured more accurately. However, their heightened sensitivity to sound pressure can result in a popping quality when transients are too loud, as might be the case when percussive materials are being recorded. Condenser mics also tend to capture sounds at greater distances; this can lead to a more detailed live or ambient recording but also makes it difficult to isolate signals in different mics. The appropriate mic for a given circumstance will depend largely on the characteristics of the source being recorded. Conventional wisdom suggests that condenser mics are more appropriate for acoustic instruments while dynamic microphones are well suited for amplifiers.

The sensitivity of a microphone to sound pressure waves entering the capsule at different angles is referred to as its polar pattern. Broadly speaking, the two patterns most useful to music production are unidirectional and omnidirectional (Fig. 9.3).[14] A unidirectional microphone is most sensitive to sources directly in front of it, with amplitude and high frequencies rolling off as the mic is moved off axis. From the rear, unidirectional mics pick up very little, a trait that can be leveraged for signal isolation. By contrast, an omnidirectional microphone is equally sensitive from all angles around the capsule. Omnidirectional polar patterns are useful when the aim is to capture multiple sources distributed in physical space, as is often the case in a live recording. They are also employed

Figure 9.3

Unidirectional and omnidirectional microphone polar patterns.

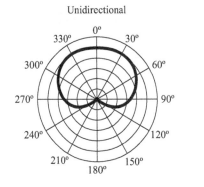

Unidirectional

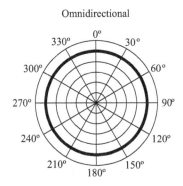

Omnidirectional

to capture room acoustics since they are sensitive to reflections entering the capsule from the sides and rear.

Placement

The position of a microphone relative to the sound source plays a significant role in the fidelity of the captured signal, with angle and proximity the two primary considerations. A directional mic will capture the broadest spectrum, and in particular, the highest frequencies, when placed on axis with the capsule pointed directly at the source. High frequencies are attenuated as the mic is moved or angled off-axis, much like turning the treble knob down on a hi-fi stereo system. It is important to make adjustments to the position and angle of the mic until a suitable spectral balance is obtained in the captured signal.

Proximity is perhaps even more critical to mic placement because close and distant positions have distinctive qualities that are difficult to alter or simulate in postproduction. It is imperative, therefore, that the right distal perspective is captured in the initial recording. Close mic positions are typically considered those up to three feet from the source, while distant positions place the mic more than three feet away. Of course, this is merely a guideline. The more pertinent distinction between close and distant miking derives from the perception of proximity in the recording, and ultimately, how that compares to a listener's expectation of what the source should sound like. For instance, mic positions that seem to place the source at distances closer than a normal listening perspective will be perceived as close, regardless of any measure of the mic's actual distance from the object. Generally speaking, a little distance between the source and the mic tends to produce a more natural listening perspective, akin to how we are accustomed to hearing object in the world. After all, how often do we listen with our ears only inches away from the source?

Stereo and Mono Sound Images

Humans localize sound based on discrepancies between the signals received in the left and right ears. The sound wave from a source positioned directly in front of a listener will arrive at the two ears at roughly the same time and sound similar in both ears. However, a source positioned off-axis will be closer to one ear than the other, so there will be timing, amplitude, and spectral differences between the two ears. Although these discrepancies are too subtle to be heard overtly, the mind uses them to determine the direction from which the sound originated.

The principle behind stereophony is that a more realistic sonic image can be captured and re-presented using two identical microphones spaced at roughly the distance separating our ears so that the same discrepancies are captured in the left and right signals. When a stereo recording is played back, the signal captured by the left microphone should be panned fully left and that captured by the right mic panned fully right to properly render the image and avoid phase cancellation. Stereo images do indeed sound more realistic than mono images. Sources can appear to be positioned within the stereo field with greater definition. For instance, it is possible for the source to appear between, and even beyond the width of the speakers, or at locations in front of or behind the speaker line. Importantly, however, a stereo image will be heard accurately only when one is listening

209

(a) (b) (c)

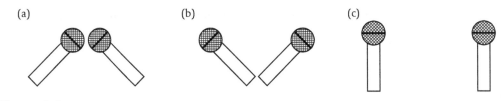

Figure 9.4
Common stereo mic placement configurations: (a) coincident; (b) near-coincident; (c) spaced-pair.

from a position that roughly forms an equilateral triangle with the two speakers, a vantage point referred to as the sweet spot.

Three basic stereo microphone placement configurations are shown in Figure 9.4. The coincident configuration places the mic capsules as close to each other as possible, while the near-coincident configuration positions the capsules at approximately the distance of two ears. In both cases, changes to the angle of the microphones will alter the width of the stereo image. The spaced pair configuration is achieved by having each microphone on its own stand so that they can be moved even farther apart. In this case, the physical distance between the two microphones can be exaggerated to magnify the stereo width, but this method is also the most susceptible to phase cancellation issues.[15]

A mono sound consists of one signal captured from a single microphone. When played back through a two-speaker sound system the same signal is sent to both the left and right speakers, which projects an image that is characteristically different from stereophony. Mono images tend to cling to the speakers, making it difficult to position a source at locations between, beyond, behind, or in front of the speaker line. While channel strips on a mixer provide a pan knob that allows the sound to be weighted more toward one speaker than the other, panning only affects the volume in each speaker, which is just one factor in sound localization. Mono signals do have advantages. First, they are easier to mix with clarity since there is not as much signal to deal with. Second, mono images offer greater consistency when one is listening to a mix from different positions off-axis, as stereo images are heard accurately only from within the sweet spot.

Other Two-Mic Techniques

A guitar might be recorded using two different microphones side-by-side in a coincident or near-coincident configuration. For instance, a dynamic microphone might be paired with a condenser mic that is better able to capture detail. Or the mics could be placed at different distances from the source: a close mic may serve as the primary track, with a distant mic capturing room reflections. Rather than focusing on a stereo image, these two-mic techniques strive to obtain tracks with unique tonal characters that can then be blended at the mixing board. Unlike a stereo image, the different mic signals are typically not panned to individual speakers. However, one must be cautious of phase cancellation issues whenever signals from distinct mics are combined, especially when they are positioned at significantly different distances from the source.

Capturing the Acoustic Guitar

It is a common misconception that the sound of an acoustic guitar projects from the sound hole. In actuality, the hole simply serves as a vent to stabilize air pressure in the body as it vibrates, and in fact, pointing a microphone at the sound hole usually yields an unsatisfactory tone. The majority of sound emanates from the soundboard. When recording an acoustic guitar, microphones are typically placed one to two feet from the instrument and directed toward the upper end of the fretboard where the neck joins the body. From this position a mic is able to capture the vibrating soundboard as well as activity over the fretboard. In the case of works that employ extended techniques or instrumental preparations, the sound projected from the fretboard is often crucial to the overall effect and a separate microphone may be required to capture it adequately. Other microphone placement tactics can be leveraged for some interesting effects. For instance, with a spaced pair configuration one mic can be pointed at the soundboard behind the bridge while the other is positioned over the fretboard, thereby providing "body" and "fretboard" signals that can be re-balanced in post-production. Alternatively, positioning two mics vertically in a near-coincident pattern spreads the strings across the stereo image, as the upper mic points down to the higher strings and the lower mic points to the lower strings. Of course, all of these suggestions merely provide starting points. The microphones will need to be moved around with a concern for angle and proximity until the proper tone and perspective are found.

Capturing the Electric Guitar

Electric guitar amplifiers typically house a 10- or 12-inch speaker with no tweeter or crossover system, and consequently, they do not project much in the way of high frequencies. Dynamic microphones—even fairly inexpensive ones—are usually a fine option when miking an amplifier. A good starting position for the mic is two to three feet in front of the speaker, with the capsule either positioned or angled slightly off-axis. Altering the position and/or angle has the effect of rolling off high frequencies. As usual, experimentation with angle and proximity is required to find the right tone.

Direct Signals

Electromagnetic pickups, piezoelectric pickups, and contact microphones offer alternative means of obtaining a signal from a guitar. While such direct signals can be useful on a concert stage, they generally yield unacceptable results in the recording studio, principally because they present an overly close and unnatural representation of the instrument. That said, an interesting practice has emerged in electric guitar recording known as reamping, in which a direct signal from the instrument is recorded and then later played back through a miked amplifier and re-recorded to achieve the actual sound. Reamping essentially separates the performance from the guitar tone, and thereby allows for significant experimentation in post-production. For instance, the entire signal chain can be reconfigured, including changes to effects pedals and the amplifier. This is primarily advantageous when the guitarist is unsure about the tone to use for a given work or inclined to experimentation.

The downside of reamping is that the performer is not able to hear the instrument's actual sound while recording since it will not have been fully formed. This can be problematic to the extent that the tone or any effects have an influence on the performance, which, arguably, is usually the case. If reamping is pursued, it is important to remember that the signal coming out of any recording equipment will likely be line level or higher and will need to be sent through a reamp box to bring it to instrument level before it is connected to an amp.

Recording Models

The mixed work format can present unique challenges to conventional recording practices. A live-oriented recording strategy is always viable, and in works with no more than a few fixed electronic indices, tracking and overdubbing may also be an option. However, in cases involving indeterminacy, real-time processing, or any significant amount of sound file triggering, it is usually not possible to track the instrument and electronics asynchronously. The two must be recorded together since their content and timing are interdependent and unique to each performance. Yet, for the engineer to have a significant degree of post-production mixing capability, the instrument and electronic components need to be isolated on separate tracks. Achieving this may require some unusual and rather cumbersome tactics. Three models are provided below that offer a range of options for recording mixed works.

Model 1: Live Recording with Room Mics

The simplest and most authentic means of obtaining a live recording is to set up the instrument and sound reinforcement system as if on a concert stage and then use a pair of high-quality condenser microphones placed in a stereo configuration in front of the staging area to capture everything. Expanding on this same principle, multiple stereo pairs could be used, providing close, distant, narrow, and wide perspectives that can be blended in post-production. A principal advantage of recording with room mics is that all components acquire the same perspective and room acoustics. Indeed, this is largely what contributes to the live recording quality. Not surprisingly, the technique yields the best results when conducted in a space with good acoustics. Fortunately, the minimal equipment requirements allow this technique to be taken to spaces outside the recording studio, such as an actual concert venue. Moreover, this method of recording is easiest on the performer(s), as the music is simply presented as normal.

The limitations of room miking become evident in post-production. Without sources isolated on separate tracks, the ability to alter the timbres of individual instruments or re-balance the mix is significantly hampered. It is, therefore, crucial to ensure that the tones and balance of sources projected during the performance are correct before recording.

Model 2: Live Recording to Separate Tracks

Greater post-production mixing potential is available when sources are recorded on separate tracks. In a live recording this generally requires that a distinct microphone be placed in front of each source. With multiple instruments in the same room, complete isolation may not be possible, but a variety of ways are available to minimize extraneous sounds in the microphones. First, more isolation will be achieved by keeping the levels at the sources as low as possible and using closer mic placements. Furthermore, barriers could be erected around sources to shield the mics from external sounds. Of course, in a large recording studio it may be possible to place the performers in separate rooms, monitoring each other through headphones.

Non-live components can be recorded direct for the sake of isolation, in which case the performer(s) will have to monitor the electronics in headphones while recording. However, it can be difficult to achieve a live sound quality in post-production when mixing direct electronics. They will often sound as if they are in a different space or are being listened to from a different perspective, usually closer than that of the live instruments. Both issues can be remedied by reamping the electronics. Here, however, a stage amp typically does not provide the frequency range required. Instead, non-live components can be projected from high-quality studio monitors or sound reinforcement speakers set up in the same room that the instruments were recorded in and then re-recorded through microphones.

Model 3: Multi-Tracking

A studio-based approach to recording strives to capture the individual components of the music one at a time so that greater care can be given to the tone and performance of each. In the context of a mixed work, this is usually possible only when the electronics are fixed and in most cases limited to a few separate indices. For pieces that adopt the single-index fixed format (i.e., instrument plus tape) the process is not unlike any other studio-based recording: the electronics track is first added to the recording session and the performer then monitors the electronics in headphones while playing along and recording to a separate track. Passages in which the instrument plays solo can be recorded freely, and a click track can be created, if needed, to count the performer back in when the next electronics index enters. As previously stated, the ability to track a mixed work is largely dependent on the music itself, and in particular, on the capacity to set up clicks, record in sections, and capture intedertminacy without compromising the interdependence of parts. Not all works are amenable to such a strategy.

APPENDIX I

The E-Standard Fretboard

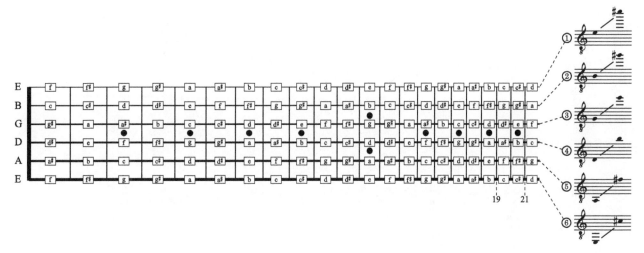

Figure A.1
Fretboard pitches in E-standard tuning, along with ranges per string.

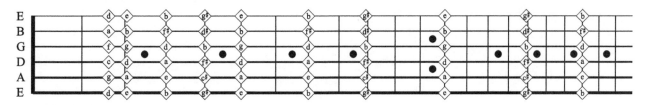

Figure A.2
Harmonics in E-standard tuning.

APPENDIX II

Bi-Tones in E-Standard Tuning

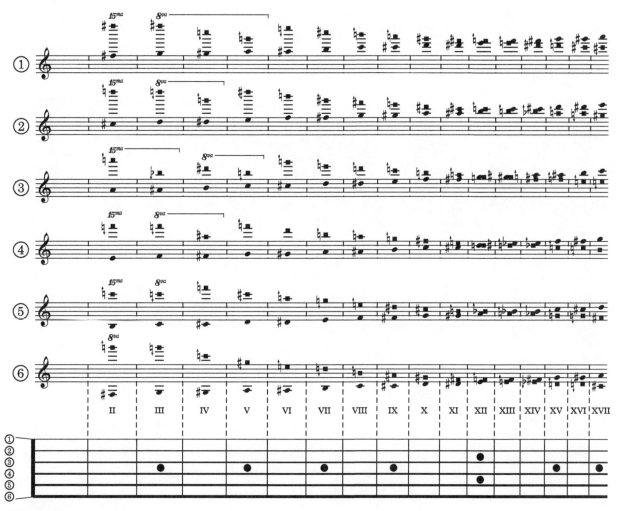

Figure A.3
Bi-tones across the fretboard in E-standard tuning.

NOTES

Preface

i. Schneider does give some attention to the electric guitar, but by and large, his book is weighted toward the nylon string instrument.

ii. In referring to techniques throughout the book, the writing assumes a right-handed player. Left-handed players will have to reverse any references to specific hands.

Chapter 1

1. Despite the name, catgut seems to never have been derived from cats but rather from various other farm animals.

2. Bracing is done to strengthen the soundboard, but it also influences how the soundboard vibrates and is therefore an important contributor to the tone of the instrument.

3. The body is only one factor in determining a guitar's utility. Other considerations include scale length, string spacing, and whether the body joins the neck at the 12th or the 14th fret.

4. The term "floating bridge" is also used to refer to particular vibrato systems on electric instruments. Those are discussed in the Bridges, Saddles, and Tailpieces section of this chapter.

5. There were earlier experiments with electronic amplification using tungsten pickups and carbon button microphones attached to the bridge, none of which resulted in commercially available instruments.

6. Steel players prefer specialized volume pedals and are adamant about the importance of this. A common guitar volume pedal will not do.

7. Some steel tunings can be difficult to obtain on a conventional instrument due to the tension they place on the neck.

8. The EBow is discussed in Chapter 4.

9. This is in contrast to the tuning peg used on a bowed stringed instrument, which is held in place by mere friction.

10. These measurements are merely generalizations and may vary with different manufacturers.

11. More accurately, it is the string spacing at the saddle that impacts the right hand technique, but the spacing at the nut is a good indication of the relative spacing at the saddle.

12. While scale length is given as a single measurement, in practice the saddle is angled so that the length increases for the lower strings. This is done to counter the varying degree of pitch change that occurs when the strings are depressed to the frets.

13. Replacing a plastic saddle with bone or ivory is an inexpensive way of improving the tone and sustain of the instrument.

14. Plastic pins, by far the most common, tend to wear, which can prevent the ball-end from sitting properly against the bridge plate. There is debate as to whether the bridge pin material affects the tone of the instrument, but most agree that worn pins have a negative effect. If nothing else, upgrading to harder materials avoids the wear issues associated with cheaper pins.

15. To maximize sustain, players sometimes lower the tailpiece until it rests on the body of the guitar and then thread the strings from the pickup side of the tailpiece and wrap them over the top—referred to as "reverse stringing."
16. Tremolo is a rapid fluctuation in amplitude. The misnomer is attributed to Leo Fender, who reversed the terms "tremolo" and "vibrato" on early amplifiers.
17. A floating vibrato bridge should not be confused with a floating fixed bridge like that found on an archtop guitar. As convention has it, they are both qualified as "floating."
18. Undersaddle transducers can easily be installed and removed, but it requires removal of the strings so that the saddle can be lifted.

Chapter 2

1. Note that the guitar is a transposing instrument, sounding one octave lower than written.
2. More is said about the relationship between tuning and spectral roughness in the discussion of just intonation later in this chapter.
3. Bands to use this version of drop-C tuning include Bullet for My Valentine, Helmet, System of a Down, and Slipknot, to name just a few.
4. The "major" descriptor is used here to distinguish these tunings from their minor and modal counterparts, but it is usually omitted when referencing major tunings.
5. The same could be said about fingered pitches, but the resonance is particularly pronounced in the case of harmonics because the player tends to lift the fingers off the strings.
6. Such tunings are sometimes referred to as "regular," referring to the regularity of a single interval between all strings.
7. The sine wave is an exception, as it contains only a single frequency.
8. Perception of timbre is more complex than this account suggests, but those details are not pertinent to the current topic.

Chapter 3

1. The sub-octave treble clef (marked by an "8" below the standard treble clef) is occasionally encountered in the literature to capture the transposition of the instrument, but this is unnecessary and could potentially be misleading.
2. The letter "o" should not be used to indicate an open string, as it can easily be confused with the symbol for a harmonic.
3. The tablature notation presented here was chosen because it is often found in both classical and popular music literature. Variants are encountered in practice.
4. There are ways of playing chords that incorporate fingers with a pick: hybrid picking and tapping with left hand fingers are two that come to mind. The notational approaches for strumming with the fingers may be better suited for these techniques.

Chapter 4

1. Of course, it would be more appropriate to think that a specific type of guitar is chosen for a particular musical style and technique.
2. Al Di Meola and John McLaughlin serve as notable examples of guitarists who play the nylon string instrument with a pick.
3. The reader might look to Mississippi John Hurt for an example.
4. It is worth noting that pieces composed for EBow in Standard Mode can be played using either model, while a piece requiring Harmonic Mode can only be played with a PlusEBow.
5. If the instrument is normally played with the volume knob at 10 it might be rolled back to 7.

6. Bowed string notation would use the word "arco" to indicate the use of a bow. However, a guitarist may not be familiar with the term.
7. Any shape note head would suffice as long as it is clearly defined in instructions that accompany the score.
8. This is not Villa-Lobos's notation. He refers to this as a "double harmonic" and accordingly, uses a triangle note head. Technically, it is not a harmonic.

Chapter 5

1. Snap pizzicato is also referred to as Bartók pizzicato, as Bela Bartók was one of the early composers to use the effect extensively, albeit on bowed string instruments.
2. In both the Charpentier and Ginastera examples the original scores used straight glissando lines. Those have been replaced with wavy lines in the transcription to remain consistent with the notational approach adopted in this book.
3. A variety of formalized trill patterns are encountered in practice, mainly associated with Baroque music. The reader is encouraged to consult any general guide to music notation for more information on these.
4. If these concepts are unclear the reader is advised to review them before proceeding, as they are important to the current discussion of harmonics.
5. The micro-fluctuations of pressure applied on the string by the finger have a damping effect, as compared to the stability of a fixed nut.
6. Front and back tones are collectively referred to as a bi-tone. However, when sounded together, the effect is multiphonic.
7. It should be noted that tapping with the right hand is somewhat difficult with long fingernails, which may be a prohibitive factor for many classical players.
8. A tambour is also a drum, from which the technique derives its name.
9. Fingerstyle players should be warned that scraping strings with the nails could roughen them up severely.

Chapter 6

1. For the purposes of this text, preparations are limited to those that are temporary and removable, as distinguished from a modified guitar that has undergone permanent alterations.
2. The technique of splitting the string length into prepared and unprepared regions can be used in the context of many preparations and is worth keeping in mind.
3. Felt is used in the figure to protect the fretboard from being scratched.
4. To collect the data in the graph, a split shot fishing sinker was attached to the fourth string (D) at the 15th fret so that the intervallic relationship between the front and back tones was roughly a perfect 4th. A series of recordings was made attacking the string at different locations, with each attack location recorded three times. Spectral analysis was performed on each recorded sound from 500 ms to 1,000 ms into the sound. The fundamentals of the three spectral components were measured as 371 Hz (front tone), 275 Hz (back tone), and 102 Hz (subtone). Three measurements were taken at each attack location and the results were averaged.
5. Needle nose pliers are recommended for pinching the sinker to ensure that it firmly grasps the string. A loose gripping weight tends to produce a blurred and noisy sounding result.
6. Objects can be placed on felt so as not to scratch the surface of the instrument, as shown in the figure.
7. Although buzzing bottle caps are effective on electric guitars, the rear pickup often restricts the position of the cap relative to the instrument's bridge.
8. In physics, this upward force is referred to as potential energy.

Chapter 7

1. Guitarists use the term "tone" to refer to the timbral quality of the instrument; it should not be confused with a sense of pitch or periodicity.
2. The amp's user manual should clarify the impedance of the inputs.
3. Assuming professional line level is 1.23 volts and consumer line level is 0.316 volts, the equation dBu = 20 × log (V/0.775) was used to calculate the level for both professional and consumer devices at unity gain and then the difference was determined, which rounds to 12 dBu.
4. The output level from magnetic pickups varies considerably, with active pickups generally having a higher output than passive pickups.
5. When performing this test, the total cable length used in each scenario should be the same in order to eliminate the effects that capacitance may have on the tone.
6. The same technique could be employed using two separate amplifiers with some interesting possibilities for the spatial distribution of sound.
7. Most passive volume pedals do degrade the signal, even when fully open.
8. See Chapter 4 for more information regarding the EBow.
9. These parameters may be named differently depending on the pedal. For instance, drive is often labeled "gain" or "distortion"; level may be labeled "volume" or "output"; tone may be labeled "color."
10. Flanger sweeps are often applied in a similar manner to an entire studio mix.
11. Some ring modulators accept a second audio input, although the modulation of two complex signals results in an extremely dense spectrum.
12. When subtracting, if the difference tone runs into the negative it wraps around 0 Hz. Consequently, we get the same result regardless of which input we subtract from the other.
13. The term "stereo" is used here solely to refer to two channels. Stereo delays do not create a stereo image.
14. Of course, the wet signal is always strictly tied to the dry, even if the perception does not suggest that.
15. I refer here to reverbs used for natural effects. When the parameters are pushed to extremes the effect does become more sound-altering.
16. Composer Denis Smalley uses the terms "intrinsic" and "extrinsic" space to distinguish the sense of space in the sound itself from the space acquired once that sound is projected into a physical space.
17. In more technical terms, compression increases the root mean square (RMS) level of the signal without increasing the peaks.
18. Terry Riley's *Reed Streams* (1966) or Brian Eno and Robert Fripp's *The Heavenly Music Corporation* (1973) provide examples using tape.

Chapter 8

1. Max is the prevailing tool in use today for audio programming and I refer to it purely for this reason. Other audio programming environments do exist, including James McCartney's SuperCollider, Native Instrument's Reaktor, and Miller Puckett's PureData, to mention just a few.
2. Accumulating hardware pedal buffers tends to degrade the audio signal. Chapter 7 presents a detailed discussion of this issue.
3. A voltmeter, oscilloscope, or other electrical measurement device can be used to get an accurate calibration. However, it is easy enough to get close with an empirical comparison.
4. Their system employs a hexaphonic pickup to isolate the six signals for each string.

5. Despite user-friendly ambitions, instrumental augmentation is technical business and some amount of software programming should be expected.

Chapter 9

1. By non-live, I refer to any electronically mediated sounds that are not realized by the performer. These include the playback of sound files, even when triggered by the performer, and real-time processing that responds to a live performer's input.
2. Composer Mario Davidovsky begins his *Synchronism No. 6* for piano in this way.
3. Composer John Cage may have disputed such an account of listening. However, for this listener, one of the more striking qualities of Cage's chance music is how often events seem coordinated, despite having been arrived at by chance operations.
4. Of course, there are works that force the listener to consider such unintentional sounds as part of the music. John Cage's *4'33"* is the classic example.
5. A more detailed examination of microphones and miking techniques is deferred until later in this chapter, where it is presented in the context of studio recording.
6. See Chapter 7 for more information regarding audio signals and direct boxes.
7. The lowest frequency canceled is dependent on the listener's angle off axis from the source. For instance, at a position 90 degrees off axis, the lowest frequency canceled would be roughly 565 Hz.
8. Instructions on how to implement a Mitchell Donut can be found on the supplemental website.
9. New instruments based on modeling technology, such as the Line6 Variax, do not have the same noise issues.
10. A noise gate can also be used to silence the instrument when the amplitude falls below a specified threshold. Chapter 7 provides a more detailed discussion of noise gates.
11. Whenever electronics are fed from an audio interface into a guitar amp they should be sent through a reamp box to convert the line-level signal to instrument level. See Chapter 7 for more details on audio signals and signal conversion.
12. The BEAST system at Birmingham University in the UK is a notable example of a large sound diffusion system. It utilizes around 100 speakers.
13. There are other mic types, but dynamics and condensers are the most common.
14. There are other mic polar patterns, most notably the bi-directional or "figure eight" pattern. Moreover, unidirectional polar patterns can be found in a range of shapes, with varying degrees of sensitivity in the rear and sides.
15. Phase cancellation will occur at the frequency with a wavelength that is double the distance of the two mics, with frequencies around it also attenuated.

REFERENCES

Anthony, M., Roth, D. L., Van Halen, E., and Van Halen, A. (1978). *Eruption*. New York, NY: Warner Bros.

Applebaum, M. (2004). *DNA*. Self-published.

Atkins, C. (1996). Waiting for Susie B. On *Almost Alone*. Nashville: Columbia Records.

Bach, J. S. (1973). Sheep May Safely Graze. On Parkening, C. (Ed.), *Parkening Plays Bach*. Chicago: Antugua Casa Sherry-Brener.

Barlow, C. (1981). *. . . Until . . . Version 7*. Self-published.

Bartetzki, A. (2007). Traces. Self-published.

Bellinati, P. (1993). Jongo. San Francisco, CA: Guitar Solo Publications.

Bello, J., Daudet, L., Abdallah, S., Duxbury, C., Davies, M., and Sandler, M. (2005). A Tutorial on Onset Detection in Music Signals. *IEEE Transactions on Speech and Audio Processing*, 13(5): 1035–1047.

Berlioz, H. (1858). *Treatise on Modern Instrumentation and Orchestration*. Cambridge: Cambridge University Press.

Biberian, G. (1969) *Prisms II*. Self-published.

Bonham, J., Jones, J. P., Page, J., and Plant, R. (1969). Heartbreaker on *Led Zeppelin II*. New York: Atlantic Records.

Brouwer, L. (1986). Paisaje Cubano Con Campanas. Milan: Ricordi.

Bryant, F. and Bryant, B. (1957). Bye Bye Love. On *The Everly Brothers: Bye Bye Love* (Single). New York: Cadence Records.

Bryant, F. and Bryant, B. (1957). Wake Up Little Suzie. On *The Everly Brothers: Wake Up Little Suzie* (Single). New York: Cadence Records.

Cage, J. (1940). *Bacchanale*. New York: Edition Peters.

Cage, J. (1948). *Sonatas and Interludes*. New York: Henmar Press.

Carlevaro, A. (1978). *School of Guitar*. New York: Boosey and Hawkes.

Carter, E. (1983). *Changes*. New York: Boosey & Hawkes.

Cash, J. (1956). I Walk the Line. Memphis: Sun Records.

Cavallone, P. (2008). Au réveil il était midi. Rome, Italy: Edizione Musicale RAI Trade.

Charpentier, J. (1974). Etude No. 1. Paris: A. Leduc.

Cobain, K. (1991). Come as You Are. On *Nevermind*. Los Angeles, CA: DGC.

Company, A. (1963). *Las Seis cuerdas*. Milan: Edizioni Suvini Zerboni.

Cornell, C. (1991). Mind Riot. On *Soundgarden: Badmotorfinger*. Hollywood, CA: A&M Records.

Cornell, C. (1994). Spoonman. On *Soundgarden: Superunknown*. Hollywood, CA: A&M Records.

Crumb, G. (1968). *Songs, Drones, and Refrains of Death*. London: Peters Edition.

Davies, P. M. (1978). *Lullaby for Ilian Rainbow*. New York: Boosey & Hawkes.

Davies, P. M. (1984). Sonata. London: Chester Music Ltd.

Domeniconi, C. (1985). *Koyunbaba*. Berlin: Edition Margaux.

Domeniconi, C. (1998). *The Bridge of the Birds*. Berlin: Germany: Chanterelle.

Elgart, M. (1990). Snack Shop. In P. Yates and M. Elgart, *Prepared Guitar Techniques.* Los Angeles, CA: California Guitar Archives.

Eno, B. and Fripp, R. (1973). The Heavenly Music Corporation. On *No Pussyfootin.* London: Island Records.

Fiore, G. (2013). *The Just Intonation Guitar Works of Lou Harrison, James Tenney, and Larry Polansky* (Doctoral dissertation, University of California, Santa Cruz).

Frampton, P. (1975). Show Me the Way. Santa Monica, CA: A&M Records.

Freeth, N., and Alexander, C. (1999). *The Acoustic Guitar.* London: Running Press.

Frengel, M. (2000). *And Then, Romina . . .* Self-published.

Frengel, M. (2004). *Slinky.* Self-published.

Frengel, M. (2010). A Multidimensional Approach to Relationships between Live and Non-Live Sound Sources in Mixed Works. *Organised Sound, 15*(2), 96–106.

Ginastera, A. (1978). *Sonata for Guitar.* New York: Boosey & Hawkes.

Graham, D. (1962). She Moved through the Fair. On *From a London Hootenanny* (EP). London: Decca Records.

Grainger, P. (1910). *Shallow Brown.* Mainz, Germany: Schott.

Greenwood, J. (1997). The Tourist. On *OK Computer.* Los Angeles, CA: Capital Records.

Guaus, E., Ozaslan, T., Palacios, E., and Lluis Arcos, J. (2010). A Left Hand Gesture Caption System for Guitar Based on Capacitive Sensors. *Proceedings of the 2010 Conference on New Interfaces for Musical Expression (NIME 2010)*, Sydney, Australia, June 18.

Harrison, L. (1978). *Serenade for Guitar and Optional Percussion.* Milwaukee, WI: Hal Leonard Music Publishing.

Hajdu, G. (1999). *Re:Guitar.* Self-published.

Haverstick, N. (2006). *Mysteries.* Paris: CPEA.

Hendrix, J. (1967) Purple Haze. On *Are You Experienced?* New York, NY: Reprise Records.

Henze, H. W. (1976). *Royal Winter Music: First Sonata on Shakespearean Characters.* London: Schott.

Henze, H. W. (1983). *Royal Winter Music: Second Sonata on Shakespearean Characters.* London: Schott.

Hjorth, D. (2007). *Let Newton Be.* Self-published.

Hopkin, B. and Landman, Y. (2012). *Nice Noise: Modifications and Preparations for Guitar.* CA: Experimental Musical Instruments.

Huber, K. (1992). *Luminescenza.* Germany: G. Ricordi & Co. Bühnen.

Hunter, D. (2004). *Guitar Effects Pedals: The Practical Handbook.* Milwaukee, WI: Backbeat Books.

Hurt, J. (1963). My Creole Belle . On *Folk Songs and Blues.* New York: Gryphon Records.

Jagger, M. and Richards, K. (1971). Wild Horses. On *The Rolling Stones: Sticky Fingers.* London: Rolling Stones Records.

Josel, S. and Tsao, M. (2014). *The Techniques of Guitar Playing.* New York: Bärenreiter.

King, K. (2004). Nails. On *Legs to Make Us Longer.* New York: Red Ink Records.

Kokoras, P. (2002). Slide. Self-published.

Koshkin, N. (2001). *Da Capo: 24 Easy Pieces.* Columbus, OH: Editions Orphée.

Koshkin, N. (1992). *The Prince's Toys.* Paris: Editions Henry Lemoine.

Lähdeoja, O. (2008). An Approach to Instrument Augmentation: The Electric Guitar. *Proceedings of the 2008 Conference on New Interfaces for Musical Expression (NIME08)*, Genova, Italy. June 6.

Lähdeoja, O. (2011). *Yonder*. Krakow, Poland: AudioTONG.

Lee, G., Lifeson, A., and Peart, N. (1980). The Spirit of the Radio. On *Permanent Waves*. Chicago: Mercury Records.

Livgren, K. (1978). Dust in the Wind. On *Kansas: Point of Know Return*. New York: Kirshner Records.

Loy, G. (2006). *Musimathics: The Mathematical Foundations of Music, Volume 1*. Cambridge, MA: MIT Press.

Mahnkopf, K. (2010). *Kurtág-Duo*. Germany: Musikverlag Hans Sikorski.

Mayer, J. (2001). Neon. On *Room for Squares*. New York: Sony Music.

Mandelbaum, M. J. (1961). *Multiple Division of the Octave and the Tonal Resources of 19-Tone Temperament*. (Doctoral dissertation, Indiana University, Indiana).

Mitchell, J. (1970). Big Yellow Taxi (Single). Hollywood, CA: Warner Bros. Records.

Mitchell, J. (2015). Speaker Directivity Modifier. http://www.tgpwebzine.com/?page_id=424.

Moore, R. (1988). The Dysfunctions of MIDI. *Computer Music Journal 12*(1): 19–28.

Murail, T. (2004). *Vampyr!* Paris: Editions Henry Lemoine.

Newton, D., and Marshall, M. (2011). The Augmentalist: Enabling Musicians to Develop Augmented Musical Instruments. TEI'11, Funchal, Portugal, January 22–26.

Page, J. (1968). White Summer. On *The Yardbirds: Little Games*. London: Epic Records.

Page, J. (1969). Black Mountain Side. On *Led Zeppelin*. London: Atlantic Records.

Polansky, L. (1997). *II—V—I*. Lebanon, NH: Frog Peak Publication.

Reboursière, L., Frisson, C., Lähdeoja, O., Mills, J. A. III, Picard, C., and Todoroff, T. (2010). Multimodal Guitar:A Toolbox for Augmented Guitar Performances. *Proceedings of the 2010 Conference on New Interfaces for Musical Expression (NIME 2010)*, Sydney, Australia, June 17.

Reboursière, L., Lähdeoja, O., Chesini Bose, R., Drugman, T., Dupont, S., Picard-Limpens, C., and Riche, N. (2011). Guitar as Controller. *Quarterly Progress Scientific Report, Institute for New Media Art Technology*, 4(3), 41–54.

Reed, L. (1964). The Ostrich. On *The Primitives*. New York: Pickwick Records.

Reed, L. (1967). Venus in Furs. On *The Velvet Underground & Nico*. New York: Verve Records.

Reed, L. (1967). All Tomorrow's Parties. On *The Velvet Underground & Nico*. New York: Verve Records.

Ribot, M. (2001). Somewhere. On *Saints*. CA: Atlantic Records.

Riley, T. (1967). *Reed Streams*. San Francisco, CA: Mass Art.

Romitelli, F. (2002). *Trash TV Trance*. Italy: Ricordi Milan.

Sandström, S. (1972). *Surrounded*. Stockholm: Nordiska Musikförl.

Schneider, J. (1985). *The Contemporary Guitar*. Berkeley: University of California Press.

Shaked, Y. (1982). *Einseitig ruhig*. Celle, Germany: Moeck Verlag.

Smith Brindle, R. (1973). *Concerto de Angelis*. London: Schott Music.

Smith Brindle, R. (1979). The Harp of David. In *Guitarcosmos 3*. London: Schott.

Smith Brindle, R. (1979). Percussion Piece. In *Guitarcosmos 3*. London: Schott.

Smith Brindle, R. (1982). *El Polifemo de Oro*. London: Schott.

Stockhausen, K. (1965). *Mikrophonie II*. Vienna: Universal Edition.

Stone, K. (1980). *Music Notation in the Twentieth Century: A Practice Guidebook*. New York: W.W. Norton.

Swayne, G. (1979). *Suite for Guitar*. Kent: Novello.

Tenney, J. (2000). *Septet*. In *New Music for Plucked Strings* (L. Polansky, Ed.). Lebanon, NH: Frog Peak Publication.

Trott, W. (2009). Edenton Played Touring Musician, but His Session Player Role Trumps All. *Nashville Musician 2009*(2): 28–29.

Verfaille, V., Quek, O., and Wanderley, M. (2006). Sonification of Musicians' Ancillary Gestures. *Proceedings of the 12th International Conference on Auditory Display*, London, UK, June 20–23.

Waters, M. (1948). I Feel Like Going Home. Chicago: Aristocrat Records.

Waters, R. (1979). Hey You. On *Pink Floyd: The Wall*. London: Harvest Records/EMI Records.

Webster, J. (1952). *The Touch System for Electric and Amplified Spanish Guitar*. New York: Wm. J. Smith Music Company.

Wessel, D. and Wright, M. (2002). Problems and prospects for intimate musical control of computers. *Computer Music Journal*, 26(3):11–22.

White, B. (1940). Aberdeen Mississippi Blues (Single). New York: Okey Records.

Worrall, H. (1860). *Sebastopol: A Descriptive Fantasy for the Guitar*. Cincinnati, OH: A. C. & J. L. Peters.

Yasser, J. (1932). *A Theory of Evolving Tonality*. New York: Da Capo Press.

Yates, P., and Elgart, M. (1990). *Prepared Guitar Techniques*. CA: California Guitar Archives.

Yoakam, D. (1987). "Little Ways" on *Hillbilly Deluxe*. New York, NY: Reprise Records.

York, A. (2003). Bach, Cello Suite No. 3 in C major. On *Into Dark*. San Francisco, CA: Gsp Records.

INDEX

232

Printed in the USA/Agawam, MA
January 24, 2017

647254.082